NOOK
Tablet

the missing manual®
The book that should have been in the box

Preston Gralla

O'REILLY®

Beijing | Cambridge | Farnham | Köln | Sebastopol | Tokyo

NOOK Tablet: The Missing Manual, Ninth Edition
By *Preston Gralla*

Published by O'Reilly Media, Inc., 1005 Gravenstein Highway North, Sebastopol, CA 95472.

O'Reilly books may be purchased for educational, business, or sales promotional use. Online editions are also available for most titles (*safari.oreilly.com*). For more information, contact our corporate/institutional sales department: 800.998.9938 or *corporate@oreilly.com*.

Editor: Nan Barber	**Indexer:** Bob Pfahler
Production Editor: Melanie Yarbrough	**Cover Designer:** Monica Kamsvaag
Copyeditor: Julie Van Keuren	**Interior Designers:** Ron Bilodeau and J.D. Biersdorfer
Illustrations: Robert Romano and Rebecca Demarest	

March 2012:   First Edition

Revision History for the First Edition:

    2012-03-09   First release

See *http://oreilly.com/catalog/errata.csp?isbn=9781449317751* for release details.

ISBN: 978-1-449-31775-1
[LSI]

Contents

PART VI **Getting Social**

CHAPTER 14

NOOK Friends, Facebook, Twitter, and Beyond **361**

CHAPTER 15

Managing Your Contacts **387**

PART VII **Advanced Topics**

CHAPTER 16

Settings **399**

The Missing Credits

About the Author

Preston Gralla (author) is the author of more than 40 books that have been translated into 20 languages, including *Samsung Galaxy S II: The Missing Manual*, *Droid X: The Missing Manual*, *Droid 2: The Missing Manual*, *Big Book of Windows Hacks*, *Windows Vista in a Nutshell*, *How the Internet Works*, and *How Wireless Works*. He is a contributing editor to Computerworld, a founder and editor-in-chief of Case Study Forum, and was a founding editor and then editorial director of *PC/Computing*, executive editor for *CNet/ZDNet*, and the founding managing editor of *PC Week*.

He has written about technology for many national newspapers and magazines, including *USA Today*, *the Los Angeles Times*, *The Dallas Morning News* (for whom he wrote a technology column), *PC World*, and numerous others. As a widely recognized technology expert, he has made many television and radio appearances, including on the CBS "Early Show", MSNBC, ABC "World News Now", and National Public Radio. Under his editorship, PC/Computing was a finalist for General Excellence in the National Magazine Awards. He has also won the Best Feature in a Computing Publication award from the Computer Press Association.

Gralla is also the recipient of a 2010–2011 Fiction Fellowship from the Massachusetts Cultural Council. He lives in Cambridge, Massachusetts, with his wife (his two children have flown the coop). He welcomes feedback about his books by email at *preston@gralla.com*.

About the Creative Team

Nan Barber (editor) has worked with the Missing Manual series since its inception—long enough to remember booting up her computer from a floppy disk. Email: *nanbarber@oreilly.com*.

Melanie Yarbrough (production editor) lives in Cambridge, Massachusetts, where she works as a production editor. When not ushering books through production, she's writing and baking whatever she can think up. Email: *myarbrough@oreilly.com*.

Bob Pfahler (indexer) is a freelance indexer who indexed this book on behalf of Potomac Indexing, LLC, an international indexing partnership at *www.potomacindexing.com*. Besides the subject of computer software, he specializes in business, management, biography, and history. He can be reached at *bobpfahler@hotmail.com*.

Julie Van Keuren (proofreader) quit her newspaper job in 2006 to move to Montana and live the freelancing dream. She and her husband M.H. (who is living the novel-writing dream) have two sons, Dexter and Michael. Email: *little_media@yahoo.com*.

Acknowledgments

Many thanks go to my editor Nan Barber, who not only patiently shepherded this book through the lengthy writing and publishing process, but provided valuable feedback and sharpened my prose. Thanks also go to Brian Sawyer, for making the introduction that ultimately led to this book.

I'd also like to thank all the other folks at O'Reilly who worked on this book, especially Melanie Yarbrough for bringing the beautiful finished product to fruition, Julie Van Keuren for excising errors, and Bob Pfahler for writing the index.

—*Preston Gralla*

The Missing Manual Series

Missing Manuals are witty, superbly written guides to computer products that don't come with printed manuals (which is just about all of them). Each book features a handcrafted index and cross-references to specific pages (not just chapters).

Recent and upcoming titles include:

Access 2010: The Missing Manual by Matthew MacDonald

Buying a Home: The Missing Manual by Nancy Conner

CSS: The Missing Manual, Second Edition, by David Sawyer McFarland

Creating a Website: The Missing Manual, Third Edition, by Matthew MacDonald

David Pogue's Digital Photography: The Missing Manual by David Pogue

Dreamweaver CS5.5: The Missing Manual by David Sawyer McFarland

Droid 2: The Missing Manual by Preston Gralla

Droid X2: The Missing Manual by Preston Gralla

Excel 2010: The Missing Manual by Matthew MacDonald

Facebook: The Missing Manual, Third Edition by E.A. Vander Veer

FileMaker Pro 11: The Missing Manual by Susan Prosser and Stuart Gripman

Flash CS5.5: The Missing Manual by Chris Grover

Galaxy S II: The Missing Manual by Preston Gralla

Galaxy Tab: The Missing Manual by Preston Gralla

Google+: The Missing Manual by Kevin Purdy

Google Apps: The Missing Manual by Nancy Conner

Google SketchUp: The Missing Manual by Chris Grover

HTML5: The Missing Manual by Matthew MacDonald

iMovie '11 & iDVD: The Missing Manual by David Pogue and Aaron Miller

iPad 2: The Missing Manual, Third Edition by J.D. Biersdorfer

iPhone: The Missing Manual, Fifth Edition by David Pogue

iPhone App Development: The Missing Manual by Craig Hockenberry

iPhoto '11: The Missing Manual by David Pogue and Lesa Snider

iPod: The Missing Manual, Tenth Edition by J.D. Biersdorfer and David Pogue

JavaScript & jQuery: The Missing Manual, Second Edition by David Sawyer McFarland

Kindle Fire: The Missing Manual by Peter Meyers

Living Green: The Missing Manual by Nancy Conner

Mac OS X Lion: The Missing Manual by David Pogue

Mac OS X Snow Leopard: The Missing Manual by David Pogue

Microsoft Project 2010: The Missing Manual by Bonnie Biafore

Motorola Xoom: The Missing Manual by Preston Gralla

Netbooks: The Missing Manual by J.D. Biersdorfer

Office 2010: The Missing Manual by Nancy Connor, Chris Grover, and Matthew MacDonald

Office 2011 for Macintosh: The Missing Manual by Chris Grover

Palm Pre: The Missing Manual by Ed Baig

Personal Investing: The Missing Manual by Bonnie Biafore

Photoshop CS5: The Missing Manual by Lesa Snider

Photoshop Elements 10: The Missing Manual by Barbara Brundage

PHP & MySQL: The Missing Manual by Brett McLaughlin

PowerPoint 2007: The Missing Manual by E.A. Vander Veer

Premiere Elements 8: The Missing Manual by Chris Grover

QuickBase: The Missing Manual by Nancy Conner

QuickBooks 2012: The Missing Manual by Bonnie Biafore

Quicken 2009: The Missing Manual by Bonnie Biafore

Switching to the Mac: The Missing Manual, Lion Edition by David Pogue

Wikipedia: The Missing Manual by John Broughton

Windows Vista: The Missing Manual by David Pogue

Windows 7: The Missing Manual by David Pogue

Word 2007: The Missing Manual by Chris Grover

Your Body: The Missing Manual by Matthew MacDonald

Your Brain: The Missing Manual by Matthew MacDonald

Your Money: The Missing Manual by J.D. Roth

For a full list of all Missing Manuals in print, go to *www.missingmanuals.com/ library.html*.

Introduction

WHAT GIVES YOU ACCESS to the world's greatest literature, today's bestsellers, tomorrow's up-and-coming authors, the world's top newspapers and magazines, TV shows and movies, great games, email, and more?

It's the NOOK Tablet—a great combo eReader and Android tablet from the bookseller Barnes & Noble.

This book will help you get the most out of your NOOK Tablet, and there's a lot you can get out of it, as you'll see. Whether you're looking just to get started or want to dig deep into the tablet's capabilities, this book's got you covered.

NOTE This book covers the features available on the NOOK Color as well as the NOOK Tablet. When the NOOK Color differs in any significant way from the NOOK Tablet, we'll let you know.

About the NOOK Tablet and NOOK Color

You likely already know that the NOOK Tablet and NOOK Color are eReaders that let you read thousands of books, magazines, and newspapers, as well as documents created with Microsoft Office and PDF files—and do all that in a nifty, lightweight, easy-to-carry, elegant piece of hardware.

But that's just the beginning of what these amazing devices can do. Even though at eight inches high, five inches wide, and less than half an inch thick, they're smaller, more portable, and less expensive than many other tablets, they do just about everything that bulkier, costlier tablets can do. And they're certainly light to carry, at just under 16 ounces.

Want to stream the latest movies and TV shows to it? Yes, it can do that. And you'll find the screen well suited for TV and movie watching, because it's crisp and clear with a high resolution. Movies and TV shows are often clearer and sharper on the NOOK's high-resolution screen than on larger tablets.

There's a lot more to the NOOK Tablet and NOOK Color than reading and watching TV and movies. Want to browse to any website? Read and compose email? Keep track of all your contacts?

Yes, it does all that as well.

How about playing Internet radio stations, playing games, sharing books with your friends, discussing books with others, borrowing books from the library?

Yes, it does all that and more. You can also download thousands of apps that do pretty much anything you want. In short, the NOOK Tablet and NOOK Color are eReaders but also powerful, very portable tablets. You don't want to wait to make use of all their amazing capabilities, though. That's where this book comes in—it will put you on the fast track to all the NOOK's magic.

Buying a NOOK

Before you can start using a NOOK Tablet or NOOK Color, you need to buy one. If you've got a Barnes & Noble store near you (and you likely do, considering how many there are), head for the NOOK section—pretty much all the stores have one, and the salespeople are more than happy to help you find it. You can hold NOOKs in your hands, try them out, and ask for advice about them. And once you do that, you'll most likely want to buy one.

As this book goes to press, the NOOK Color costs $169, and the NOOK Tablet costs either $199 or $249, depending on the amount of storage. Why the price difference? For starters, the NOOK Tablet comes with a 1 GHz dual-core processor and 1 GB of RAM, while the NOOK Color has a 800 Mhz single-core processor and 512 MB of RAM. What does that mean in real-world terms? The NOOK Tablet will do things faster for you than will the NOOK Color. That doesn't mean the NOOK Color isn't fast, because it is. It means that that the NOOK Tablet is super-fast. In addition, the $249 NOOK Tablet comes with twice the built-in memory (16 GB for the NOOK Tablet versus 8 GB for the NOOK Color). The $199 NOOK Tablet comes with 8 GB of built-in memory.

Those prices may change, though. So be on the lookout for the special deals that Barnes & Noble occasionally runs. For example, in one special, you could buy a NOOK Color for $99 if you also purchased a one-year subscription to the digital versions of either *The New York Times* or *People* magazine to read on the NOOK Color. Deals like this come and go, so make sure to ask whether any specials or discounts are available before you buy. Barnes & Noble is pushing the NOOK Tablet and NOOK Color heavily, so there's a good chance you'll be able to find some kind of deal. Do a web search for terms such "NOOK deals" to see if any are available. Also make sure to head to *www.barnesandnoble.com* or *www.bn.com* on the Web, and then click the NOOK icon to see if there are any specials in effect.

TIP Barnes & Noble stores aren't the only retail outlets where you can buy a NOOK Tablet or a NOOK Color—other stores have them as well. For example, many Best Buy stores also stock them.

If you're not near a Barnes & Noble store or other retail outlet that stocks NOOKs, or if you just prefer buying over the Internet, the *www.bn.com* website is a great place to buy. Shipping is typically free, so you won't pay extra for the convenience of buying online. And you can also buy at some other online outlets, such as *www.bestbuy.com*.

Finally, if you plan to use the NOOK outside your home, strongly consider buying a cover or case. A cover protects your NOOK and its screen from damages, so they're well worth the small investment. They typically range in price from $15 all the way up to $90 for designer-name leather ones. Some covers are great for commuters, because you can just flip open the top, start reading, and then flip the top down when you're done. You'll find a good selection at Barnes & Noble and other retailers.

About This Book

There's an entire world to explore in the NOOK Tablet and NOOK Color, and the little leaflet that comes in the box doesn't begin to give you all the help, advice, and guidance you need. So this book is the manual that should have accompanied the NOOK Tablet and NOOK Color. This book refers to the NOOK Tablet, or the NOOK generally, but that information also applies to the NOOK Color. The book indicates those few instances in which the NOOK Tablet and NOOK Color work differently.

The brain running the NOOK Tablet and NOOK Color is a piece of software from Google called Android. Barnes & Noble then tweaked Android quite dramatically to turn it into an eReader and tablet. So the NOOK doesn't look like or work like other Android tablets you may have seen—but underneath it all, it's an Android.

There's a chance that since this book was written, there have been some changes to the NOOK Tablet and NOOK Color. To help keep yourself up to date about them, head to this book's Errata/Changes page, at *http://nooktab-mm*.

About the Outline

NOOK Tablet: The Missing Manual is divided into eight parts, each of which has several chapters:

- Part 1, **The Basics**, covers everything you need to know about using the NOOK as an eReader and a tablet. It gives you a guided tour of the hardware, shows you how to set up the NOOK so it works just the way you like, and then shows you how to use it for the first time. By the time you finish you'll be a pro.

- Part 2, **Reading Books, Newspapers, and Magazines**, shows you everything you need to know about reading using your NOOK. You'll become an instant expert at using all of its remarkable reading tools, including using bookmarks and notes, changing font and text size, and searching inside books and publications. And it also has an entire chapter devoted to kids' books, including how you can record your voice reading a book to your children.

- Part 3, **Buying, Borrowing, and Managing Your Library**, covers how to buy books, newspapers, and magazines, and then track them in your own personal library. You'll find out how to find what you want to buy fast and get the lowdown about it, and then keep track of everything in a customizable library. And you'll also see how you can borrow books from friends, and lend to them as well—and how you can borrow books for free from the library.

- Part 4, **Apps, Movies, TV Shows, Music, Photographs, and Files** lets you take advantage of many of the NOOK's most remarkable features. You'll see how to find, download, install and use thousands of apps, and get recommendations for some of the best ones on the planet. You'll also see how you can watch movies and TV shows, as well as listen to streaming Internet radio stations—or play your own music collection. Also included is how to transfer files to your NOOK, and how to use the NOOK's built-in music player.

- Part 5, **The Web and Email**, covers the NOOK as a great Internet device. You'll find out how to browse the Web and send and receive email using any email account.

- Part 6, **Getting Social**, shows you how to use the NOOK's many social features, such as sharing books, reviews, and recommendations with friends, as well as using the NOOK in concert with Facebook and Twitter. And it covers how you can use the NOOK to keep track of your contacts as well.

- Part 7, **Advanced Topics** shows you how to tweak the NOOK's features. It also reveals how to *root* your NOOK, which means changing its software to run like a standard Android tablet.

- Part 8, **Appendixes**, has three reference chapters. Appendix A, Maintenance and Troubleshooting, offers plenty of help troubleshooting issues with the NOOK's operation, and a rundown of accessories you can use with it. Appendix B, File Formats, lists the file formats your NOOK can handle. Appendix C, Visiting B&N with Your NOOK Tablet, covers some nifty things you can do with your NOOK when you visit a Barnes & Noble store, such as read books free for an hour.

About→These→Arrows

In this book and the entire Missing Manual series, you'll find instructions like this one: Tap Settings→Sounds→Mute. That's a shorthand way of giving longer instructions like this: "Tap the Settings button. On the screen that opens, tap Sounds. And from the screen that opens after that, tap the Mute option."

It's also used to make it easier to understand instructions you'll need to follow on your PC or Mac, such as File→Print.

About the Online Resources

As the owner of a Missing Manual, you've got more than just a book to read. Online, you'll find example files so you can get some hands-on experience, as well as tips, articles, and maybe even a video or two. You can also communicate with the Missing Manual team and tell us what you love (or hate) about the book. Head over to *www.missingmanuals.com*, or go directly to one of the following sections.

Missing CD

So you don't wear down your fingers typing long web addresses, the Missing CD page offers a list of clickable links to the websites mentioned in this book. Go to *http://missingmanuals.com/cds/nooktablettmm.com* to see them all neatly listed in one place.

Registration

If you register this book at *www.oreilly.com*, you'll be eligible for special offers—like discounts on future editions of *NOOK Tablet: The Missing Manual*. Registering takes only a few clicks. To get started, type *www.oreilly.com/register* into your browser to hop directly to the Registration page.

Feedback

Got questions? Need more information? Fancy yourself a book reviewer? On our Feedback page, you can get expert answers to questions that come to you while reading, share your thoughts on this Missing Manual, and find groups for folks who share your interest in the NOOK. To have your say, go to *www.missingmanuals.com/feedback*.

Errata

In an effort to keep this book as up to date and accurate as possible, each time we print more copies, we'll make any confirmed corrections you've suggested. We also note such changes on the book's website, so you can mark important corrections into your own copy of the book, if you like. Go to *http://tinyurl.com/nooktab-mm* to report an error and to view existing corrections.

Safari® Books Online

Safari® Books Online (*www.safaribooksonline.com*) is an on-demand digital library that delivers expert content in both book and video form from the world's leading authors in technology and business. Technology professionals, software developers, web designers, and business and creative professionals use Safari Books Online as their primary resource for research, problem solving, learning and certification training.

Safari Books Online offers a range of product mixes and pricing programs for organizations, government agencies and individuals. Subscribers have access to thousands of books, training videos and prepublication manuscripts in one fully searchable database with publishers like O'Reilly Media, Prentice Hall Professional, Addison-Wesley Professional, Microsoft Press, Sams, Que, Peachpit Press, Focal Press, Cisco Press, John Wiley & Sons, Syngress, Morgan Kaufmann, IBM Redbooks, Packt, Adobe Press, FT Press, Apress, Manning, New Riders, McGraw-Hill, Jones and Bartlett, Course Technology and dozens more. For more information about Safari Books Online, please visit us online.

With a subscription, you can read any page and watch any video from our library online. Read books on your cellphone and mobile devices. Access new titles before they're available for print, and get exclusive access to manuscripts in development and post feedback for the authors. Copy and paste code samples, organize your favorites, download chapters, bookmark key sections, create notes, print out pages, and benefit from tons of other time-saving features.

O'Reilly Media has uploaded this book to the Safari Books Online service. To have full digital access to this book and others on similar topics from O'Reilly and other publishers, sign up for free at *http://my.safaribooksonline.com*.

The Basics

CHAPTER 1

Getting to Know Your NOOK Tablet

WELCOME TO THE NOOK Tablet, the easy-to-carry, do-everything device that lets you read books, newspapers, and magazines; watch TV and movies; listen to music; browse the Web; check your email; run countless apps...and that's just for starters. In this chapter, you'll find out everything it can do, and get a guided tour of the NOOK Tablet (and NOOK Color) so you can get up and running quickly.

NOTE This book covers the NOOK Color as well as the NOOK Tablet. When the NOOK Color differs in any significant way from the NOOK Tablet, we'll let you know.

What Your NOOK Tablet Can Do

To say that the NOOK Tablet is a do-everything device is not hyperbole. Take a gander at this list of everything it lets you do:

- **Read eBooks.** The NOOK Tablet has been designed from the ground up to be a great eReader. It's easy on the eyes, lets you carry thousands of books in its thin frame, and adds many reading extras, such as bookmarking, note taking, and more. It lets you get books from the world's largest bookstore—2.5 million titles and counting—with most under $10 for the NOOK version.

- **View multimedia inside books.** With a NOOK Tablet, books really come alive, because music and video can be embedded right in the book. (Try that with a paperback!) See a recipe you like, and want details about how to make it? A NOOK cookbook can contain videos showing you exactly what to do.

NOTE Books with additional content like this are called *enhanced* books. You'll see that label when you shop for books, so you'll know when you're getting multimedia goodies.

- **Read interactive kids' books.** Interactive kids' books can include video and music, and the NOOK Tablet can read them aloud to kids. In fact, you can record your own voice doing the reading. For details, see page 125.

- **Borrow and lend books.** Just like you can borrow and lend books with your friends, you can do that same thing with many books on your NOOK Tablet, using the LendMe feature. You'll even be able to borrow library books on it.

NOTE There are some restrictions on borrowing and lending books. For details, see page 182.

- **Read newspapers and magazines.** You can read countless newspapers and magazines on your NOOK Tablet, usually by springing for either a subscription or a single copy (if, for example, the swimsuit issue is all you want).

- **Watch TV, movies, and other videos.** The NOOK Tablet's spectacular screen lets you watch TV and movies on built-in Hulu Plus and Netflix apps. (The apps are free; you have to pay for the services.) There's also a video player for playing other videos.

NOTE As this book went to press, the NOOK Color didn't have Hulu Plus or Netflix capabilities. A free software update will eventually let the NOOK Color play them, so check for updates regularly. (See page 435 for details about how to upgrade your NOOK Color's software.)

- **Play music, audiobooks, podcasts, and other audio content.** The built-in music player and reader apps do all the work for you, and the NOOK Tablet makes it easy to find all the audio content your ears desire.

- **Browse the Web.** The NOOK Tablet has a web browser built right in, so you can visit any website on the Internet and view all of its contents, including videos.

- **Download and use apps.** Dying to play the latest game (Angry Birds, anyone?) or run the latest cool app? The NOOK Tablet lets you do that, with its built-in Apps store. Many are free, and even for-pay apps are often quite, er...cheap.

NOTE   Techies may want to know that the NOOK Tablet is based on Google's Android operating system, which also runs many smartphones and tablets. Many of the apps written for smartphones and tablets also run on the NOOK Tablet.

- **Keep track of your contacts.** With the NOOK Tablet's Contacts app, you can keep track of friends, family, and business acquaintances, and even sync contacts with your Google account.

A Quickie Look at the Hardware

If you're the kind of guy or gal who loves specs, read on, because here's where you'll learn what's under the hood. (Don't care about hardware? Skip on to the next section.)

The NOOK Tablet is powered by a 1 GHz (gigahertz) dual-core processor and comes with plenty of RAM to run the tablet and all its apps. Not sure what that means? Simple: The NOOK Tablet is super-fast.

> **NOTE** The NOOK Color has an 800 Mhz single-core processor and 512 MB of RAM. No, it's not quite as fast as the NOOK Tablet, but that's still more than enough power to do most everything you want it to do.

You can get two versions of the NOOK Tablet. One, which costs $249, comes with 16 GB of memory, of which 13 GB is available for your stuff (the other memory is used by the operating system.) Of that 13 GB, 12 GB is reserved for Barnes and Noble content. You can also buy a MicroSD card with an additional 32 GB of memory.

The other version costs $199, and comes with 8 GB of memory, of which 6GB is available for content, with 5 GB of that reserved for Barnes and Noble content. As with the more expensive NOOK Tablet, you can buy a MicroSD card with an additional 32 GB of memory. Both versions measure 8.1 by 5.0 by 0.48 inches, and weigh a mere 14.1 ounces. They've got great battery life: Up to 11.5 hours for reading, or 9 hours for video.

> **NOTE** The NOOK Color has 8 GB of memory and 6 GB for content, with 5 GB of that reserved for Barnes & Noble content. It measures 8.1 by 5.0 by 0.48 inches and weighs 15.8 ounces. Its battery life is good for 8 hours of reading.

The NOOK Tablet also comes with a built-in WiFi card for connecting to hotspots and WiFi networks, as well as all the hardware you'll read about in the next section.

Headphone Jack

Power Button

Volume Controls

Micro SD Slot (on back of NOOK)

Nook Button

USB Port

The NOOK Button

Down at the bottom of the NOOK Tablet, you'll find the NOOK button, which just happens to be in the horseshoe shape of the NOOK symbol. If the tablet is sleeping (see page 21), pressing the NOOK button wakes it up. If the tablet is already awake, pressing the button opens the Quick Nav bar that lets you take advantage of all of the tablet's features. (For more details, see page 49.) Pressing the NOOK button twice in a row brings you to the tablet's Home screen (page 27).

When the NOOK Color received a software update, it began working just like the NOOK Tablet. That update, numbered 1.41, was released at the end of 2011 and the beginning of 2012. There's a chance that your NOOK Color hasn't yet received the update. If that's the case, the NOOK Color will operate somewhat differently than you read here. Fear not, though: If you don't have it yet, the software update is on the way.

If the Quick Nav bar is showing and you press the NOOK button, you'll be sent to the Home screen.

Speaker and Volume Buttons

Turn over your NOOK Tablet, and you'll see the speaker near the bottom. Many apps have built-in volume controls, but the NOOK Tablet has physical volume buttons as well. Find them on the right-hand side of the tablet, up near the top. Pressing the top button increases the volume; pressing the bottom button turns it down.

Headphone Jack

Near the upper-right corner of the NOOK Tablet, you'll see a headphone jack. There's no magic to how it works—plug in headphones or an external speaker, and you're ready to go.

Power Button

In the NOOK Tablet's upper-left corner lives the power button. Hold it for a second or two to turn off your NOOK Tablet; hold it again for a second or two to turn it back on.

TIP If your NOOK Tablet is sleeping, pressing the power button will wake it up. For details about sleep, see below.

Sleeping, Locking, and Waking from Sleep

If your NOOK Tablet's screen stayed on all the time, it'd burn up battery life pretty quickly. So if the tablet detects that you haven't used it in a while, it blacks out the screen and locks it. In other words, the NOOK Tablet goes to sleep.

Normally, if you're not using your tablet for 2 minutes, the screen blacks out. But if you'd like, you can increase that interval. Press the NOOK button and select Settings→Screen→"Screen timeout," and from the screen that appears, select the interval you'd like, anywhere from 2 minutes to 1 hour.

When the screen blacks out, to make it come to life again, press either the NOOK button or the power button. The tablet wakes from its slumber. Slide the green NOOK button onscreen over the to the right, and you'll unlock it.

Anyone can wake your tablet like this, not just you. If you're worried about security, though, you can lock your tablet so that only someone with a password can use it. Press the NOOK button and select Settings→Security→"Device lock passcode." Then type the password you want to use. From now on, the only way to unlock the NOOK Tablet will be to first enter the passcode after waking it from sleep.

USB Port, Connector, and Charger

At its bottom, the NOOK Tablet has a small USB port, and it serves double duty. The tablet comes with a USB cable; plug the cable's mini connector into the USB port, plug the other end of the cable into a power adapter, and then plug the power adapter into a wall outlet. That's how you charge your NOOK Tablet.

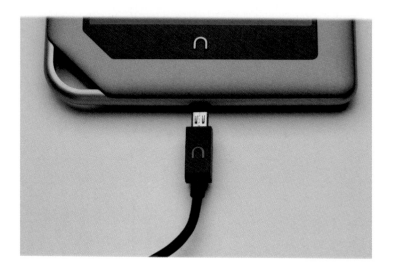

But the USB port and cable do more than just drink in power. If you plug the other end of the cable into your PC or Mac instead of a wall, it lets you transfer files between your computer (either PC or Mac) and the NOOK Tablet. As you'll see in Chapter 11, it's a great way to transfer music or other media files from your computer to your tablet.

Keep in mind, though, that when you connect your NOOK Tablet to a computer in this way, you won't be able to use the NOOK for anything else. It's in *USB mode*, and you can only transfer files between your computer and your NOOK Tablet when it's connected like this.

To transfer files, open up Windows Explorer on your PC, or Finder on your Mac. The NOOK Tablet looks like any other USB drive, so move files just as you would normally between a USB drive and your computer.

NOTE In order for your PC to transfer files between the NOOK Tablet and your PC, your PC needs to install a small piece of software called a *driver*. The installation should happen automatically when you plug in your NOOK. If it doesn't, you might need to do a bit of work. See page 435 for details.

Microphone

Up at the top of the NOOK Tablet, just to the left and in front of the power button you'll see a tiny hole. That's the microphone. Yes, it's small, but it does the job very well.

VividView Color Touchscreen

Use your NOOK Tablet for more than a few moments, and you'll notice that the 7-inch screen is nice and bright, with high-resolution. Barnes & Noble's marketing department calls it a VividView touchscreen. It's also fully laminated to help reduce glare. If you're a techie, you'll like to know that it's got a resolution of 1024-600. That's a lot of pixels packed into a small space.

Unlike other eReaders, the NOOK Tablet comes with a slot where you can add plenty of extra storage—up to a whopping 32 GB. All you need to do is buy a microSD card, available in pretty much any electronics store as well as online. Prices vary, of course, but if you shop around you should be able to find one for under $50. As you'll see on page 277, it's easy to install.

Turn over your NOOK Tablet, and look down at the bottom, just behind the funny little notch. Lift up the small plastic rubber flap with the NOOK logo and insert the card right there. You're ready to go.

Home Screen

On the NOOK Tablet, just like in *The Wizard of Oz*, there's no place like home. Get used to the Home screen because you'll be spending plenty of time there, finding books to read, navigating your tablet and checking its status, and much more. Press the NOOK button to get there.

You'll explore the Home screen in much more detail in Chapter 3, but here's a brief rundown of what you'll find:

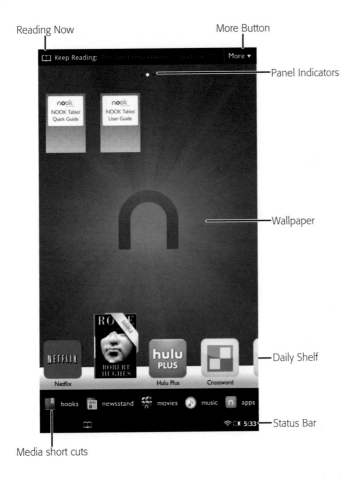

Reading Now

More Button

Panel Indicators

Wallpaper

Daily Shelf

Status Bar

Media short cuts

- **Reading Now.** At the top left of the screen you'll see an icon of a book, with the words "Keep Reading," followed by the name of the most recent book you've been reading next to that. Tap it and you'll open the book to the last page you were reading.

- **More.** At the top right of the screen there's a More button. Tap it to see the most recent books, newspapers and magazines, files, movies, and TV shows you've been viewing. Tap anything to jump to it.

- **Panel indicators.** With the NOOK Tablet, you get three different Home panels, not just one. Why more than one panel? You get more room to put books, apps, and icons on the screen. The white button indicates which of the three Home screens you're currently viewing. Swipe to the left or right to get to another one.

- **Wallpaper.** Your NOOK Tablet's Home screen has wallpaper on it, just like a computer does. And just as on a computer, you can change the wallpaper. See page 65 for details.

- **Daily Shelf.** Across the bottom of the Home screen is the Daily Shelf, which holds the books, apps, magazines, and newspapers that you've recently bought (or borrowed or downloaded). The shelf is bigger than it looks. Swipe it, and you'll reveal more content. Tap any book, newspaper, or magazine you want to read or app you want to run.

- **Media shortcuts.** Just below the Daily Shelf you'll find shortcuts to the various types of media on your NOOK Tablet: Books, Newsstand, Movies, Music, and Apps.

- **Status bar.** As the name says, this area tells you what you need to know about your NOOK Tablet's status—whether you're connected to a WiFi network, the time, and your battery life. Any notifications you get appear on the left side of the Status bar. The Status bar also gives you shortcuts to books you're reading. Depending on the app you're using, it may also have buttons that when tapped perform a function for the app, such as launching a search bar.

NOTE The Status bar is visible no matter what you're doing on the NOOK Tablet—whether you're on your Home screen, reading a book or magazine, or even watching a video.

The seven buttons on this bar, which appears when you press the NOOK button, let you get to the Home screen, open your Library, go shopping, search the NOOK Tablet, access apps, browse the Web, and change your settings. See Chapter 3 for more details on how to Quick Nav.

CHAPTER 2

Setting Up Your NOOK Tablet

NOW THAT YOU'VE TAKEN the guided tour of your NOOK Tablet, it's time to get started. So in this chapter, you'll charge your tablet, connect to a network, register with Barnes & Noble, and then be on your merry way.

Charging Your NOOK Tablet

First things first—before doing anything else, charge your NOOK Tablet. It'll likely already have some kind of charge, but that's not good enough; you want it to be charged completely so your reading (and watching and playing) won't be interrupted.

Get out your USB cable and power adapter (page 23). Plug the larger end of the USB cable into the power adapter, and then plug the power adapter into a wall outlet. Then connect the mini USB connector on the cable to the small USB port at the bottom of your NOOK Tablet. Your NOOK will start charging immediately. The little NOOK icon on the USB cable near the mini connector will turn orange, showing that your NOOK is charging. When it's fully charged, it turns green. It takes about 3 hours to fully charge a NOOK Tablet, but if your NOOK Tablet already has a charge, it may take less time.

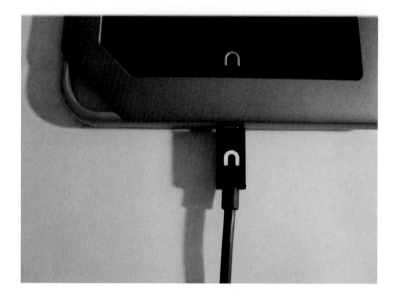

As you'll see in Chapter 11, you can use the USB cable to connect your NOOK Tablet to your computer and then transfer files between them. Unlike some smartphones and Android tablets, though, your NOOK Tablet doesn't charge when it's connected to a computer.

By the way, you don't need to wait for your NOOK Tablet to charge while you're going through setup. You can set it up while it's charging. So plug it in and keep this book open while you get it set up to go.

Initial Setup and Connecting to a Network

When you turn on your NOOK Tablet for the first time, you'll be welcomed by a video. It's worth watching if you have the patience, since it covers the basics of using the tablet. But if you're not in a video kinda mood, don't worry, because this book covers everything in the video and more.

At the end of the video, you wind up on the Terms and Conditions page (if you skip the video, you go straight there). It's got the usual legal rigmarole you can expect from such things. Unless you're a lawyer with the time and inclination to read it, you'll likely just tap the green Agree button. On the next screen, select your time zone, and then tap Next.

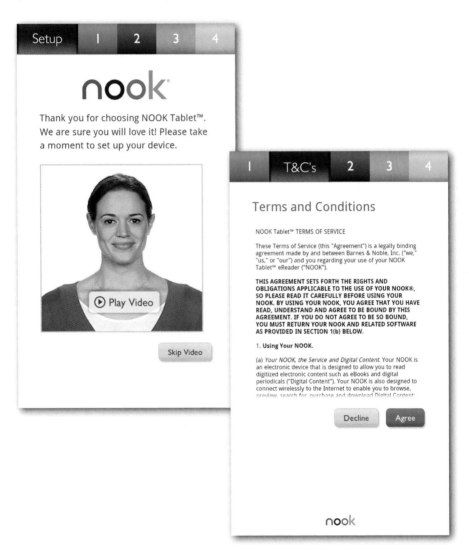

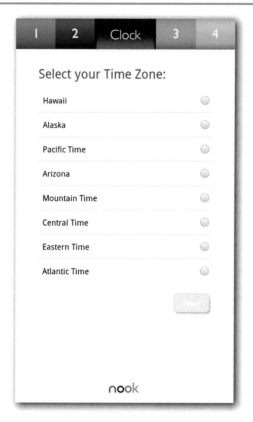

Now the fun begins. Your NOOK Tablet looks around in search of a WiFi network. It lists any that it finds. If you're at home, you see your home WiFi network listed; if you're at a B&N, that network is what you see. If any public WiFi hotspots are nearby, you'll see them in the list as well.

TIP If you have a home network and haven't turned on its security, do it. Do it right now. Having an unsecured home network is like leaving your front door open and posting an invitation saying, "Come right in! What's mine is yours, so take what you'd like." Check your router's documentation for turning on security.

Tap the network to which you want to connect—your home network, or whatever network you're near—and on the screen that appears, enter your password and tap Connect. If you're worried that someone will steal your password, turn on the "Hide password" box first.

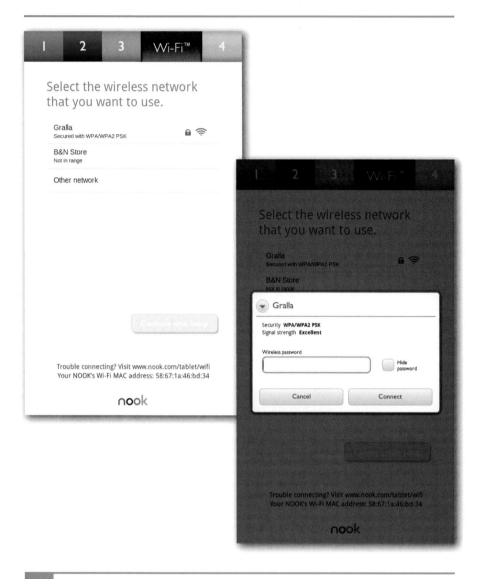

TIP Having trouble making your WiFi connection? Go to *www.nook.com/tablet/wifi* to seek help for your particular problem (scroll down to the Connectivity heading). If you can make the connection, but then run into problems, check out this chapter's troubleshooting section on page 38.

After a moment or two, you'll see a connection icon next to the network you tapped, and the indication beneath it, "Connected to the internet." Tap "Continue with Setup" to move on.

Your NOOK has a number assigned to it called a MAC address, a unique identifier, like an ID, that identifies your NOOK Tablet to the Internet. No two devices have the same MAC address, so what you see is unique in the world. It's not likely that you'll need to know your MAC address, but if you ever need it, like if you're asking for tech support, you can easily find it out. After you've registered the NOOK, press the NOOK button and select Settings→"Device Info"→"About Your NOOK" and you'll find it listed at the bottom of your screen.

Register Your NOOK Tablet

Before you can go any further, you have to register your NOOK Tablet and log in with a Barnes & Noble account. If you've ever ordered anything from *www. barnesandnoble.com* (or, to save your fingers, *www.bn.com*) or if you have a Barnes & Noble Member card, you already have an account. Enter your email address and password for the account (hint: the address that Barnes & Noble is sending you email to). If you don't already have an account, create one now by tapping the notification at the bottom of your screen.

TIP If you'd like, you can set up a Barnes & Noble account on the Web using your PC or Mac at BN.com.

When you register, you also have to provide a credit card and a billing address for your Barnes & Noble account. That's so you can pay for all the goodies you're about to buy.

After a moment or two, the screen tells you that your registration was successful and whisks you off to a Get Started page. From there you can check out tutorials for learning more about your NOOK Tablet; start shopping for books, movies, and music; or simply explore your tablet. To start exploring, press the NOOK button, and you'll come to the main screen. (As for what to do next, turn to Chapter 3, "Using Your NOOK Tablet for the First Time.")

Using and Troubleshooting WiFi

You'll probably use your NOOK Tablet in more than one place—your home, a public WiFi hotspot in a café or airport, or at a Barnes & Noble location, to name just a few. In those cases, you need to connect to a WiFi network other than the initial one you used when you set up your tablet.

It's simple. Just follow these steps:

❶ **With your NOOK Tablet turned on, press the NOOK button.** The Quick Nav bar appears.

❷ **Tap the Settings icon and select Wireless.** From the screen that appears, make sure that the button at the top right is On, rather than Off.

❸ **Tap the WiFi hotspot you want to connect to.**

❹ **Type the password, if the hotspot requires one, and then tap Connect.**

That's all it takes; you're connected.

Troubleshooting WiFi

The vast majority of the time, you should have no problems making a WiFi connection. But wireless technology can be finicky sometimes, and when that happens, you might need some help. The technology is confusing enough that you may feel the need to consult a local witch doctor or magician to help, but this book is really all you need. Don't go looking for your wizard hat yet.

One problem you may come across when making a connection to your home network is that your network name doesn't show up on the NOOK Tablet's WiFi list. If that's the case, the likely hitch is that your home network is set up to be a *hidden* network; that is, it doesn't broadcast its presence to the world.

TIP Are you the techie type who has a burning desire to know all there is to know about the WiFi network to which you're connected? It's easy to do. On the Wireless connection screen, tap the network's name. A screen appears with details that will warm the cockles of any geek's heart, including the signal strength, exact speed of connection, type of security being used, and even the IP address your NOOK Tablet is currently using.

One way to solve the problem is to unhide your network; check your router's documentation for details. But there's another way to solve it as well. When you get to the Wireless connection screen, as outlined in the previous section, tap Other Network. On the screen that appears, type the network name (called a *service set identifier* or SSID) and tap Save. (You'll of course first need to know the name of the hidden network to do this.) From then on, that network will show up on your network list. If the network requires security, tap the down arrow in the Security box, and choose the type of security the network uses. (If you're at a hotspot, ask for the security type and password; if you're at home, check your router or its manual for details.) After you select the security method, type a password, tap Save, and you're all set.

You may come across other WiFi problems that need solving as well. Here's a quick rundown on how to fix some of them:

- **If a WiFi network shows up but you can't connect to it,** try turning off your NOOK Tablet, and then turning it back on. That often solves the problem.

- **If you keep having problems connecting to a WiFi network,** on the Wireless connection screen, tap the network name, and then tap Forget from the screen that appears. Back on the Wireless connection screen, try connecting to it again.

- **If all else fails,** call the NOOK technical support line at 1-800-THE-BOOK. You'll be able to get help from a technical wizard who can help troubleshoot whatever ails your NOOK Tablet.

Using Your NOOK Tablet at a Barnes & Noble Store

You can use your NOOK Tablet at any WiFi hot spot, but it really shows off its stuff when you use it at a Barnes & Noble store. When you go into the store, your NOOK Tablet automatically connects to its WiFi hotspot (if you've got the tablet and WiFi turned on, of course).

Now the fun begins. Tap Shop. You'll come to a special page at the top of which is a "More in Store" section that offers you free extra content you won't find anywhere else, such as articles by authors of popular books, review roundups, and more.

Better yet, you can spend an hour reading any eBook for free—that's right, any book that B&N sells as an eBook, you can read for up to an hour, and you won't have to pay a penny—a great way to find out whether you like a book before you commit to buying it.

If you have any questions about the NOOK Tablet, or need help of any kind, you'll find out that you have a friend as well, because stores offer free in-person technical support and advice.

CHAPTER 3

Using Your NOOK Tablet for the First Time

YOU'VE FIRED UP THE NOOK Tablet, you've got it charged and set up, and you've registered it. Now the real fun begins. In this chapter, you'll get down to brass tacks, using the NOOK Tablet for the first time. You'll find out how to control it using gestures and the keyboard, and learn the ins and outs of the Home screen and all its nooks and crannies, including how to customize it.

Using Gestures to Control the NOOK Tablet

You control the NOOK with nothing more than your fingers, whether you're reading a book, watching a movie, downloading an app, or navigating around the screen. Here are the gestures you need to master:

- **Tap.** Tap something on your screen with your fingertip—don't push, don't press, just a light tap will do. It performs the most basic of actions, like selecting an app to run, or switching to your Library.

- **Double-tap.** Tap not once but twice on your screen in quick succession to perform a wide variety of shortcuts. Double-tap the Home screen, and it'll clean up the screen and arrange all the covers of your books, magazines, and newspapers in a grid. Double-tap in Shop (page 146) or Library (page 159) on a book or periodical cover and a new window opens that provides details about it.

TIP With all the tapping, pressing, swiping, and sliding you'll do on your NOOK, the screen tends to get fingerprints on it. Your best bet for cleaning it is to use a soft cloth, like the kind used to clean eyeglasses.

- **Press and hold.** Press your finger on something and hold it there for a couple of seconds to perform a variety of functions. Most often, you'll get a pop-up menu that offers a number of choices about the image you've got your finger on. So, for example, press and hold a book cover, and a menu pops up with choices like opening the book to read it, recommending it, deleting it, archiving it, and so on. Press and hold your finger on a word in a book, then lift your finger, and the Text Selection toolbar appears, giving you a variety of choices about what to do with the text.

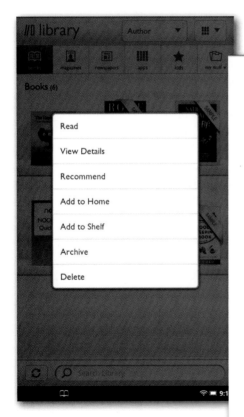

- **Swipe.** Slide your finger across the screen to the left or right, and you'll accomplish any one of similar tasks—like moving forward or backward in a book or scrolling through a list or collection. For example, swiping is how you scroll through a row of book covers on your Daily Shelf (page 56).

- **Scroll.** Slide your finger up or down on the screen to scroll through any list that displays a scrollbar. Think of it as a vertical swipe.

NOTE The scroll gesture is useful when browsing web pages—use it to scroll up and down a page.

- **Drag.** Place your finger on an object and drag it to another location; it's like using your mouse to drag an object on a computer. Once you've dragged the object to its new location, lift your finger to let it go.

- **Pinching in and spreading out.** Pinch two fingers together—your thumb and forefinger are the best bet—and you'll get to see more of the image; in other words, you zoom out. Move your two fingers away from each other and you zoom in.

NOTE Double-tapping on a picture of magazine page often zooms in on it. Double-tap again to zoom back out.

Using the Secret Back Gesture

If you've used other Android tablets, you might have gotten used to the Back button—a button you can tap or press that sends you to the last thing you were doing. For example, if you were in the Library and then opened a book, tapping the Back button would bring you back to the Library.

There's no Back button on the NOOK, and you won't find a Back gesture documented anywhere. But that doesn't mean it's not there. In fact, there is one, even though it doesn't work in all circumstances. (But that's better than none.)

To go back to a previous location, swipe your finger from right to left along the Notification bar at the bottom of the screen. If you're reading a book, and had previously been in the Library, you'll get sent to the Library. If you're in the Library and had previously been on the Home screen, you'll return to the Home screen. Try it whenever you can. It doesn't work in every circumstance, but when it does, you'll find it a great shortcut.

The Keyboard

Most of the time you'll be tapping, swiping, scrolling, and pinching while using your NOOK, but sometimes you'll be using a keyboard as well—a virtual, onscreen keyboard rather than a physical one.

You don't need to do anything special to make the keyboard appear. Tap anywhere you need to enter text—in a search box on a website or in the body of an email message, say—and it automatically appears.

Use the keyboard as you would a physical one, except tap instead of type. To switch from the letter keyboard to the number and symbol one, tap the ?123 icon . You'll find plenty of numbers and symbols—but there's even more. Tap the Alt key ALT to find them. The keyboard has a very nice timesaving shortcut—the

Go  button to the right of the space bar. When typing in text for a search on the Web, tap that button rather than tapping the search button on a web page. Don't waste your precious time hunting and pecking for a search button.

When you're in the number and symbol keyboard, click the ABC icon <img> to switch back.

Your fingers may get a bit cramped tapping on the small screen, so if you want to feel more expansive and get a bit more room as you tap away, turn the NOOK sideways, and the keyboard expands to fill the extra space.

To make the keyboard disappear, tap the keyboard icon <img> in the lower-left corner of the screen.

Accented and Special Characters

What? You say you're not satisfied with those symbols and want even more? Well, you're in luck. If you want to enter accented or special characters, such as those used in foreign languages (é, for example) it's simple to do. Press and hold your finger on a key such as the letter "a." A palette of accented characters appears. Tap the one you want to insert. The following chart shows which keys let you enter special characters.

KEY	ACCENTED AND SPECIAL CHARACTERS
A	á, à, â, ã, ä, å, æ
C	ç
E	3, è, é, ê, ë, ē
I	ì, í, î, ï, ī, 8
N	Ñ
O	ò, ó, ô, õ, ö, ō, œ, ø, 9
S	ş, ß
U	ù, ú, û, ü, ū, 7
Y	´y, ÿ, 6
O	ⁿ, ø
%	‰
-	-, —
+	±
(	[, {, <
)	], }, >
"	", ", «, », ⊠
?	¿

The Quick Nav Bar

Wherever you are on your NOOK Tablet, it's easy to get anywhere else. Press the NOOK button, and voilà, the Quick Nav bar appears. It pops up over whatever else you're doing. You can then use the Quick Nav bar to hop to wherever you want to go on your NOOK.

Here's what each of the buttons on the Quick Nav bar does:

- **Home.** Heads you to the Home screen (page 27) with all its features, such as the Daily Shelf (page 56) and any books, magazines, or newspapers you've put on the Home screen.

- **Library.** Tap and you go to your Library (page 159), which has all your books and magazines.

- **Shop.** Takes you to the Barnes & Noble NOOK Store (page 146), for buying books, periodicals, and apps.

- **Search.** Tap to launch the NOOK's very nifty search feature, which performs a global search all of your books, magazines, newspapers, and files. It also has a little bit of extra searching magic, and searches the Web and the Barnes & Noble NOOK Store.

- **Apps.** Shows you all your NOOK's built-in apps, such as Contacts, Email, Netflix, Hulu Plus, NOOK Friends, plus any apps you've downloaded.

NOTE Depending on when you bought your NOOK Color, it may or may not have come with the Netflix app. Before the late 2011 and early 2012 NOOK Color update, the NOOK Color couldn't run this app, and so it wasn't included. If your NOOK Color lacks the Netflix app, you can download it for free from the NOOK Store. As of this writing, Hulu Plus doesn't work on the NOOK Color, but it may by the time you read this. To find out, search for *Hulu Plus* in the NOOK Store. If it shows up as available, you can download and use it. If not, you can't.

- **Web.** Opens up the NOOK's browser so you can surf the Web. (See page 291 for details.)

- **Settings.** Tap to change every single setting on your NOOK, including your WiFi network settings, the sounds, security options, screen brightness, Reader settings, and plenty more.

The Status Bar

At the very bottom of the NOOK screen, you'll find the Status bar, which keeps you up to date with the state of your NOOK, and any alerts and notifications. For example, if you're having a problem with your WiFi connection, you get an update from NOOK Friends (see page 361). The Status bar is visible no matter what you're doing—even when you're reading a book.

The Status bar is divided into two sections. The one on the left sends you alerts and notifications. Way over on the far right, you see details about the state of your NOOK, such as its battery level.

Over on the right, what you'll generally see is straightforward:

- An icon that tells you whether you've got a WiFi connection.

- A battery life indicator.
- The time, displayed on a 12-hour clock. If you prefer having it displayed on a 24-hour clock, change it via the Time Settings screen (page 410).
- A mute symbol, if you've muted the NOOK (page 53).

Over on the left side, the Status bar has a lot more action. Plenty of different icons may appear there. Here's a list of the most common:

- An open-book icon, when tapped, brings you to the page of the book, newspaper, or magazine you most recently were reading.

- An envelope icon with an @ sign means you've got new email.

- A green NOOK symbol indicates that your NOOK has been updated with the latest software.

- An icon of two friends appears to tell you that there's been action in the NOOK Friends app, such as a new contact added.

- A yellow caution symbol warns you that you've got problems with your WiFi connection.

- A downward-pointing arrow tells you that an app, book, newspaper, or magazine is downloading.

- A letter P appears when the Pandora streaming music app is in the background; tap to return to the app.

- Red musical notes indicate that the Music Player is in the background; tap to return to it.

- A red circle that has a number in it tells you the number of LendMe notifications you've received (page 182), recommendations, and software updates.

To see more details about the alerts, tap that area of the Status bar. A Notifications screen pops up with details about each alert—like the number of new email messages. On this screen, you can tap any of the alerts to get even more information about it or to jump to a screen where you can take action on an alert. For example, tap the email alert, and you go straight to your email inbox.

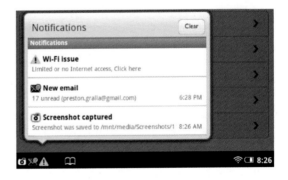

Quick Settings

The Status bar does one more thing for you: It launches the Quick Settings screen, which lets you fiddle with the NOOK's most important settings. Tap the right-hand side of the Status bar, and the Quick Settings screen launches. The screen has these five options:

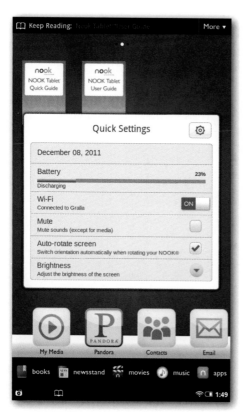

- **Battery.** Shows how much battery life you've got left. If the NOOK is charging, you see the word "Charging" beneath it, and if the NOOK isn't plugged in you'll see the word "Discharging."

- **WiFi.** This toggle switch tells you whether WiFi is turned on or off. Tap the switch to turn it on—or off if it's already turned on. The toggle appears green when it's turned on. If you're connected to a WiFi network, its name appears here as well.

- **Mute.** Turn on this checkbox to mute all sounds except for music, video and other audible media.

- **Auto-rotate screen.** When this box is turned on, the NOOK's screen orientation changes to either horizontal (landscape) or vertical (portrait). You can see this behavior when you're reading some magazines, or browsing the Web. If you don't like this behavior, tap to uncheck the green box.

- **Brightness.** Tap, and a slider appears that lets you change the brightness of your screen.

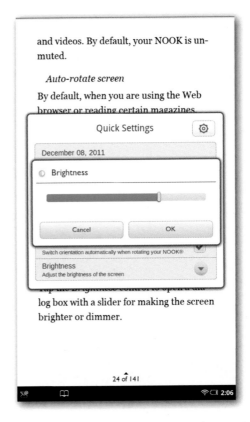

To make the Quick Settings screen go away, tap anywhere outside it. And if you want to change even more settings—literally every single one on your NOOK—tap the little gear icon on the upper right of the Quick Settings screen. (See Chapter 16 to learn how to change all the NOOK's settings.)

NOTE Quick Settings also shows you the current date at the top of the screen.

The Keep Reading and More Menus

Your NOOK, above all, is designed for reading books, and it always keeps them front and center. And that's what the Keep Reading and More menus, at the top of the Home screen, do for you.

In the upper-left part of the Home screen, you see an open-book icon followed by the words "Keep Reading" and the name of the last book, magazine, or newspaper you were reading. Tap that icon, and you jump to the most recent page. If you're new to the NOOK and have yet to read anything on it, you see the sad phrase "Keep Reading None." (If that's the case, get reading real fast; that's what the NOOK is for, after all.)

What if you want to see more than just the last book, newspaper, or magazine you were reading? Glad you asked—that's where the More menu comes in. Tap the More button, and a menu drops down with lots more than just the last book you were reading. It lists:

- Titles and authors of the last three books you've read.

- Titles and publication dates of the last three newspapers or magazines you've read.

- Names and file types of the last three files you've opened in the My Files folder.

- Three Netflix recommendations. If you're logged into Netflix, the recommendations are based on the kinds of movies and TV shows you have in your Netflix queue. If you're not logged in, the recommendations are based on what's currently popular, and there's a link you can tap to log in.

To open anything on the More menu, just tap it. To close the menu without opening anything, tap anywhere outside the More menu.

The Daily Shelf

The NOOK is a smart little companion. It knows what kinds of things you're likely to do—what books or magazines you want to read, what apps you plan to launch, and so on. You find them on the Daily Shelf—a list of books, publications, and apps running across the bottom of the Home screen. It's like a virtual version of the little table beside your favorite chair where you keep all the things you like to use every day. There are more items than you can see on a single screen—flick your finger to the left or right to see more. Tap any to read it or run it.

To put items on the Daily Shelf, simply drag them from the Home screen (page 59). Also, every time you do one of the following, a new item is added to the far left, and the old items slide over to the right:

- Buy a book, publication, or app.

- Download a free book.

- Receive a LendMe offer (page 199).

- Get a recommendation from a friend for a book or periodical to read.

- Get sent the latest issue of a newspaper or magazine to which you've subscribed.

- Run an app.

The Daily Shelf can hold up to 50 items. When you reach 50 items and add a new one, it's added at left, and the oldest item—the one furthest to the right—is kicked off the Daily Shelf.

NOTE All items in your Daily Shelf are also in your Library, so if you're looking for an item that seems to have fallen off the shelf, tap the Library button in the Status bar.

The NOOK puts items in the Daily Shelf in chronological order, but you're not stuck with them that way. You can easily rearrange them. To move an item to a different spot, press it, drag upward about an inch, and then drag it to the left or right, just above where you want it to place it. The other items part like the Red Sea and leave an empty space for the item. Drag the item to its new location, and it nestles in nicely.

Customizing the Daily Shelf

What if you don't want certain kinds of items to show up on the Daily Shelf—apps, say? No problem. You can easily control which items show up and which don't. Press the NOOK button to display the Quick Nav bar. Then tap Settings, and in the App Settings area of the screen, tap Home. The Daily Shelf Items section lets you choose which items should show up and which shouldn't. Turn off the boxes next to those items you don't want to appear.

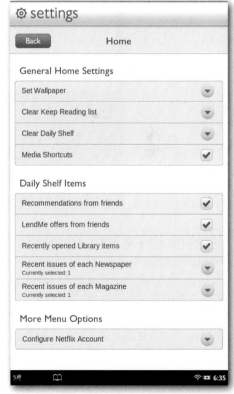

Some items show up on the Daily Shelf no matter what you do. Books you've bought or downloaded, for example, always appear.

If you'd like, you can also have more than one issue of a newspaper or magazine show up. In the Daily Shelf Items section, tap either "Recent issues of each Newspaper," or "Recent issues of each Magazine," and select none, 1, 2, 3, or all.

Deleting Items from the Daily Shelf

If there's an item on the Daily Shelf that you don't want there, press and hold it, and from the window that pops up, select "Remove from Home." That removes it not just from the Daily Shelf, but from your Home screen as well. (See page 59 for how to place items onto your Home screen.)

NOTE When you delete an item from your Daily Shelf, it's still available on your NOOK and appears in your Library.

Moving Items Between the Daily Shelf and the Home Screen

Since items on the Daily Shelf shift about as you add and remove them, you may have some items that you'd prefer to keep in a permanently fixed location on the Home screen. Just drag an item to the Home screen and then release it. It appears on the Home screen, and vanishes from the Daily Shelf as items to its left and right slide together to close the gap between them.

You can also move an item from the Home screen to the Daily Shelf—just drag it. Keep in mind, though, that it will behave just like any other Daily Shelf item and get moved to the right as newer Daily Shelf items are placed over on the left.

Media Shortcuts

Just below the Daily Shelf are five small icons: Books, Newsstand, Movies, Music, and Apps. They're a quick and simple way to see a list of the most recent books, newspapers, apps, and so on that you've recently read or used—and get recommendations on others you might be interested in.

NOTE The NOOK Color doesn't have media shortcuts.

Tap any icon, and you see a list of the items in that category you've recently read or used, along with recommendations—the B&N top-selling 100 books, for example. Tap the icon of any item to go to it.

Customizing Your Home Screen

The Daily Shelf's main talent is putting an always-changing selection of books, magazines, newspapers, and apps within easy reach. But that selection isn't permanent; it changes as you use your NOOK.

You may, though, want to have some items always within easy reach: for example, the books and magazines you're currently reading; Netflix so you can quickly jump to watching your favorite movies; and so on. Fortunately, you can easily move items on and off your Home screen, anchor them at specific locations, and if things get too messy arrange them in a neat grid.

As explained in the previous section, to move an item from the Home screen to the Daily Shelf, just drag it where you want it. If you'd like, you can even stack books by dragging one over the other. Just make sure that you don't completely obscure a book with what you drag over it.

And it's not just books you can stack. You can do so with any item, including magazines, newspapers, and apps.

If you're the tidy sort, you can even arrange all the items into a neat grid. To do it, just double-tap any open area of the Home screen, and they magically rearrange themselves. Any stacked items are unstacked and distributed on the grid.

If you prefer, press your finger on an open area of the Home screen, and from the pop-up menu, tap "Clean up this panel."

Remember, also, that you've got three Home screen panels, so you can use all of them to place items on. To move from one panel to another, just swipe over to it. As you do so, the white dot on the panel indicator moves to show you which panel you're currently on.

To move an item off the Home screen, hold your finger on it, and from the menu that appears, select "Remove from home."

NOTE When you remove an item from the Home screen, you're not actually deleting the item. It's still on your NOOK and accessible from elsewhere—the Library or the Apps menu, for example.

When you hold your finger on an item, though, you can more than just remove it from the Home screen:

- **Read** opens a book or periodical for reading.

- **Open** runs an app.

NOTE If a book or app on the Home screen has not fully downloaded, a Download indication on the cover or icon tells you so.

- **View Details** shows details about an item—for example a book description along with its ratings, price, and so on. In the case of an app, you'll see a description, the developer's name, its age-appropriateness, and similar information.

- **Recommend** lets you tell your friend the book or periodical via Facebook, Twitter, or NOOK Contacts.

- **Remove from home**, as explained previously, removes the item from the Home screen.

Also, as described in the previous section, you can move items from the Home screen to the Daily Shelf, and vice versa.

Changing Your Wallpaper

There are times in life when you want a change in the way things look—a new paintjob on your house, a new set of furniture, a different haircut. You may feel that way sometimes about your NOOK. You can't give the NOOK a new hairdo, but you can change its *wallpaper*—the background picture on your Home screen and its panels.

Here's how to do it:

❶ **Press and hold an empty area of the Home screen or a panel.** A pop-up screen appears.

❷ **From the screen that appears, select "Change wallpaper."** A new screen appears with two tabs on it: Wallpapers and Photo Gallery. Wallpapers are pictures that have been designed to look nice as wallpaper background. The Photo Gallery (page 267) contains all the photos and pictures on your NOOK, any of which you can also use as wallpaper.

❸ **Tap either the Wallpapers or the Photo Gallery tab.** You'll see a list of six choices. But there are more than what you see. Flick down through the list to see more choices. When you come to a choice you want, tap it.

What happens next depends upon whether you choose a picture from Wallpapers or from Photo Gallery. If you choose a wallpaper, you'll see a preview of it.

❹ When you've found a background you like, tap Set Wallpaper. You go to the Home screen with your new wallpaper there in all its shining glory. Otherwise, tap Cancel, in which case you end up back on the Home screen, old wallpaper intact.

If you instead choose a photo from the Photo Gallery, you see the photo with a highlighted box inside it. (On the NOOK Tablet, the box doesn't have a color outline; on the NOOK Color, the box is outlined in orange.) That box shows you the dimensions of the NOOK wallpaper. Everything inside the box will become the wallpaper.

❺ **Drag the box around until you have what you want to show up as wallpaper. Then tap Save.** Voilà—your photo becomes your new wallpaper. Tap Discard and you get sent to the Home screen, with no changes made.

There's another way to set one of your photos as wallpaper as well, starting from the Gallery rather than the Home screen:

❶ **First go to the Gallery: Press the NOOK button, and then tap Apps→Media.**

❷ **Browse until you find the photo you want to use as your wallpaper.**

❸ **Tap the photo you want to use as your wallpaper.**

❹ **When the photo appears onscreen, tap it anywhere on it.** A menu appears.

❺ **Tap the Wallpaper button.** The screen appears for cropping the photo so you can use it as wallpaper. Make your selection as you would normally.

Returning Home

No matter where you are or what you're doing on your NOOK, there's an easy way to return to the Home screen—and you don't even need to click your ruby slippers to get there. Press the NOOK button twice. You're there.

Searching your NOOK

Here's another of the many great things about your NOOK: Even though it's chock-full of books, magazines, newspaper, apps, and more, finding what you want is a breeze. That's because the NOOK has a great built-in search tool...in fact, it has not just one, but two search tools, one for searching the Library, and one for searching everywhere on the NOOK, launched from the Quick Nav bar.

Searching from the Quick Nav Bar

On the Quick Nav bar, tap the Search button, and start typing your search terms. The NOOK immediately displays results, and as you type more letters, it narrows down the search.

The keyboard at the bottom of the screen hides some of the search results, so when you want to see all the results, tap the icon on the keyboard that makes it go away (page 47). You see all the results of your search by category, such as Library or Apps. Tap any item to go to it—a book, a newspaper, or magazine, an app, results from the Web, and so on.

Here are the categories you'll search when you do a search from the Quick Nav bar:

- **Library.** Your books, magazines, and newspapers that match the search.

- **Apps.** The apps whose name or first letter combination in the name matches your search.

- **Music.** Artists, albums, and tracks that match your search.

- **Shop.** Books, magazines, and newspapers that match your search, but from the B&N store, not from your hard disk.

- **Web.** Searches your bookmarks and history.

If the search pulls up more matches than can fit in any category, it shows a See More button. Tap it to see more results in that category. At the bottom of the screen, you also see buttons that let you tap to Search Web and Search Wikipedia.

What if you want to search only Apps, or Music, or the Library? Simple—up at the top right of the screen there's a Show menu. Tap the down arrow and choose the category you want to search. That way, you'll limit the results to that one category.

There's also a way to limit the kinds of searches you do to only a few selected categories. At the far right of the Show menu there's a gear-shaped Settings button. Tap it and you get a screen where you can select which items to search whenever you launch a search from the Quick Nav bar. Uncheck any items you don't want to search. You can always go back and change your selections.

NOTE You can't turn off searching the Library or Shop—the NOOK always searches them when you search from the Quick Nav bar.

Searching the Library

Searching the Library is a bit more basic. In the Library, tap the Search button at the bottom of the screen. You'll search through the Library by author, title, and subject, although the NOOK also searches for the names of apps as well. If it doesn't find any results, it searches the Store, figuring that you're looking for a book, newspaper, or magazine.

Reading Books and Periodicals

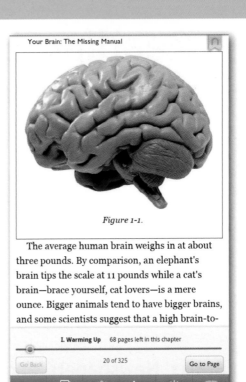

Figure 1-1.

The average human brain weighs in at about three pounds. By comparison, an elephant's brain tips the scale at 11 pounds while a cat's brain—brace yourself, cat lovers—is a mere ounce. Bigger animals tend to have bigger brains, and some scientists suggest that a high brain-to-

CHAPTER 4

Reading Books, Newspapers, and Magazines

YOUR NOOK TABLET DOES many things, but above all it's a great eReader for books, newspapers, and magazines. You'll find countless tools that make your reading experience efficient and enjoyable—and you'll learn all about them in this chapter.

Opening a Book

To open a book, simply tap its cover, or else hold your finger on the cover and select Read from the pop-up menu. Here are the main places you'll find a book cover to tap:

- On your Home screen, if you've placed one there
- On the Daily Shelf
- In your Library
- In the Books media shortcut at the bottom of the Home screen (page 59)

TIP When browsing or searching the NOOK Store, when you come across a book that you already have on your NOOK, the green button below it displays "Read" rather than a price. Tap it to read the book.

There are other ways to open a book without even hunting around in the Library for them. If you want to jump to the last book you were reading, tap the book icon at the bottom of the screen in the Notification area, or tap the Keep Reading book icon at the top of the Home screen. The Keep Reading feature is particularly handy, because it also shows the title of the book you're reading—which you'll appreciate if you have multiple books going at a time.

If you want to read a book that you've recently been reading, but not the most recent one, tap the More button at the top right of the Home screen. Down drops a long list of recent books and periodicals you've read, files you've opened, and movies and TV shows you've watched (or that have been recommended to you). Books are at the top of the list.

A Tour of the Book Reader

Tap a book cover, and you get sent to the first page of the book, or if you've been reading it, you go to the last page you read. You'll get a simple, uninterrupted view of the book page—text along with any illustrations, photos, and so on. At the very bottom of the page, you see the page number you're on and the total number of pages in the book. You may also see icons that look like blue notepads along the right side of the page—these indicate notes that you or another reader has added to the book. Tap a note to read it. (For the full story on notes, see page 103.)

2

Augustus

Until the advent of photography and then of TV, which effectively replaced them, propaganda statues were indispensable when it came to perpetuating the iconography of leadership. They were produced in mass numbers all over the world to celebrate the virtues and achievements of military heroes, political figures, wielders of every sort of power over all kinds of people. Most of them are wretched kitsch, but not all, and one of history's more successful icons of power is a marble statue exhumed in a villa that once belonged to the Empress Livia, wife of Octavian and mother of the future Emperor Tiberius, near the site of the

NOTE The page numbers at the bottom of the page are for the NOOK version of the book, not the print version.

To move ahead one page, tap any spot along the right edge of the screen, or swipe your finger to the left. To move back one page, tap any spot along the left edge of the screen, or swipe your finger to the right.

That's just the basics, though. To unleash the full power of the NOOK's reader, tap anywhere in the center of the page or at the bottom of the page to bring up the Reading Tools menu. This menu does all kinds of nifty things—hops to the interactive table of contents, searches the book, changes the font size and brightness, and more.

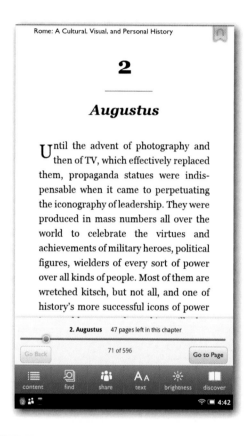

TIP You may need a bit of practice bringing up the Reading Menu. If you tap too far to the right, you'll go forward one page, and too much to the left you'll go back a page. Aim for square in the middle.

Here are the six reading tools:

- **Contents.** Jumps you back to the book's table of contents, with the current chapter highlighted. It's interactive—tap a listing in the table and you'll jump to that location in the book. Separate tabs show notes, highlights, and bookmarks and let you jump to them as well.

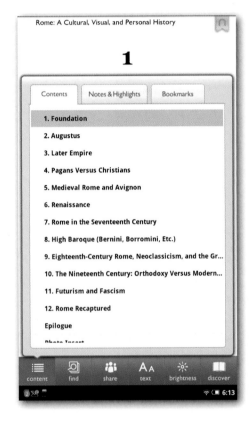

- **Find.** Pops up a search box and keyboard so you can search the book you're reading.

- **Share.** Tap here and you can share information about the book with others—recommend it, review it, "Like" it on Facebook, and more. See page 92 for details.

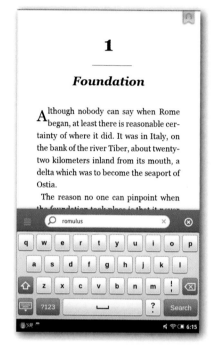
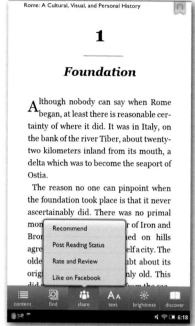

- **Text.** Lets you make the text just right—not too large, not too small, just the right font, and with just the right background color. See page 96 for details.

- **Brightness.** Tap to launch a slider that lets you adjust the screen brightness. Slide it to the right to make the screen brighter, and to the left to make it dimmer.

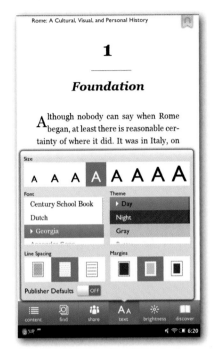
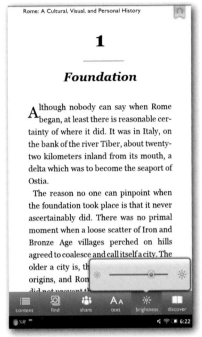

- **Discover.** Tap here to see books related to the one you're reading—for example, books by the same author. You'll often see unrelated books as well, such as the B&N Top 100. As with everywhere else on the NOOK, tap a book to see details.

NOTE If you download a book to your PC or Mac, and then transfer it to your NOOK (page 282), the Discover feature may not be available; in that case the icon will appear dimmed.

Look at the top-right corner of the screen when you bring up the Reading Tools menu, and you see a gray NOOK icon. That's for creating a bookmark. Tap the icon: It turns blue and elongates. You've just added a bookmark, and it stays there even when the Reading Tools menu disappears. Tap it again and it disappears—you've just deleted a bookmark.

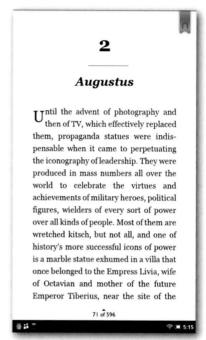

Just above the Reading Tools menu, you'll find some handy tools for navigating through the book. Tap the "Go to Page" button, and a screen appears that lets you type in a page number to head to. Tap in the page number, tap Go, and off you go.

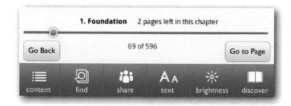

After you do that, to get to the page you were just reading, tap the Go Back button.

There's also a nifty slider that shows you your current location in the book, including the chapter number and title, and how many pages remain in the chapter. Drag the slider to move forward or back in the book. As you drag the slider, the page number and chapter number and title appear to show the location you're moving through.

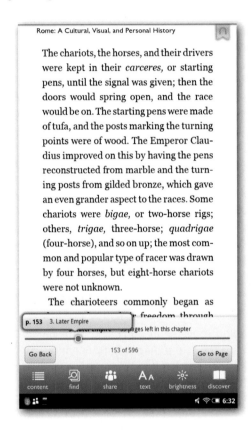

Using the Table of Contents

A book's table of contents does a lot more than just let you navigate by chapter title. It's also your gateway into three great NOOK features—Notes, Highlights, and Bookmarks. (You learned how to create a bookmark on page 87; for help on creating notes and highlights, turn to page 103.)

Tap Contents on the Reader Tools menu, and you come to a page with three tabs: Contents, Notes & Highlights, and Bookmarks.

Tap the Notes & Highlights tab and you'll see the list of all the notes and highlights you've added to your book. To jump to any, tap it.

Tap a listing, and you go to the page with the note or highlight. The text that you highlighted or attached a note to is highlighted in green. If there's a note, you see a small blue note icon in the right margin. Tap the icon to read or edit the note.

Rome: A Cultural, Visual, and Personal History

ply of grain. His armies completed the conquest of Spain. He also had military failures, the worst of which was undoubt-

Contents	Notes & Highlights	Bookmarks

p.72	He made short work of avenging Caesar's death... *last edited 12/15/11, 7:22 AM*
p.76	Trajan... *last edited 12/15/11, 7:24 AM*
p.79	Claudius ... *last edited 12/15/11, 7:25 AM*
p.83	Two aqueducts started by the Emperor Caligula ... *last edited 12/15/11, 7:26 AM*
p.84	At its height, the Roman Empire included fifty to sixty million people... *last edited 12/15/11, 7:27 AM*

Clear all   Show Notes & Highlights ON

content   find   share   A A   text   brightness   discover

1:16

> **NOTE** The list in the table of contents doesn't distinguish between notes and highlights, so you won't know what you're tapping until you get there.

Claudius in 52 C.E.; certainly the aqueduct
whose construction created the most difficulty was the Aqua Marcia, begun in 144
B.C.E. under the praetorship of Quintus
Marcius, with a total run of ninety-one ki-
lometers of which eighty ran under-
ground.

Aqueduct maintenance was a never-
ending occupation, done in the main by
slaves. The channel or *specus* of each
aqueduct was constantly being narrowed
by the buildup of "sinter," the common
German term for deposits of calcium car-
bonate (CaCO3), carried in the water and
deposited on the channel walls. How fast
it built up depended on several variables:
the "hardness" or lime content of the water, the texture of the channel (rough sur-
faces encouraged buildup, which rough-
ened the surface more, increased friction,
and so trapped more sinter), and the
speed of water flow. Research done on the

Claudius in 52 C.E.; certainly the aqueduct
whose construction created the most difficulty was the Aqua Marcia, begun in 144
B.C.E. under the praetorship of Quintus
Marcius, with a total run of ninety-one ki-

📄 **Note**   12/15/11, 7:25 AM

See if the PBS series is available on Netflix

Cancel   Edit

ter, the texture of the channel (rough sur-
faces encouraged buildup, which rough-
ened the surface more, increased friction,
and so trapped more sinter), and the
speed of water flow. Research done on the

Julia (33 B.C.E.) and the Aqua Virgo (so
called because its source outside the city
was pointed out to his surveyors by a
young girl). Between them they brought
some 150,000 cubic meters a day into
Rome. Two aqueducts started by the
Emperor Caligula (the Aqua Claudia in 38
C.E., the Aqua Anio Novus in the same
year) had to be finished by the Emperor
Claudius; between them, they gave Rome
a further 380,000 cubic meters a day. All
in all, the eleven aqueducts provided
some 1.13 million cubic meters of water to
meet the daily requirements of about a
million people, which averaged out at
about 1.13 cubic meters of water per person per day.

Not all this water was used for drinking,
cooking, and washing. Water also had a
strong—indeed,   essential—decorative
and metaphorical aspect in ancient
Rome, as it does today. Not every house

Tap the Bookmarks tab, and you see a list of your bookmarks. Tap any to go to one. If you'd like to delete all your bookmarks, tap "Clear all" at the bottom of the tab and they all vamoose.

If you're looking at the table of contents and decide not to use it, tap on the page behind it. The table of contents vanishes.

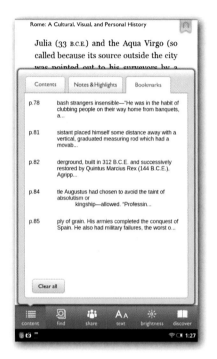

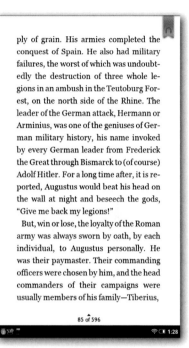

Sharing Your Reading

For many people, reading is more than a solitary pleasure; it's one that they enjoy sharing with others as well. That's where the Share icon on the Reading Tools menu comes in. Tap it, and a menu pops up that lets you share your thoughts about the book you're reading with others. You can even write book reviews. Think of it as your own personalized book club.

NOTE If you download a book to your PC or Mac, and then transfer it to your NOOK (page 282), the Share feature may not be available; in that case the icon will appear faint instead of bright.

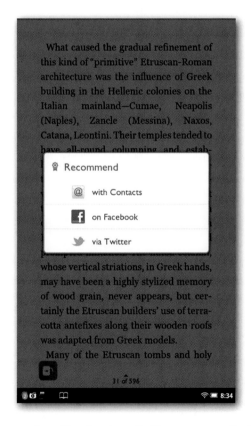

If you already hang out on Facebook or Twitter, you may find that the easiest way to share what you're reading. You can link your NOOK account to your existing Facebook or Twitter account; to learn how, flip to page 376. You can also share by email with your NOOK Contacts.

Once you've linked your accounts, you're ready to start sharing. Tap the Share button, and here's what you can do:

- **Recommend.** Tap to launch and you'll be able to recommend your book to others using Facebook or Twitter, or to your contacts. The exact form you fill out depends on which sharing method you choose.

  When you select Contacts, for example, an email-like screen appears that lets you select the contacts to whom you want to recommend the book. The NOOK thoughtfully enters all the basic information for you about the book—title, description, author, and so on—so that you don't have to do it yourself. There's a place on the form to add a message of your own, but there's a 420-character limit.

When you send a recommendation, there's also a link to the book so people can buy it, and a photo of the cover. In addition, if the person to whom you've sent the recommendation uses a NOOK, he gets a small notification in the shape of a medal or ribbon on his Notification bar. Tapping that icon and then tapping the screen that appears opens up the full recommendation, book cover and all. He can then download a sample of the book, view all the details about it, or remove the recommendation.

- **Post Reading Status.** Lets the world know via Facebook or Twitter not only what book you're reading, but what percentage of the book you've read. It calculates that by looking at where you are in the book when you tap the Share button, so no cheating and jumping ahead.

- **Rate and Review.** How good or bad is the book you're reading on a one-to-five star scale? What do you have to say about it? Tap here to share your views. Your review is posted on BN.com and appears when people browse the book; it also shows up when people view the book on their NOOK. You can also post the review to Facebook or Twitter.

- **Like on Facebook.** Tap here and you instantly add a "Like" to the book on your Facebook account.

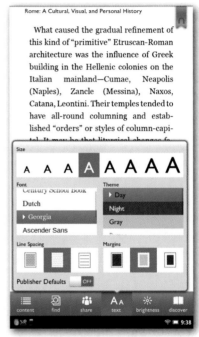

Changing the Text and Display

Want to make the text of the book larger or smaller, change its font, spacing, and more? Simply tap the Text icon in the Reading Tools menu. Here's what you can customize:

- **Size.** Yes, when it comes to reading, size does matter. Just tap any one of the eight font sizes. The text behind the menu changes so you can see a preview.

- **Font.** Scroll through the list and make your choice. As with all other selections, the text behind the menu changes so you can see how the font you chose will look.

- **Line spacing.** Changes how much space there is between lines of text. The leftmost choice puts the least amount of space between the lines, the rightmost choice puts the most, and the one in the middle is somewhere between the two. With this choice, you want to seek a balance between more lines on a page (so you do less page turning) and the potential eye strain of having lines too close together.

- **Theme.** Changes the background and text color combination. Out of the box, the NOOK uses the Day theme, which has black text against a white background; Night has white text against a black background. Other choices include different colored text, such as black text on a sepia background.

- **Margins.** Do you like wide margins? Narrow ones? Somewhere in the middle? Make your choice here.

As you can see in the nearby figures, the changes you can make are quite dramatic—one figure shows the text and display as out of the box, the other after it's been customized.

Superbus, whom the patricians expelled and refused ever to replace, a system evolved that was designed never to put such authority in one man's hands again. Supreme authority was granted not to one but to two chosen figures, the *consules* (consuls). Their powers were exactly equal, and one could overrule the other: thus the Roman state could take no action on any issue unless both consuls agreed on it. This at least saved the Roman state from some of the follies of autocracy. From now on, the prospect of "kingship" would be a political bogey to Romans; the consul Julius Caesar, to take the outstanding example, would be assassinated by a cabal of republicans who feared that he might make himself a king. Meanwhile, the religious powers of the kings were hived off and invested in a supreme priest, known as the *pontifex maximus.*

Every Roman citizen not a patrician was

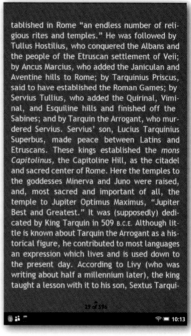

tablished in Rome "an endless number of religious rites and temples." He was followed by Tullus Hostilius, who conquered the Albans and the people of the Etruscan settlement of Veii; by Ancus Marcius, who added the Janiculan and Aventine hills to Rome; by Tarquinius Priscus, said to have established the Roman Games; by Servius Tullius, who added the Quirinal, Viminal, and Esquiline hills and finished off the Sabines; and by Tarquin the Arrogant, who murdered Servius. Servius' son, Lucius Tarquinius Superbus, made peace between Latins and Etruscans. These kings established the *mons Capitolinus,* the Capitoline Hill, as the citadel and sacred center of Rome. Here the temples to the goddesses Minerva and Juno were raised, and, most sacred and important of all, the temple to Jupiter Optimus Maximus, "Jupiter Best and Greatest." It was (supposedly) dedicated by King Tarquin in 509 B.C.E. Although little is known about Tarquin the Arrogant as a historical figure, he contributed to most languages an expression which lives and is used down to the present day. According to Livy (who was writing about half a millennium later), the king taught a lesson with it to his son, Sextus Tarqui-

Changing Back to Your Original Text and Display Settings

What if you prefer the way the text and display were out of the box? Tap the Publisher Defaults button at the bottom of the screen so it's switched to On, and you'll change it back to that default. To change it back to the last set of your customizations, tap the button again so it's switched Off.

Selecting Text, Taking Notes, Highlighting Text, and More

One of the niftiest things about the NOOK Tablet—and what sets it apart from reading a paper book—are the extras it gives you: notes, text highlighting, and the ability to select text and then do something with it—look up a word in a dictionary, say, or share it with others via email or social networking sites like Facebook.

It all starts with selecting text. Press and hold your finger on a word. As you hold your finger on it, the word gets highlighted and appears magnified inside a balloon so you can more easily read it.

murdered his twin brother for committing it. History does not tell how Romulus may have felt about slaying his only brother over a perceived threat to his sovereignty, but it is perhaps significant that the sacred group that ran around the *pom* **Luperci** s to assure the fertility of Roman flocks and women in later years was known as the Luperci or Wolf Brotherhood.

So the embryo city, rooted in an unexplained fratricide, had one founder, not two, and as yet no inhabitants. Romulus supposedly solved this problem by creating an asylum or a place of refuge on what became the Capitol, and inviting in the trash of primitive Latium: runaway slaves, exiles, murderers, criminals of all sorts. Legend makes it out to have been (to employ a more recent simile) a kind of Dodge City. This can hardly be gospel-true, but it does contain a kernel of symbolic truth. Rome and its culture were not "pure." They were never produced by a single ethnically homogeneous people. Over the years and then the centuries, much of Rome's popula-

26 of 596

10:32

murdered his twin brother for committing it. History does not tell how Romulus may have felt about slaying his only brother over a perceived threat to his sovereignty, but it is perhaps signifi  round the ility of Roman flocks and women in later years was known as the Luperci or Wolf Brotherhood.

So the embryo city, rooted in an unexplained fratricide, had one founder, not two, and as yet no inhabitants. Romulus supposedly solved this problem by creating an asylum or a place of refuge on what became the Capitol, and inviting in the trash of primitive Latium: runaway slaves, exiles, murderers, criminals of all sorts. Legend makes it out to have been (to employ a more recent simile) a kind of Dodge City. This can hardly be gospel-true, but it does contain a kernel of symbolic truth. Rome and its culture were not "pure." They were never produced by a single ethnically homogeneous people. Over the years and then the centuries, much of Rome's popula-

26 of 596

10:33

When you release your finger, two vertical bars appear at each end of the word, and the Text Selection toolbar pops up as well. If you want to select more than the single word you just highlighted, drag one or both of the bars to highlight more text. The Text Selection toolbar stays above the highlighted section.

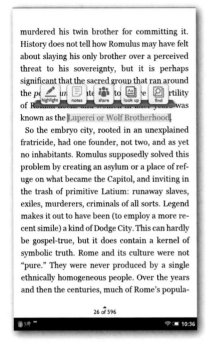

Now tap an icon on the toolbar to do one of the following:

- **Highlight.** Does what the name says. After you highlight the text, as explained earlier, you can see a list of all your highlights by tapping Reading Tools→Contents.

- **Notes.** Highlights the text and adds a note, as explained on page 103. As you read a book, you see a blue note icon where you've added a note. Tap a note to read and edit it. As with highlights, you can see a list of all your notes by tapping Reading Tools→Contents.

- **Share.** Tap and you can share the highlighted text (what the NOOK calls a quote) with your contacts, or with others on Facebook or Twitter. You'll have to first link your NOOK account to your Facebook and Twitter accounts (page 376) if you want to share on those services. When you share via Contacts, a window opens where you can choose a contact or multiple contacts with whom to share the highlighted text via email; tap the Add Contacts button to select them. When you select Facebook, a window pops up that lets you post the highlighted text along with a note to your (or a friend's) Facebook Wall. When you select Twitter, a window pops up letting you post it to your Twitter account.

NOTE When you share the quote, there's also a link to the book on the BN.com website. Keep in mind that Twitter only lets you post messages of 140 characters or less, so your quote and any comment have to be shorter than that. In fact, they'll have to be even shorter, since the link included in the Tweet uses some characters. Check the number in the lower-right corner of your Twitter window, which tells you how many characters you have left. If you see a negative number, you've gone over the limit, so you'll have to delete some text.

NOTE If you've copied the book you're reading from your computer to your NOOK, you may not be able to share the highlighted text with other people, and the button may be grayed out.

- **Look up.** Searches the Merriam-Webster Collegiate Dictionary built into the NOOK, and shows you the results. But it does more than that as well. Down at the bottom of the screen is a search box with three icons to its right. To change or edit your search term, simply change it in the box. The first of the three icons is for the dictionary. You're already using it, so don't bother tapping it. (The only time you may tap the dictionary icon is if you enter a new search term and want to look it up in the dictionary.)

The other two icons may look familiar—they're for Google (the colorful letter g in the middle) and the online encyclopedia Wikipedia. Tap either icon and you'll go to Google or Wikipedia in the NOOK's browser and see the results of your search there.

TIP If you've launched a search that leads you to the Web and want to get back to your book, simply tap the icon of an open book in the Notification bar.

- **Find.** Tap this to search the book for other mentions of the term. For details about how use the Find feature, see page 107.

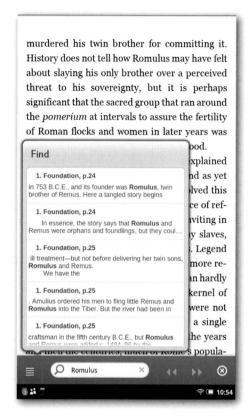

If you decide to call the whole thing off and don't want to do anything with the text you just highlighted, tap anywhere on the screen; the Text Selection toolbar vanishes. The toolbar will also vanish if you don't tap anything on it for 10 seconds.

NOTE If you've disabled the NOOK Tablet's browser (page 325), you won't be able to search for text via Google or Wikipedia.

Handling Notes

When you tap the notes icon on the Text Selection toolbar, a note-writing screen appears. You've got up 512 characters, so you can be more expansive than when using Twitter, with its 140—character limit. You can't write the Great American Novel in the text box, though—or even the Great American Short Story.

When you're done writing the note, tap Post. The Text Selection toolbar vanishes, and you're sent back to the book. The text you've just highlighted is in green, and there's a blue note icon on the right margin of the page next to it.

To read the note, tap it. If you then want to edit it, tap Edit. You go back to the note-writing screen.

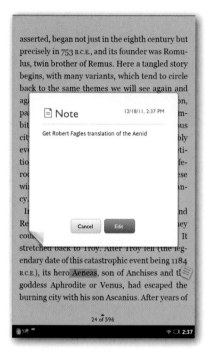
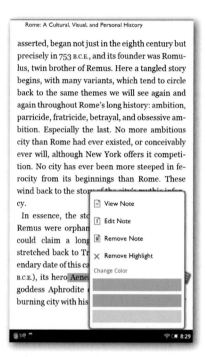

Want to do more with the note, such as changing its color? There's a simple way to do it. Tap the highlighted text (not the note icon), and a screen appears with these options:

- **View Note.** Does the same thing as tapping the note icon—you read the note.

- **Edit Note.** Takes you to the now-familiar note-editing screen.

- **Remove Note.** Deletes the note but keeps the text highlighted

- **Remove Highlight.** Deletes both the note and the highlight.

- **Change Color.** Tap the color you want your notes to be, and that's what they'll use from now on.

To see all your notes, go to the book's table of contents from the Text Selection toolbar, and then tap the Notes & Highlights tab. You'll see them all listed by the highlighted text associated with them. To jump to the note itself, tap the listing. Remember, the list of notes and highlights doesn't distinguish between the two, so from that tab, you can't tell which listings are merely highlighted text and which have a note attached.

When you're on the Notes & Highlights tab, you can also hide all of your notes and highlights for a clutter-free reading experience. Turn off the Show Notes & Highlights button at the bottom of the screen. You can still see your notes and highlights on the Notes & Highlights tab; they just don't show up in the text itself.

Handling Highlights

You handle highlights in the same way you handle notes. Create them by using the Text Selection toolbar, and view the list by going to the Notes & Highlights tab of the table of contents. Tap any highlight to see a menu of options similar to the one you get when you tap a note, although it's more limited. You can add a note to the highlight, remove the highlight, or change its color. If you add a note to the highlight, it then acts like any other note.

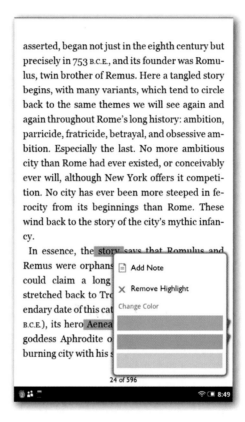

Searching in Books

One of the most useful things you can do on your NOOK Tablet is search for a word or phrase in it. Try that with a printed book! You have two convenient ways to do it—the Reading Tools menu or the Text Selection toolbar.

To search using the Reading Tools menu, bring up the menu by tapping anywhere in the center of the screen; then tap Find. A search box and the keyboard appear. Type your search word or term, and then tap the Search button.

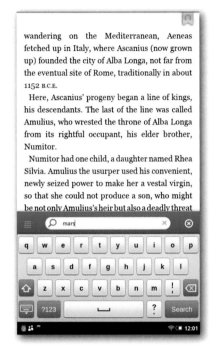
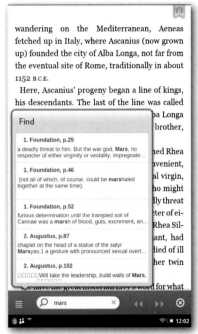

TIP When the search box appears, you see two X's at its right—one inside the box, and one to the far right outside the box. Tap the X *inside* the box to delete the search term already in the box. Tap the X *outside* the box to make the search box and keyboard disappear.

After a little while, a screen pops up showing you the results. You'll see the chapter and page number, the text surrounding your search term, and the search term itself. Scroll through the results and tap any of them; you jump to that spot in the book with the search term highlighted.

Underneath the results screen, you see a Search toolbar. You can type a new search in its search box, or tap the double forward arrow to jump to the next search result, or tap the double back arrow to jump to the previous search result. Tap the small Table of Contents icon ☰ to the left of the search box to make the search results screen disappear or to make it appear again if you've made it go away.

When you select text and choose Find from the Text Selection toolbar, that does the exact same thing as choosing Find from the Reading Tools menu. The NOOK searches the book for the term you highlighted, and it shows the results in the same way.

Reading Mode and Zooming in on Images

Most of the time, you'll read books with the NOOK Tablet held vertically—the standard reading mode. But there may come a time when you'd prefer to read in landscape mode—with the NOOK held horizontally. For example, you may come across a picture or photo that's best viewed horizontally, or a table that looks best that way. Or you may just be in the mood for some widescreen reading—you renegade! No matter the reason, all you have to do is turn your NOOK so the longest side is at the bottom, and your NOOK automatically orients the book that way. Meanwhile, a small lock icon appears in the right corner of the screen and stays there for a few seconds. Tap it, and you lock the screen to the new orientation for any books you read (the icon changes to a locked lock). So even if you turn your NOOK back vertically, it still displays books in landscape mode. To let the NOOK change the book's orientation as you change the orientation of the NOOK, turn the NOOK to another orientation, and when the locked icon appears, tap it so the lock opens.

NOTE Turning the NOOK horizontally doesn't *always* put it into landscape mode. For example, you'll never see the Home screen in landscape mode. If you put the NOOK into landscape mode while reading a book, when you go back to the Home screen, sure enough, it's vertically oriented.

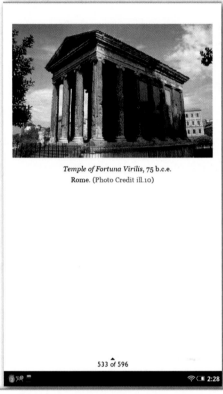

Temple of Fortuna Virilis, 75 b.c.e.
Rome. (Photo Credit ill.10)

533 of 596

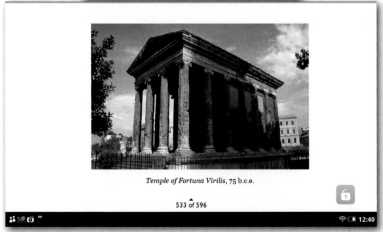

Temple of Fortuna Virilis, 75 b.c.e.

533 of 596

When you're viewing graphics or photos, the NOOK gives you an awesome power—the power to zoom. Tap the picture twice to zoom in. Tap the Close button at upper right to return to the normal view.

If you want to make sure your NOOK *never* changes orientation, tap the gear icon on the Notification bar so the Quick Settings screen appears. Then turn off the "Auto-rotate screen" checkbox. That way, the NOOK always stays in landscape mode. To let it change its orientation, check the box.

Video Inside Books

Reading a book on the NOOK Tablet is more than a text-based experience; you can enjoy videos embedded in books, too. When you come across a video, tap its triangle to play it. Control the video using the usual controls at bottom for stopping and resuming, and dragging the bar to go forward or backward.

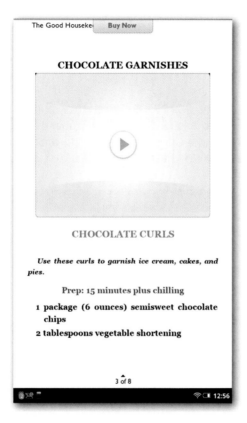

If you'd like to see the video taking up the full screen, tap the icon that has four outward-pointing arrows. You'll see video controls for a few seconds, but then they vanish. To make them reappear, tap the screen. To get back to the page you were just reading, tap the Back button at upper left.

Tapping Links

Some books include links in them, for example, from text to footnotes or end-notes. Links aren't underlined as they often are on the Web. Instead, they're in blue. Tap to follow the link. Generally, when you tap a link and go to its destination, there's also a link you can tap to get you back to where you were before you followed the link.

Reading PDFs

When you buy books for your NOOK Tablet, they're in a format called EPUB. NOOK books you borrow and lend are in that format as well. But your NOOK is a do-everything device when it comes to eReading, and it can handle more than EPUB books—it can read PDF files as well.

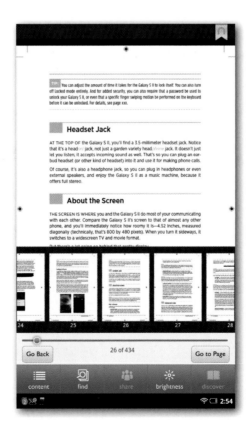

You typically get PDF files by copying them to your NOOK from your computer, as described on page 282.

NOTE When you tap a PDF in your Library to read it, you'll be asked whether you want to open it in Quickoffice Lite (page 273) or the Reader. The Reader has more reading features than Quickoffice Lite, so it's your best bet. If you want PDFs to always open in the Reader (or Quickoffice Lite), turn on the checkbox next to "Use by default for this option" before making your choice.

Reading a PDF is much like reading a book, with some important differences:

- At the top of the Reading Tools menu there's a thumbnail viewer that shows thumbnails of every page in the PDF. Swipe through the thumbnails, and when you find a page you want to read, tap it. Tapping it also closes the Reading Tools menu.

- Zoom in on a page by double-tapping it; zoom out by double-tapping it again.

- Not all the tools on the Reading Tools menu are available for PDFs. You can't share quotes or reviews of the PDF, use the Discover feature to find related books, or change the display of the pages.

NOTE To return to reading a PDF, tap the More button from the Home screen, but remember that you'll find it listed in the Files section, not in the Books section (page 55).

Reading Magazines

The NOOK Tablet is great for reading magazines as well as newspapers, with plenty of features designed specifically for magazines. Some tools are similar—like the way you turn the pages—but others are entirely new, like ArticleView, where you see only the text of an article, without illustrations.

NOTE Magazines come in a variety of formats, and so the features in each magazine may vary somewhat. This section covers the format used by most popular magazines.

乳制品
Dairy

CHANGING CHINA
By ORVILLE SCHELL

AND VICE
VERSA

You can read a magazine in two different views:

- **Page View.** In this view, the magazine looks exactly like the printed version of the magazine, including the page layout, photos and graphics, and advertising.

- **ArticleView.** In this view, you see only the text of articles, with no layout, photographs, graphics, or advertising to get in your way.

Using Page View

Just as with a book, you get around a magazine in Page View by swiping your fingers or tapping on the right or left edges of the screen to go forward one page or back one page.

> **NOTE** The Text Selection tools don't work in magazines.

You can use regular (portrait) or landscape mode when reading a magazine. Depending on the magazine's layout, one or the other may look better. Photo spreads or the beginning of highly designed articles often look better in landscape than portrait mode, as do certain photographs.

In Page View, text may be small and difficult to read. If that's the case, spread your thumb and forefinger outward to zoom in; pinch them in to zoom back out. You can also double-tap to zoom in and then zoom out, but pinching gives you finer control over the level of zoom. (For a refresher on gestures, see page 43.)

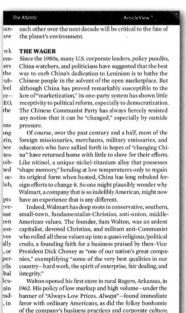

Magazines also have their own specialized Reading Tools menu. Tap the center of the screen to make it appear. It doesn't have the full complement of tools you'll find in the Reading Tools menu for books—no sharing, no changing the display. But it does the job, and it also has a feature that you won't find in books: A row of small thumbnails of every page in the magazine. Swipe through the pages, tap the one you want to read, and you're there.

NOTE When you read a magazine, you don't see the Notification bar at the bottom of the screen.

There's also a Table of Contents icon. Tap it to see the magazine's table of contents, which lists every article, along with its title and part of the article's first sentence. To jump to the article, tap its listing.

In the table of contents, tap the Bookmarks icon to see any bookmarks you've placed in the magazine. Adding a bookmark is simple: There's a very small plus sign at the top right of each magazine page. Tap that plus sign, and it turns into a dog ear—you've just bookmarked the page. To remove the bookmark, tap the dog ear and it turns back into a plus sign.

You can also change the brightness of the screen by tapping the Brightness button.

Using ArticleView

When you're getting down to serious article reading, you may want to use ArticleView. Although you won't see the layout or pictures, the text is larger and appears in a long, scrollable window—no distractions. You can also adjust the text size and font in ArticleView, something you can't do in Page View.

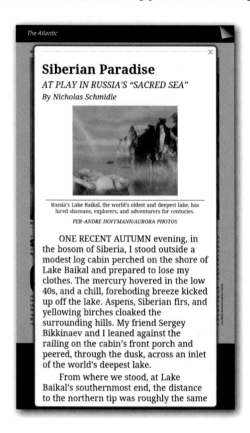

NOTE Not all magazines let you use ArticleView.

To use ArticleView, when you're in Page View, tap the ArticleView button at the top of the screen to open the scrollable text window. The entire article is in that window, so you don't have to turn pages. Sometimes there'll be a photo or graphic at the very beginning of the article, but apart from that, there are no pictures.

To read the article, just scroll. To close ArticleView and return to Page View, tap the X at the top of the ArticleView screen or tap outside the ArticleView window.

ArticleView has its own Reading Tools menu. Tap the center of the screen, and you'll find not just the Content and Brightness buttons, but also a Text button that lets you change the size of text, font, line spacing, margins, and so on (black on white, white on black, black on gray, and so on), in the same way you can do it in books.

Navigating isn't as easy in ArticleView as in Page View, because each article is its own self-enclosed world and there's no thumbnail display. So to get around in ArticleView, tap the middle of the page to open the Reading Tools menu, tap the Content icon to get to the table of contents, and then tap the next article you want to read. When you get there, though, you'll be in Page View, so if you want to read in ArticleView, tap the ArticleView icon again.

Reading Newspapers

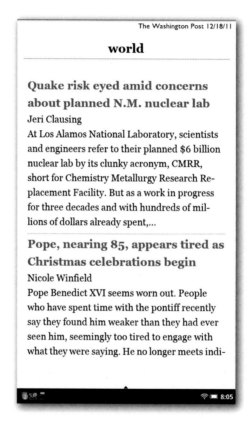

Reading newspapers is much like reading books, and even includes the same Reading Tools menu. You open a newspaper in the same way you do a book or a magazine—by tapping its cover. The NOOK newspaper won't look like its print counterpart. Instead of laid-out newspaper pages, you'll see scrollable lists of stories.

NOTE The NOOK version of a newspaper may not include *everything* that's in the paper-based version. It may not have all the photos, comics, or puzzles, for example.

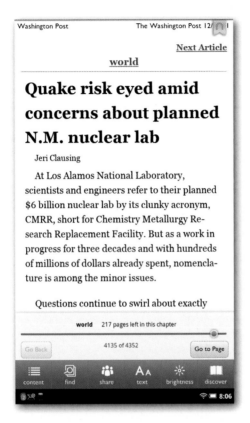

Tap any story to read it. Navigate through the story just as you do in a book, by swiping your finger or tapping the page edges. You get one additional navigational gesture: If you swipe your finger from the bottom of the screen toward the top, you go to the next page, and if you swipe it from the top of the screen down, you move to the previous page. Tap anywhere in the center of the page to bring up the Reading Tools menu, which works just as it does in books (page 83). To bookmark a page, tap in the upper-right corner. The Text Selection toolbar works the same way as well (page 99), but it may be a bit tricky to manage when you're reading the newspaper on the subway.

Reading Comic Books

The NOOK Tablet also lets you read comic books. You navigate the same way as with books, and you can use the Reading Tools (page 83) the same way. The Text Selection toolbar doesn't work, however.

The Elephant's Child: How the Eleph...

CHAPTER 5

Reading NOOK Kids Books

KIDS' BOOKS TRULY COME alive on the NOOK, with interactive activities and features—you can even record yourself reading the book, so your child can listen to you reading even when you can't be there. You'll learn how to do all that and more in this chapter.

What Can NOOK Kids Books Do?

Kids aren't like adults, and the books they read aren't the same as adult books, either. NOOK Kids books are different from NOOK books for adults, with plenty of additional features. They're specifically formatted for high-resolution touch-screen displays, and they're designed to be read in landscape mode (horizontally) rather than most books' vertical orientation. That way, you can see an entire two-page spread at a time—the way children's books are designed to be read.

A NOOK Kids book can also read itself aloud, or, as mentioned earlier, you can record your own voice doing the reading. What could be more comforting to your child when you're not around?

Beyond all that, many NOOK books for kids also have interactive features, including games and educational play.

The Elephant came upon his aunt, the Hippo. "Auntie," he asked her, "why are your eyes so red?"

"SHHHH!" she snorted. "So many questions! Take your nosy-nose somewhere else!"

So the Elephant did exactly that.

Buying a NOOK Kids Book

A NOOK Kids book can have any number of features, such as inter-activity or the ability to record your voice reading the book to your child. Not all kids' books have all the available features. When you open a book, you can see its capabilities, which may include the following:

- **Read by Myself.** The child can read the book to herself onscreen. Every children's book falls into this category.

- **Read to Me.** The book includes narration so the child can hear the book read aloud.

- **Read and Play.** The book includes narration as well as interactive features, such as playing games or drawing on the screen.

- **Read and Record.** You can record your voice reading the book aloud, so your kid can listen to it whenever he wants.

Before buying a kids' book, carefully read its description to make sure you're getting the features are most important to you and your children.

When you browse the Kids section of the NOOK Store, look for the Read and Play and Read to Me sections. The Read and Play section has books that are interactive, and the Read to Me section has books that will read themselves to your kids. Many Read and Play books frequently have the Read to Me feature as well.

No matter which section you choose, it's also a good idea to read the book description, because that may have more details, including what types of interactive features are included.

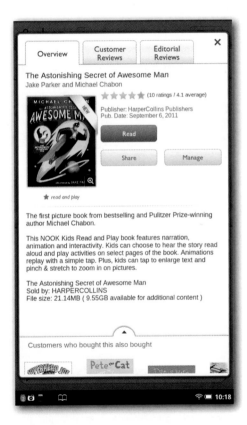

Reading a NOOK Kids Book

Open a NOOK Kids book as you do any other book—tap its cover. The book opens to landscape mode, so turn the NOOK to match its orientation. On the right-hand side of the screen you see the book cover, and on the left you find square buttons, letting you choose in which mode to open the book—Read by Myself, Read and Play, Read to Me, and Read and Record. The exact buttons that appear depend upon the capabilities built into the book.

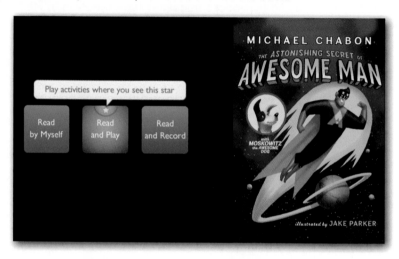

Read by Myself

If you and your child (or your child alone) want to read the book without narration, tap the Read by Myself button. That opens the book without using the audio track or narration, although the activities are still available—tap the white star when it appears at the top of the screen.

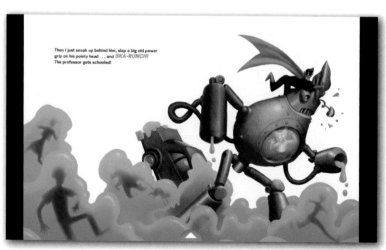

Go forward or back in the book as you would normally in a book: Swipe to the left or right to move forward or back a page, or tap the right (forward) or left (back) side of the screen.

If the text in a book is too small to read, double-tap it and you zoom in. Double-tap again or tap anywhere on the page to zoom out. If the book has an audio track, when you enlarge the text, you see a Play button in the shape of an orange triangle in the top-left corner. Tap that button to play the audio—and, yes, you can play it even if you've opened the book in Read by Myself mode. If there are any animations associated with the audio, they'll play as well.

NOTE When you turn the page after you've enlarged text, you see normal-size text on the next page, not the enlarged size. And if you've played audio on the page, the next page won't automatically play audio.

You can also zoom in on pictures by pinching out, as you normally do on the NOOK. When you're zoomed in you can also move the page around to get a better look at the picture you've zoomed in on, for example, moving it toward the center of the screen. Double-tap anywhere on the screen to zoom out and to return the page to its normal position.

When you come across a page with a star on it, that means you can play an activity, which can be just about anything—changing the colors on the page, drawing on the page, and more. Tap the star to run the activity. Arrows appear at either side of the page, the star turns into a square, and a narrator tells you about the activity and how you can play it—for example, tapping anywhere on a page to add mutant alien slime (thankfully it's onscreen only; no cleanup required).

To move to the next or previous page, tap either arrow. That's right, when you're playing, you tap arrows, rather than the screen margins. That's because, when you do an activity, the screen becomes active, so touching it spurs an action of some kind, like adding color instead of turning pages. If you want to stay on the same page but would like the activity to end, tap the square, and you go back to normal reading mode.

Listening to Read to Me and Read and Play Books

If you'd prefer to have the book read aloud to your child, tap the Read to Me or Read and Play button when you open the book. (Not all books have activities; if you open one that doesn't, there's no Read and Play button.)

At this point, nothing could be simpler: The book opens, and a narrator starts reading. The narration plays only for that page, and stops when the full page is read. To go on to the next page or back to the previous page, use your favorite page-turning gesture. When you get to the new page, the narration starts. If you want to go to the next or previous page in the middle of a page being read, just turn the page; the narration stops, and then begins reading the page to which you've turned.

Everything in the books works just like Read by Myself mode—you can zoom in and out of text and graphics, do activities when you see a star, and so on. When you do activities, the narration stops, but it continues if you zoom in and out of graphics and text.

Navigating Kids Books

When you're reading a NOOK Kids book, the Reading Tools menu doesn't work as it does in typical NOOK books. Tapping the center of the page does nothing. But if you tap the small up arrow at the bottom of the screen, you see a navigation toolbar with thumbnails of every page in the book. Swipe through the thumbnails, tap the page you want to read (or have read to you), and there you go. If you decide you don't want to go to another page, tap the down arrow or anywhere on the page to make the thumbnail navigation disappear.

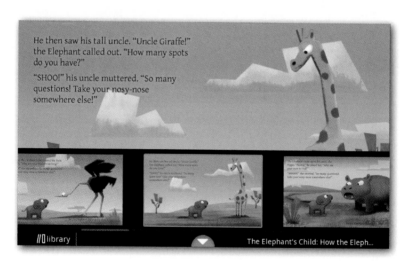

The thumbnails don't display the star that tells you whether pages have activities on them. So the only way to know whether there's an activity on a page is to go to it.

You can also get to the Kids Books section of your Library from the navigation toolbar; simply tap the Library icon. When you head there, the screen orientation changes to vertical.

Because there's no Reading Tools menu in Kids books, there's no way to get to a table of contents, no way to change the text display or brightness, and so on.

Record Reading a NOOK Kids Book for Your Kids

It's an unfortunate fact of parenting that you can't always be there to read to your kids when you want to be there. The NOOK offers the next best thing—the ability to record yourself reading a NOOK Kids book, so that you child can listen to you reading the book to her when you're not there. Whey she listens to you reading the book, it works just like listening to the normal reading of the book, except it's your voice. And, of course, you don't need to stick to the text of the page; you can add inside jokes, asides, and anything else you want to your recording. (We won't tell.)

As a way to encourage your child to read, you might want to record him reading the book. That way, he can listen to himself read the book afterward, and even read along with himself if he wants.

To record yourself reading a book, open the book and tap the Read and Record button. The first page of the book opens. Tap the green Record button to start recording your voice; the green button turns red, and an indicator appears, showing that you're reading. Tap the red Stop button to finish your recording.

The Elephant's Child
How the Elephant Got His Trunk

Read by Myself | Read to Me | Read and Record

by Rudyard Kipling

Adapted by Karen Baicker
Illustrated by Davin Cheng

Long ago, elephants had no trunks. They had only blackish, bulgy noses as big as boots. Their noses were suitable for sniffing and for wriggling side to side—but absolutely useless for picking things up.

In these far off times, there was one Elephant's Child in Africa who was born with endless curiosity. He asked ever-so-many questions, which got him ever-so-much trouble!

Done | Record | Move

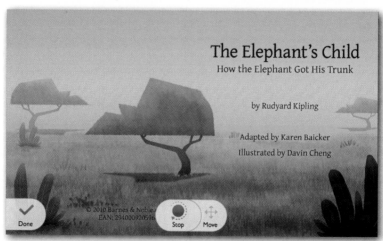

The Elephant's Child
How the Elephant Got His Trunk

by Rudyard Kipling

Adapted by Karen Baicker
Illustrated by Davin Cheng

Done | Stop | Move

The buttons on the bottom of the screen change. Tap Play to listen to your recording. While it's playing, you can pause it by tapping the Pause button. If after you listen to it you're not satisfied, tap Re-record and try again. When you're finished, move on to the next page using the normal way of moving through NOOK books.

Sometimes as you're trying to record yourself reading the book, the Record and other buttons may cover up the text. If that happens, put your finger on the Move button and drag the set of buttons somewhere else.

NOTE If you're recording yourself reading a book and for some reason you switch away from the book, for example to read another book, the NOOK automatically saves your recording. For details about editing a recording, see page 137.

Keep recording yourself until you've finished recording the entire book, or until you want to stop recording for now. As you'll see on page 137, you can always come back later and finish the book or re-record what you've already read.

When you're ready, tap Done. A window appears that lets you name the recording and choose a picture associated with it. This name and picture will appear when your child opens the book, so choose words that mean something to her. Keep it short and easy for your child to read.

The next time your child (or you) opens the book, your recording will be listed on a button at the bottom left of the screen. All he'll need to do is tap it. If he'd prefer to hear the original recording rather than you (no dessert for him if he does!), he can tap the Read to Me button instead.

You can have more than one recording for each book. After you've recorded one, when you open the book, tap Read and Record and record a second one, giving it a different name and picture. So you might record one, your spouse another, and your kids yet others.

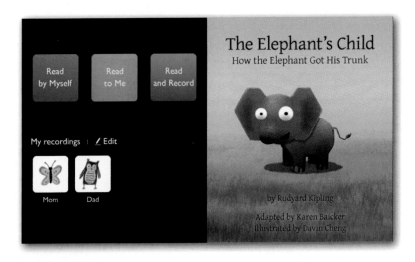

TIP Unlike the audio track that comes with a NOOK Kids book, your recording is not saved as part of the book itself. Instead, it's saved as a separate audio file in the device's My Files section. For details about how to handle that recording, and even listen to it separately from the book itself, see page 139.

Editing or Deleting a Recording

It's easy to edit or delete a recording. After all, even professional voice artists rarely get it perfect in the first take. When you open the book, tap the Edit button, and gray Edit buttons appear beneath all of your recordings. Tap the Edit button next to the recording you want to edit or record, and here's what you can do:

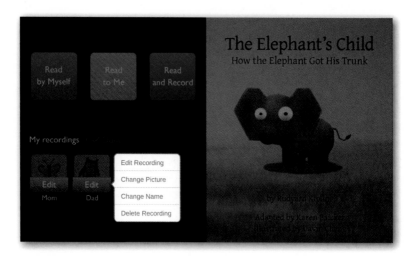

- **Edit Recording.** Sends you to the first page of the book with the Re-record, Play, and Done buttons visible.

- **Change Picture.** Takes you to a window where you can choose a new picture for the recording.

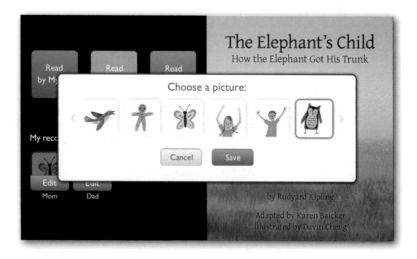

- **Change Name.** Takes you to a window where you can choose a new name for the recording.

- **Delete Recording.** Deletes the recording, but not immediately. Instead, you'll be asked whether you really, truly do want to delete it.

Tips for Better Recording

When your kids hear you reading to them, you obviously want them to hear your voice as clearly as possible, instead of sounding as if you were talking into a tin can. So follow these tips, and they should hear you loud and clear:

- **Speak slowly and distinctly.** Most people talk too quickly when they record audio. Remember, this isn't a race; it's something you want your kids to enjoy.

- **Practice reading each page a few times before recording it.** That way, you'll learn what words and syllables to emphasize, and what kind of emotion you want to put into your voice.

- **Make sure there's as little background noise as possible.** Car horns and emergency sirens don't make for the most pleasant listening experience.

- **Hold your NOOK between a foot and a foot and a half from your face.** That's the optimum distance so that your voice will be recorded clearly with no distortion.

- **Don't cover the microphone with your fingers.** The microphone is a small hole on the upper-right side of the NOOK, to the left of the sound jack. If you cover it up, your voice won't be heard.

Backing Up Your Recordings

When you record yourself reading a book, it isn't saved along with the book itself, as is the book's original audio track. Instead, it's saved on your NOOK's internal storage, and a bit of programming magic merges the audio track with the book when you play it.

NOTE Your NOOK Tablet stores your recordings on its internal storage, not on an SD card if you've installed one.

Why should you care? If you ever erase all of your NOOK's content and deregister it (see page 44) you can copy the files to your computer so that you'll always always have them. Otherwise, when you deregister your device, the recordings will be lost forever. You can also listen to them in the NOOK's Media Player, rather than in the book itself. (Is this a useful or practical thing to do? Not really. Then why do it? Because you can.)

To do it, first browse to see the audio files themselves. In the Library, tap the "My stuff" button at top right and select My Files. Then tap NOOK Kids Recordings. You'll come to a folder named something really useful and enlightening, like 2940000920596. Tap it and you'll come to more folders with even longer and more confusing names. Each of those folders contains all of your recordings for an individual NOOK Kids book.

Back these up to a personal computer if you want to preserve them.

If you want to listen to them on your NOOK Tablet's Media Player, tap any folder, and then look for any files that end in .m4a—1.m4a, 2.m4a, and so on. Tap any of the recordings. It opens in the NOOK's Media Player and you hear the recording. (For details about using the NOOK's Media Player, see page 254.)

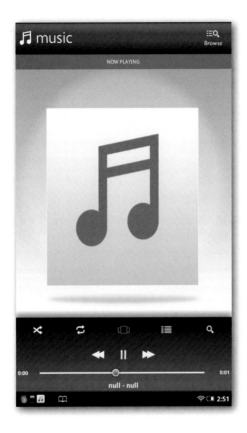

Buying, Borrowing, and Managing Your Library

CHAPTER 6

Buying Books, Magazines, and Newspapers and Managing Your Library

THE NOOK TABLET IS your entrée into the world of books, magazines, newspapers, and apps—literally millions of them. And you get them all through the NOOK Store. Once you've downloaded books, they live in your NOOK's Library. In this chapter you'll learn how to buy books and periodicals in the NOOK Store and how to manage your Library.

NOTE When you buy a book, newspaper, or magazine, it's available not just on your NOOK, but also to a NOOK app if you have one on another smartphone or tablet, as well as on a personal computer. See page 177 for details.

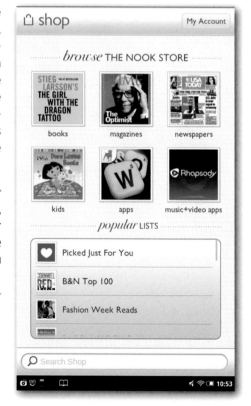

Browsing and Searching for Books in the NOOK Store

To get to the NOOK Store, tap Shop from the Quick Nav bar, or tap a Shop icon if you've placed it on one of the panels in your Home screen. You go straight to the NOOK Store.

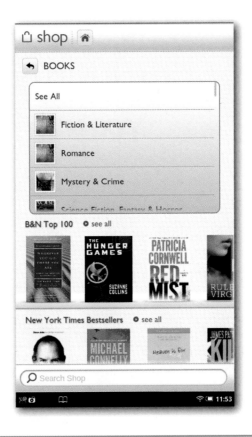

NOTE You can get to the NOOK Store only when you're connected to a WiFi network.

Toward the top of the page are categories—Books, Magazines, Newspapers, Kids, Apps, and so on. Just beneath that there's a scrollable changing set of lists of books and more, such as B&N Top 100, Cool NOOK Books, Picked Just For You (based on your previous purchases), and more. Then at the very bottom of the page, there's a search box so you can look for specific books.

TIP Here's another quick way to find books to buy—tap the Books media shortcut toward the bottom of your Home screen. The screen that appears shows you not just books you've recently been reading, but also a link for browsing the B&N top 100–selling books.

Tap Books, and you come to a page with a scrollable list of categories at the top (Fiction & Literature, Romance, Mystery & Crime, and so on), and several types of lists beneath it, including B&N Top 100, New York Times Bestsellers, and more.

To see a category, tap it and you arrive at a screen with a scrollable list of sub-categories at top, and bestselling books in that category at bottom. Tap a sub-category, and you either see a list of books, or come to yet another subcategory list, and so on, until you've finally gotten to the precise sub-sub-sub...(you get the idea)...category of book you're interested in. For example, you may start off with Books, then get to the Fiction & Literature category, then to the Mystery & Crime subcategory, then to the Women Detectives – Fiction sub-subcategory.

If a book has a banner (which the NOOK calls a *badge*) with LendMe across it, it means that after you buy the book, you can lend it to your NOOK Friends. See page 182 for details.

When you get there, you see a scrollable list of books in that subcategory, with the bestselling book in that subcategory at the top, then the next bestselling, and so on. You see the title, cover, description, price, and customer rating for each book. Tap the book to see more information about it (for details, see page 152).

No matter where you are in the NOOK Store, you can get to the store's opening screen, its front door. Tap the icon of the house at the top left of the screen.

What if you want to look at a list of titles in a different order? Up at the top of the screen, tap the drop-down arrow next to Best Selling, and you can choose to see the books in a different order—the newest first, oldest first, in alphabetical order, reverse alphabetical order, by price, and so on.

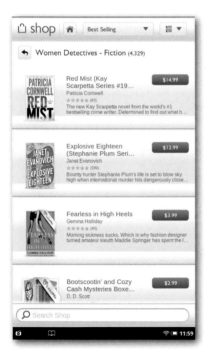

You can even change the way the list looks. Tap the down arrow at top right, and a drop-down list appears that lets you display the books in a grid instead of a list, or lets you see the books in list form with small icons or large icons.

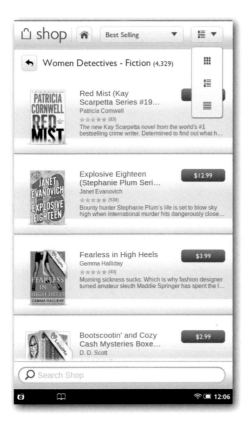

Searching for Books

If you're on a more targeted mission than leisurely browsing—if there's a particular book, author, or topic you're interested in—tap in a search term (or a few terms) into the search box at the bottom of the screen. As you type, the search results narrow down. Tap a result to launch that search, or finish typing your search terms and then tap the Search button on the keyboard.

When you first tap into the search box, you see a list of previous searches you've launched. Tap any to launch it again.

TIP The NOOK Store has many, many books you can download and read for free, ranging from the classics from authors like Charles Dickens and Jane Austen to reference books and contemporary novels. You won't find them in any one category, though. So if you're looking for free books, search for "free books for nook" in the store and you'll pull up a massive list.

After you do a search, your results appear in a moment or two. Handle the results list just like any subcategory list—reorder the results and change the way they're displayed to your heart's content.

Sampling and Buying Books

Now that you're done searching and browsing, it's time to take the plunge and buy a book. As you're browsing or searching, you'll see a green button next to any book you can buy, marked with the price. If there's no green button, then you've already bought the book, and you instead see a gray label with the word "Purchased" where the price would normally be.

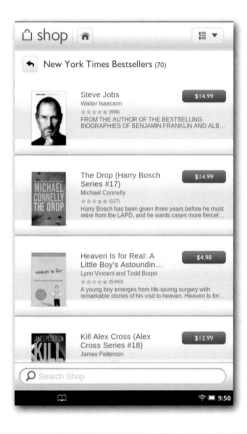

NOTE You can also preorder a book that hasn't yet been released. If the book hasn't been released yet, the word "Preorder" appears on the green button instead of the price.

You can buy the book by tapping the green button with the price on it anytime—but you don't have to commit yet. Say you want more information before you're ready to buy. Rather than tapping the green button, tap anywhere else in the book description. A screen appears with plenty of information about the book. It's divided into three tabs:

- **Overview.** Provides a good deal of information about the book, including customer ratings on a five-star scale (and the total number of people who have reviewed it), a lengthy description of the book, and buttons for getting a free sample or sharing the book. (For more details about sharing, see page 92.)

- Down at the bottom of the screen, there's a small up arrow. Tap it, and a screen rolls up showing you a list of the books that other purchasers of this book have bought, and a list of other books the author has written. Tap the down arrow, and the screen rolls back down.

TIP If you think you may want to buy the book at some point but not just yet, add it to your NOOK wish list by tapping "Add to Wishlist" on the Overview Tab. You can get to the list at any point when you tap the My Account button in the upper-right corner of the Shop (page 179). Keep in mind, though, that your NOOK's wish list is separate from your wish list on the BN.com website. The BN.com wish list contains items that you can't buy on your NOOK (paper-only books and paper-only newspapers and magazines), while the NOOK contains only items you can buy on the NOOK, which includes apps, not just books and periodicals.

- **Customer Reviews.** Here's where you can read the reviews. You can also rate each review as to how helpful it was, and report the review if you think something is fishy about it the author rating his own book, perhaps or if it contains material that violates B&N terms of conduct.

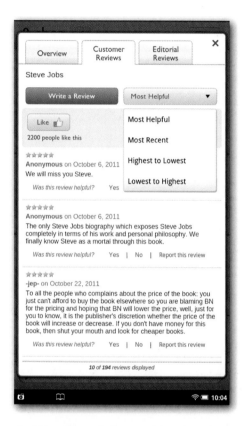

It can be tough sifting through the useful and useless reviews, so the NOOK has thoughtfully given you a tool to help find the useful ones. Toward the top of the screen there's a Most Helpful drop-down menu that lets you view reviews starting with the most helpful, the most recent, the highest ratings, or the lowest ratings.

- **Editorial Reviews.** Want to know what professional reviewers have said about the book? Tap this tab, and if there are any professional reviews, you'll see them here.

Sampling Books

Say you've gone through all this material and you're still not quite sure you want to buy. You're interested but not yet sold. Tap back over to the Overview tab, and tap Free Sample. You can then read a section of the book before deciding whether you want to shell out for it.

After a few moments the sample downloads, and you'll see the word "New" on the book cover. To read the sample, tap the Read Sample button.

The book now also shows up on your Daily Shelf (page 56) with the word "New" on the cover. Tap it to read the sample.

You can now read the book as you would normally. The difference, of course, is that you won't be able to read the entire book. The other difference is that a Buy Now button appears on all the pages.

> **TIP** What if the sample you've downloaded isn't sufficient for you to make a buying decision, and you want to read even more? Head over to your closest Barnes & Noble store. When you're in a B&N store, you get an hour of reading any NOOK book for free.

Buying Books

Time to buy the book. Whether you're browsing a book and tap the green button, tap the green button on the Overview Tab, or tap Buy Now when you're reading a sample, you'll buy it essentially the same way, with some variations:

- If you tap the green button when browsing or on the Overview tab, a Confirm button replaces the green price button.

- If you tap Buy Now when reading a sample, you'll get sent back to the Overview tab, where you can tap the green price button to buy.

NOTE After you buy a book or a magazine, Barnes & Noble will send you an email confirming your purchase.

When you tap to buy, what happens next depends upon whether you've customized the Shop (page 416). If you haven't done any customization, and just left the Shop set up as is, then when you tap the Confirm button, the book downloads, and the credit card you had on file when you registered the NOOK is charged. If you've told the Shop to first ask you to enter your B&N account password before you buy anything, enter your password. Either way, your credit card is charged, the book downloads, and you can start reading. The book shows up on your Daily Shelf and in your Library.

Browsing and Buying Magazines and Newspapers

You browse, search for, and buy magazines and newspaper from the NOOK Store the same way you do books. At the top level of the store, just tap Magazines or Newspapers instead of Books and start browsing. Same for searching.

There are only a few minor differences between buying magazines and newspapers instead of books:

- You generally can't download samples of magazines.

- When you buy a magazine or newspaper, you can buy a single issue (the current one), or else subscribe to the periodical.

- New NOOK customers can get free 14-day subscriptions to magazines and newspapers.

Using the Library to Manage Your Books and Periodicals

When you buy books, magazines, and newspapers, they show up on the Daily Shelf, and you can read them from there, or drag them to your Home screen so they're always available. But after a while the books and periodicals vanish from the Daily Shelf because new items are continually added (page 56). And you can't put *all* of your books and periodicals on the Home screen, because it will quickly fill up.

That's where the Library comes in. It's the central location for all your books, newspapers, magazines, and more. Get there by tapping the Library icon on the Quick Nav bar. Here's what you can access from the Library:

- All the books, newspapers, magazines, and other materials you bought from the NOOK Store.

- Books you've borrowed from NOOK Friends or your local library. (See Chapter 7 for details.)

- Files such as music files, Microsoft Office files (Word, Excel, PowerPoint), PDF files, and books in the EPUB format that you've transferred to your NOOK from your PC or Mac. (See page 282 for details.)

- Files (the same ones as mentioned in the previous point) that you've stored on your SD card, if you've installed one. (See Chapter 11 for details.)

The Library is divided into several sections to make it easier to find and manage everything:

- **Media bar.** This row of icons across the top of the screen sends you to different areas of the Library, based on their content—Books, Magazines, Newspapers, Apps, and so on. Tap any icon to get to that section. (For more details about the Media bar, see the next page.)

- **Library content.** Here's the reason you go to the Library in the first place—for the content you have there. This section changes according to what area of the Library you're in—Books, Magazines, Newspapers, Apps, and so on.

- **Search box.** Tap here and search the Library. No matter what area of the Library you're in, you'll search the entire Library, not just that section (page 74).

- **Sync button.** If you've bought books, publications, or other items for the NOOK from another device such as a tablet, computer, or smartphone, tapping this button downloads them to your NOOK.

- **Sorting and viewing options.** Up at the top of your screen there are two buttons for sorting and viewing your books in a variety of different ways (page 165).

There's lots to know about the Library. First, you'll start with the Media bar.

The Media Bar

The Media bar is the main way you'll navigate through your Library and see all your content. Here are the areas it lets you go to on your NOOK:

- **Books** shows all the books you've downloaded from the NOOK Store.

- **Magazines** shows all the magazines you've bought from the NOOK Store.

- **Newspapers** shows all the newspapers you've bought from the NOOK Store.

- **Apps** shows all the apps on your NOOK. Not only does it show the apps that come preloaded, such as for email and Netflix, but also all the apps that you've downloaded. (See Chapter 9 for more details on apps.)

- **Kids** shows children's books and magazines you've bought, including NOOK Kids Books.

- **My stuff,** which drops down a menu that lets you navigate to even more areas, including My Shelves (your personalized bookshelves); My Files (shows files that you've transferred to your NOOK from your personal computer, including to an SD card if you've installed one); LendMe (lets you borrow and lend books and shows your borrowed and lent books; as discussed on page 182); Everything Else (shows a variety of items that can't be displayed on your NOOK, such as the NOOK Study eTexbooks that are in your BN Lifetime Library); and Archived, which are books and periodicals that you've archived into the B&N Lifetime Library.

NOTE You see the Everything Else section only if you have items in your B&N Lifetime Library that the NOOK can't display.

The Content Area and Badges

The content area is where you'll spend most of your time in the Library. After all, that's the whole reason you're there. Using it is straightforward: Tap a book or periodical you want to read, an app you want to run, and so on, depending upon what area of the Library you're in. That's all there is to it. If any area has more content on its shelves that can fit in a single screen, flick to see more shelves.

When you're in the Books area, you'll see the books' covers, but no further description. In the magazine area, you'll see the magazines' covers, plus their issue dates. When you're browsing newspapers, you'll see the front page of each newspaper, as well as the headline of the lead story, and its beginning text.

If you buy a book or periodical and it isn't fully downloaded yet, there's a Download banner (which the NOOK calls a *badge*) on it. You also see a bar on the cover that shows how much of the book has been downloaded, and how much is left to go.

There are plenty more badges on book and periodical covers you'll likely come across in the Library, most notably these:

- **Download.** Indicates that the book or periodical hasn't yet been downloaded, or is in the process of downloading. If it hasn't been downloaded, tap to do the deed.

- **New.** The item has recently been downloaded to your NOOK and is anxiously waiting to be read.

- **Sample.** A free excerpt of a book or periodical. These samples generally don't time out and will live forever, but they're only a portion of the book or publication.

- **Recommended.** A NOOK Friend has recommended the item to you. For details, see page 93.

- **LendMe.** You can lend this to a friend. For details, see page 182.

- **Lent.** You've borrowed this item from someone or from a library. The badge indicates how many days are left in the borrowing period. Typically you can borrow something for up to 14 days.

- **Pre-order.** The item isn't yet available for sale, but if you want it as soon as it's released, you can order it ahead of time.

NOTE Books that you've copied to your NOOK Tablet's SD card don't have badges on them. However, they have a small NOOK icon in their lower-right corner to show that they're stored on your SD card.

Nifty Options for Items in Your Library

To read a book or periodical, or to run an app, just tap it. But there's plenty more you can do with your books, magazines, and newspapers (and apps) in the Library. Press and hold your finger on a book, and you get the following choices:

- **Read.** Opens the book, newspaper, or magazine to read. Why open this menu rather than simply tapping the book? Only you can answer that.

NOTE When you press and hold on an item, the menu shows you only appropriate choices—for example, Read, Add to Shelf, and other bookish options don't show up when you hold your finger on an app, and Open doesn't appear when you hold your finger on a book.

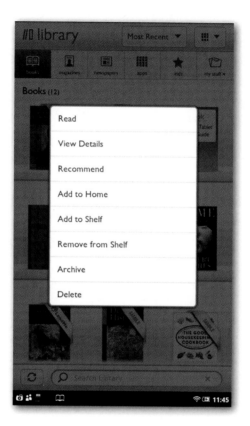

- **View details.** Shows you details about the book or periodical. It's the same information you saw on the screen before buying.

- **Open.** Runs an app.

- **Recommend.** Lets you recommend the book or periodical to a friend. Turn to page 93 for details.

- **Add to Home.** Puts a shortcut to the item on your Home screen.

- **Add to Shelf.** Lets you add it to a shelf that you've created in My Shelf. (See page 161 for details.)

- **Remove from Shelf.** Lets you remove it from a shelf.

- **Archive.** Moves it off of your NOOK, but still keeps it accessible whenever you want. See page 171 for details.

- **Delete.** Deletes the item from your NOOK. Be careful when choosing this, because unlike with archiving, you can't retrieve the item if you change your mind later. If you decide at some later point you want to read it again, you'll have to buy it again.

Changing the Library View and Re-Sorting the Library

At the top of the Library, you'll find two large buttons for changing the order in which the Library displays your items and the way they're displayed:

- **Change the sort order.** Tap this button, and you can change the order in which items are displayed. The options available here vary according to what section of the Library you're in. In Books and Kids, you can sort by Most Recent, Title, and Author. In Magazines and Newspapers, you can sort by Most Recent and Title. In Apps, you can sort by Most Recent, App Name, and Category.

- **Change the display.** Gives you control over how the items are displayed. Out of the box, the NOOK displays them on a grid of shelves, with large pictures and very little detail about each item—for example, in Books, just the book cover.

The second choice from the top also only shows the book cover, but labels the shelves, so there are fewer items on each shelf.

The third choice from the top shows a detailed list of the items, including, in the Books area, author, rating, review summary, and description.

The bottom choice shows a simple list with fewer details. In the Books area, for example, you'll see the title and author only.

Organizing Your Library by Using Shelves

If you buy enough books or periodicals (which of course you do—why else do you have a NOOK?) you may find that the Library's organization options aren't enough. What if you want to browse your collection of literary novels, mystery novels written by women, or books about footwear in 17th century France? (OK, maybe that last collection isn't big enough to *browse* through, but you get the idea.)

There's a simple solution: Organize your books (or other Library items) into shelves, just as you would on a physical bookshelf. You get to decide which books to keep together so you can find them easily.

To organize your books into shelves, tap the "My stuff" icon in the Library, and then choose My Shelves. Here's what to do next:

❶ **Tap Create New Shelf.**

❷ **On the My Shelves screen that appears, type the Name for your new shelf. Tap Save.** You end up back on My Shelves screen again, with the new (and still empty) shelf on it.

> **NOTE** You're limited to 100 characters when naming a new shelf. In a world in which you're limited to 140 characters for messages in Twitter, that should be no problem.

> **NOTE** The NOOK automatically creates a shelf for you called Favorites. Put items in that shelf the same way you put items in any shelf that you create.

❸ Tap the Edit button next to the shelf where you want to put items. A screen appears with all the items in your Library. Tap the box next to any item you want to put on the shelf. A checkmark appears next to it. If you've already got items in the shelf, those items also have checkmarks.

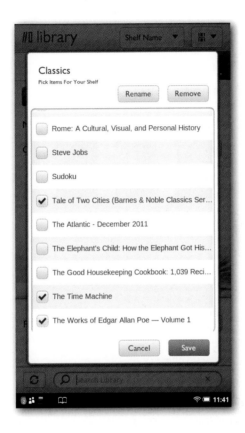

NOTE Your shelves can hold any item you've got in your Library, so you can mix apps, with books and periodicals. So, for example, if you're a crossword fan, you can create a Crossword shelf, and put in it crossword puzzle books, dictionaries, and crossword apps.

❹ **When you're done, tap Save.** You arrive back on your My Shelves screen, and the new shelf displays your items.

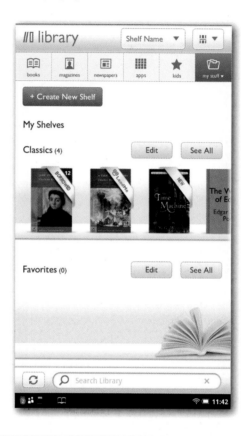

NOTE You can put items that you've borrowed onto a shelf. However, when the borrowing period expires, the item disappears there.

Once you've created a shelf, it's easy to add or remove items from it, or edit its name. Go back to the My Shelves area from the "My stuff" menu, and then tap Edit next to the shelf you want to edit. Tap Rename to rename the shelf, and add and remove items in the usual way.

You can also remove an entire shelf. When you tap the Edit button next to the shelf you want to delete, tap Remove. This removes the Shelf, but all the items in it remain on your NOOK.

Archiving Books and Periodicals

Your NOOK Tablet has plenty of storage space, and if you add an SD card, you get even more. Still, there may come a time when you begin to run out of space—or feel as if you are. In that case, you can archive books and periodicals. When you archive them, the books are still stored in your Barnes & Noble account on the Web, and you can have them sent to your NOOK Tablet whenever you wish by a simple process called unarchiving.

> **NOTE** Have you ever heard the terms *cloud* or *cloud storage*? If you read technology news, you probably have. The cloud refers to storage space on the Internet that you can access whenever you want, from any Internet-connected device. You don't need to store the item on any computer or gadget. When you archive items, you're using your own personal cloud, courtesy of Barnes & Noble. Welcome to the cloud.

Basic information about your archived items stays on your NOOK, including its cover, title, author, and description. This information stays in your Library, on your shelves, and it's searchable so you'll always be able to find things you've archived, and get them back on your NOOK at a moment's notice. As you can see, archiving is an easy way to save on storage space.

To archive an item, head to the Library. Press and hold your finger on an item, and choose Archive from the menu. The item is immediately archived. It disappears from the content area of the Library, but shows up in a shelf labeled Archived in the My Files area. To get to it, tap "My stuff"→Archived.

If you've created any personal shelves, the item also shows up there. And if you do any searches, you'll find it as well.

> **NOTE** You can't archive items that you've copied to your SD card.

To unarchive an item, hold your finger on it and select Unarchive. It's sent back to your NOOK, and appears just as it always did, no harm done.

Using The Wishlist

When you're browsing and searching for books, magazines, apps, and newspapers, you'll often come across items that you're not quite ready to buy yet, but you might want to later. That's where the NOOK's wishlist comes in. When you come across something you think you may want to buy at some point, add it to your wish list.

NOTE The wish list on your NOOK is separate from the wish list on your BN.com account. The wish list on your BN.com account includes printed books and periodicals for your NOOK, and other items you can buy on BN.com, while your NOOK's wish list only has items for your NOOK.

To add a book, newspaper, or magazine to your wish list, when you tap its cover and come to the Details page, simply tap the box next to "Add to Wishlist" so the box turns green. It's been added to your wish list.

To view your wish list, go to the top screen of the Shop. The wish list is accessible only from the top screen, so if you're browsing, searching, or doing anything else in the Shop you'll have to get to the top screen. To get there, tap the Home button at the top of any screen when you're in the Shop.

Once you're on the top screen, tap My Account and select My Wishlist. From here, you can buy books, periodicals, and apps as you would normally.

Accessing Content on Your SD Card and NOOK Tablet's Built-in Storage

The Library also offers an easy way to view files and content you've transferred to your SD card or to the NOOK's built-in storage—use the Library's My Files feature. (See Chapter 11 for details about how to transfer files to the SD card.)

To get there, tap the "My stuff" button and select My Files. You'll come to a screen with two sections, My NOOK, and Memory Card.

> **NOTE** If you haven't installed an SD card, the Memory Card option doesn't appear.

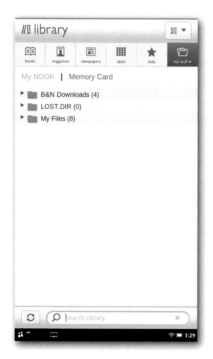 

You see the folder structure on your SD card, most likely with three sections: B&N Downloads, LOST.DIR, and My Files. B&N Downloads are for any downloads that you've moved to your SD card, and My Files is the folder you'll use for other files that you move to your SD card from your computer. As for LOST.DIR, you can generally ignore it. If the NOOK determines that you've moved any files that are corrupted or have other kinds of problems, it moves them or copies of them here.

Even if you don't have an SD card, you can still transfer files to your NOOK. If you want to see files and books you've transferred to your NOOK, tap the My NOOK button. Go to the My Files folder, just as on the SD card.

Tap the folder you want to browse, such as My Files. You see either the files themselves, or subfolders. Under My Files, for example, you see a variety of folders, including Books, Documents, Magazines, Music, Newspapers, and so on.

Tap the folder that has the files you want to read or view. In the list that appears, tap any to open it. For more details about what files you can view on your NOOK, see page Appendix B.

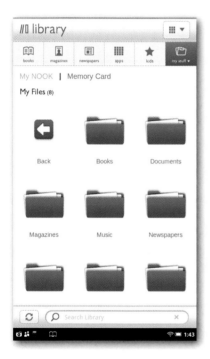

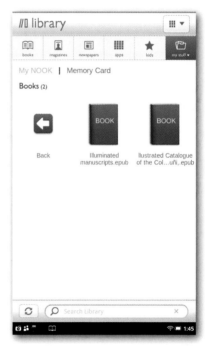

You can change the folder structure on your SD Card—deleting folders, renaming them, adding them, and so on. You do that not on your NOOK, but by connecting your NOOK to your PC or Mac using the USB cable (page 23). From your PC or Mac, you can then edit the folders just as you can any folder on your computer.

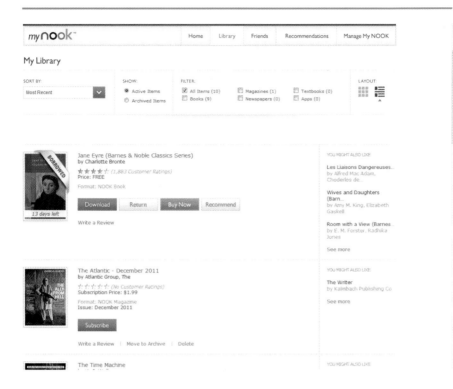

SD Cards and Your Library

When you read a book using your NOOK, you're reading it in a format called EPUB. If you transfer EPUB files to your SD card from your computer, those files show up in your Library. They likely won't have their cover, but they'll show up like other books, with their title, author, and so on. The covers are plain gray, and there's a small NOOK icon on the lower right. You can put them in shelves and search for them, just like other books. But you can't archive them or recommend them to others.

The Library on BN.com, PCs, Macs, and Mobile Devices

One of the many great things about the NOOK is that it's not a literary island. When you download a book to your NOOK, you can read it other places as well—on the Barnes & Noble website, your PC or Mac, as well as on Android phones and tablets, and on iPhones and iPads.

To view your Library and read books on the Web, head to *www.bn.com* and click the My NOOK button at the top of the page. Once you're logged in, click the Library tab, and you'll come to your NOOK Library. From here you can manage books, read them if you've downloaded a NOOK reader, recommend them, and so on.

The site offers additional features, including getting recommendations, interacting with NOOK Friends, and so on.

To read books on your PC or Mac, you need to download Barnes & Noble's free eReader app. The NOOK app does more than just let you read books—it offers a NOOK-like experience, including browsing and searching your Library.

Search in the Apple App Store or in the Android Market for the NOOK app. You can also go direcly to the BN.com download page by typing this address into your browser: *http://bit.ly/vBjE2B*. The app looks and works a bit differently for different devices, but on all of them you can browse your Library, and download and read books.

Managing your NOOK Account

Every NOOK has a NOOK account on it, with important information—your credit card number, any gift cards you've received, and so on. If you want to change your credit card, view your wish list, add a gift card, or look at items you've recently viewed, your NOOK account is the place to go.

To get there, go to the top screen of the Shop. The wish list is accessible only from the top screen, so if you're browsing, searching, or doing anything else in the Shop, you must get to the top screen. To get there, tap the Home button at the top of any screen when you're in the Shop.

Once you're there, tap the My Account button. You then have the following four choices:

- **My Credit Cards.** Here's where you find your credit card information, and where you can change it. Tap this option, and from the screen that appears, tap Change Default Credit Card to change the credit card you use when you buy things on the NOOK. You can have only one credit card on your NOOK.

NOTE Your BN.com account can have more than one credit card associated with it, but not your NOOK.

- **My Gift Cards.** If you've gotten any NOOK gift cards, here's where you find them. They don't get added to your NOOK automatically; you have to enter them manually. So when you get a NOOK Gift Card, head here and enter the information.

- **My Wishlist.** Here's where to manage your NOOK's wish list. See page 172 for details. Keep in mind that the NOOK wish list is separate from your BN.com wish list, so head to BN.com on the Web if you want to see your BN.com wish list.

- **Recently viewed.** Tap here to see the items you've recently viewed in the Shop.

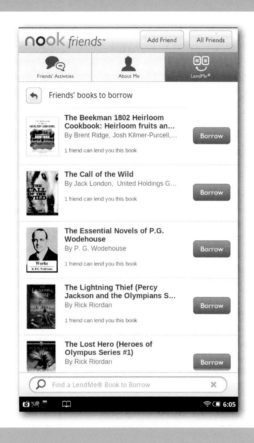

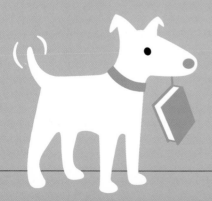

CHAPTER 7

Borrowing and Lending Books with LendMe and Your Local Library

WITH YOUR NOOK TABLET, you can borrow books from friends and lend them books, and also borrow books from your local library. In fact, in some ways it's even easier to share books with the NOOK Tablet than with printed books, because you don't need to physically hand off or collect a book. All it takes is a few taps on your NOOK Tablet.

But how to do it? Which books can and can't you lend? How long can you borrow and lend them for? Read on; this chapter has all you need to know.

Both a Borrower and a Lender Be

You have two ways to lend and borrow books with your NOOK Tablet: Using the NOOK Tablet's LendMe features to borrow and lend books with your NOOK Friends, or borrowing books from the library.

Keep in mind that you can't lend out every book you own, or borrow every book your friends own. The same holds true with library books: You can borrow books that the library assigns for borrowing.

Borrowing and lending may strike you as an odd concept when it comes to NOOK books, because there's no physical object to hand over or take in. In fact, though, an eBook is a physical object of sorts, even though it's made up of bits and bytes rather than paper and print.

When you buy a book using your NOOK, you're downloading an eBook, but that eBook is very different from a physical book on one important way: eBooks are protected with DRM (see the tip on page 81), while physical books aren't.

DRM essentially links a book to your use on the NOOK Tablet, or any NOOK reader, such as one for a PC, smartphone, or tablet. So you can't simply lend any NOOK book to anyone, or borrow any NOOK book from anyone. The book has to be coded to let it be lent, and not all books have this coding embedded in them.

Why is that coding necessary? Without it, any eBook could literally be given free of charge to millions of people, by someone simply posting it on the Internet, and other people downloading it. If all books were available for free like this, publishers couldn't stay in business, and authors couldn't make a living (including yours truly).

Bottom line: There are certain restrictions and rules about which books can be lent, how they can be lent, and for how long.

With that background out of the way, it's time to take a look at how to borrow and lend books, first from your local library, and then between friends.

Lending and Borrowing Books with LendMe

The NOOK Tablet's LendMe feature is available directly from the Library as well as through NOOK Friends, so it's always within easy reach. Before getting started with it, here are some things you need to know:

- **Only some books can be lent and borrowed.** Those that can be lent will have a LendMe badge across their cover. That way, you know before buying or downloading a book whether it can be lent out. And when it's in your Library, you can easily see which books you can lend. You'll see the badge when you're browsing in the Library as well as on the detail page you come to when you tap the cover.

TIP
You may think that all books you can download for free from the NOOK Store are lendable. After all, they're free. That's not the case, though; some free books are blocked from lending. So if you're planning to download a free book and want to lend it out, check to see whether there are multiple editions of the book. Sometimes, particularly with classic fiction from authors like Dickens, there are many free editions of a single book, some of which are lendable, and some of which aren't.

- **A book can be lent out only once.** Once you've lent the book, you can't lend it again.

- **You can't read a book while it's lent to someone.** Only one account at a time has access to a book, so during the time you've lent it to someone, you can't read it.

- **Loans last for 14 days**. At the end of that time, it's no longer available to the person to whom you've lent it. If you've borrowed a book, you can only use it for 14 days. As soon as the time expires, it's again available to the lender.

- **You can lend a book only if you've registered your NOOK Tablet or NOOK Color.** The lending feature doesn't work on an unregistered NOOK Tablet or NOOK Color.

- **Someone borrowing a book must have a Barnes & Noble account with a valid credit card.** No account, no book.

- **Borrowing is free.** No money is charged to either the lender or the borrower.

- **You can lend only one book at a time.** You have to wait until a book is returned to you before you can lend another book.

- **You can't lend a book that someone has lent to you.**

- **You can't copy a borrowed book to your microSD card.**

Seeing Your List of Lendable Books

You have several ways to find which of your books are available for lending. One is to browse around the Library: The LendMe sash appears on any books available for lending.

Depending on whether you've lent and borrowed books before, you'll see the following sashes:

- **LendMe.** As explained on page 182, you can lend this book.

- **Borrowed.** A book you've borrowed from someone. Tap to read it. When you read it, a Buy Now button appears at the top of the screen, in case you decide you want to buy the book at any point while you're reading it.

- **Lent.** A book that's currently lent to someone, or that you've offered to lend, but the potential borrower has yet to accept or decline.

- **Lent to You.** A book that someone has offered to lend to you, but you haven't yet accepted or declined. Tap it to accept or decline.

There's an even better way to see them all in the Library, so that you'll see only books available for borrowing or lending. In the Library, tap "my stuff"→LendMe. You'll find several shelves of books there:

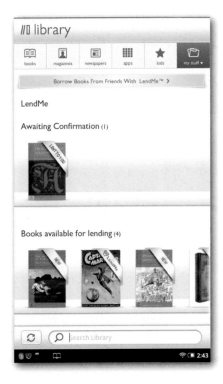

- **Borrowed.** Books you're currently borrowing. A number next to the Borrowed sash shows how many days you've got left before the book gets returned to the lender.

- **Awaiting Confirmation.** Books someone has offered to lend you. Tap to borrow the book or decline it.

- **Books available for lending.** All your books that can be lent.

NOTE Books you've already lent out don't show up in the Borrowed shelf.

- **Lent to others.** All the books that are currently on loan to other people.

The one last place to go to see what books you can lend is NOOK Friends (Chapter 14). In the NOOK Friends app, tap LendMe. There you'll see four shelves:

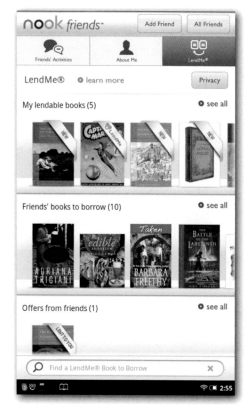

- **My lendable books.** All the books you have that can be lent.

- **Friends' books to borrow.** A great place to go if you're looking to borrow books. It lists all the lendable books from your friends. Tap any to request it. (See page 194 for details.)

- **Offers from friends.** The books that friends have offered to lend you. Tap to accept or decline.
- **Requests.** Requests from friends who've asked to borrow a book. Tap to lend the book or to decline the request.

Lending a Book

There are two ways you can lend a book to someone—offering to lend it on your own, because you think someone may want to read it, or by responding to a friend's request to borrow a book. The following sections cover both scenarios.

Making an Offer to Lend a Book

Let's say you've just read Dickens' *Nicholas Nickleby* for the first (or seventh) time and you have a friend who you know will enjoy the book. You'd like to recommend and lend the book to her.

There are three—count 'em, three—ways you can get to a screen that lets you lend a book to a NOOK Friend. Here's how to get to the screen, and what to do once you get there:

- **Launch the NOOK Friends app (page 362) and tap the LendMe button.** Then tap any book in the My Lendable Books section. A screen appears that lets you send an offer to lend the book via Contacts or Facebook. If you choose Contacts, a screen appears that lets you select your contact and type a message to her. The offer is sent via email. Your friend can then click a link in the email to accept or decline the offer.

If you choose Facebook, select the Facebook contact to whom you want to lend the book, and then type in a message. The message will be posted on your friend's Facebook Wall, and Facebook will also send a notification to her via email about the offer to lend. She can click the message on her Wall to accept or decline the offer.

TIP Someone doesn't have to be a NOOK Friend in order for you to send her an invitation to borrow a book. However, if you want to send her an offer to borrow a book via email or Facebook, you must make sure that you can contact her on your NOOK. So before making an offer to lend her a book, put her in your Contacts list, (page 392) or make sure she's a Facebook friend, and then link your NOOK account to Facebook (page 376).

Whichever way you choose, your NOOK Friend is notified via email or Facebook and has seven days either to accept the offer or decline it.

- **In the Library,** or if the book is on your Home Screen or Daily Shelf, hold your finger on a book and a pop-up menu appears. Select LendMe. The same screen appears as when you make an offer to lend a book from the NOOK Friends app.

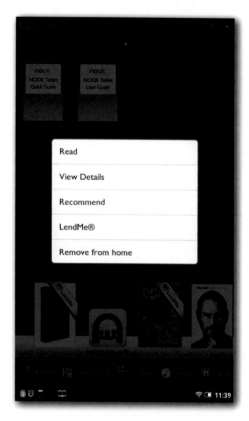

- **Double-tap a book's cover** in the Library or on the Daily Shelf or Home Screen, and the details page opens. Tap LendMe. You see the now-familiar screen for lending a book via Contacts or Facebook.

As soon as you make the offer to lend the book, the Lent badge appears across the book cover wherever it appears on your NOOK Tablet. The badge appears even if your friend hasn't yet accepted the offer, because you can't rescind the offer. If your friend accepts the offer, a number appears next to the badge, to show how many days are left in the 14-day lending period. If your friend rejects it, the Lent label disappears and is replaced with the LendMe badge.

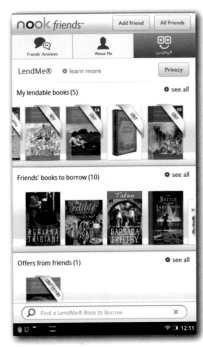

Responding to a Borrowing Request

Making an offer to lend a book is only one way to let a friend borrow a book. Sometimes a friend will ask to borrow a book as well. How does he know what books you've got to borrow? As explained on page 374, the NOOK Friends app shares a list of all the books you have available for lending to your friends (and vice versa).

You'll find out when a friend has requested to borrow a book in any of three ways:

- **You get a notification in the Notification bar.** Tap the Notification bar when you get the request, and you'll see the note "Your friends would like to borrow a book." Tap that notification, and you come to a screen that shows you who's made the request and which book he wants to borrow.

- **The book shows up on the Requests shelf in the LendMe section of the NOOK Friends app.** It's the bottom shelf, so scroll down to get there. Tap the book and a screen appears with details about who's made the request and which book he wants to borrow.

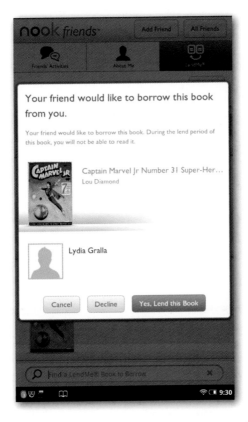

When you get to that screen, tap "Yes, Lend the Book" to lend it, "Decline" if you decide you don't want to lend it (feeling selfish, are we?), and Cancel if you simply can't make up your mind and need more time to decide.

NOTE Remember, when you lend a book to someone, you can't read it while it's being lent—14 days unless it's returned sooner. So before agreeing to lend the book, make sure you don't need access to it during that time.

- **You get an email with the request**. The email shows you the book's title and who has asked to borrow it. Tap Yes to agree to lend it; or No, Maybe Later to decline the offer for now.

Borrowing a Book

It may be better to give than to receive, but admit it, receiving is pretty nice, too, especially when it comes to borrowing books. So you'll want to take advantage of book borrowing on your NOOK, especially since it's so easy to do.

As with lending a book, there are two ways to borrow a book—ask a friend to borrow a book, and agree to borrow one when a friend recommends a book and offers to lend it to you.

Suppose you want to borrow a book from a friend. NOOK Friends is the way you do it, so make sure anyone from whom you want to borrow a book is a NOOK Friend. Then open the NOOK Friends app by pressing the NOOK button, selecting Apps, and tapping NOOK Friends.

Once you're in the NOOK Friends app, tap LendMe and go to the shelf labeled "Friends' books to borrow." There may be more than are visible, so scroll horizontally through the shelf to see them all.

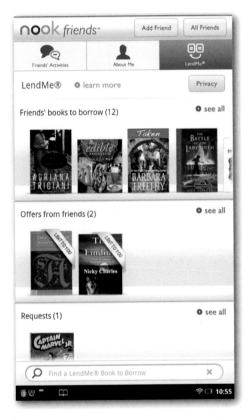

Tap any book you want to request. A screen appears with the book's title and author, and the name of the person who has it available for lending. Tap Request. A screen appears with the person's name in the Recipient field. Type a message ("pretty please" is usually effective) and then tap Send. The request goes off on its merry way via email.

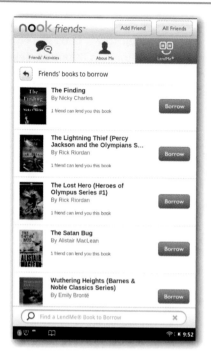

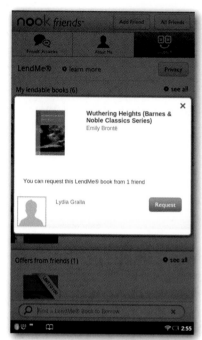

Want to see some details about any of the books on the list? On the bookshelf, tap See All. A vertically scrolling list appears. Tap a book cover, and you see the usual details screen. If you decide you want to borrow it, go back to the vertical list and tap Borrow to request it.

If you've got lots of friends with plenty of lendable books (lucky you!), it may take quite a while to scroll through them all. So if you have a specific book in mind that you're looking to borrow, head to the bottom of the LendMe screen and type a book title or author. As you type, the list of books that matches your search narrows. When you've typed in the name or title, you see a list of matching books. Tap any cover to see details, or tap Borrow to ask to borrow the book.

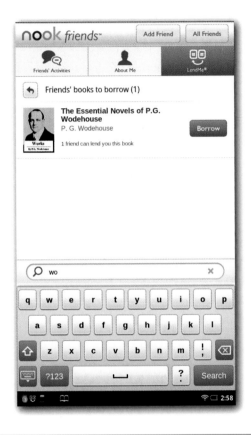

TIP You can also see the list of books you can borrow from friends in your Library. Tap "my stuff"→LendMe and then tap the bar at the top of the screen that reads Borrow Books From Friends With LendMe.

You may have a friend whose taste in books is impeccable (or matches your own, which may or may not always be impeccable). So there's a simple way to see a list of all the books a specific NOOK Friend has available for lending. In the NOOK Friends app, tap All Friends at top right. Then tap LendMe to the right of any friend whose list of lendable books you'd like to see. Tap a book cover to see its details, and tap Borrow to ask to borrow it.

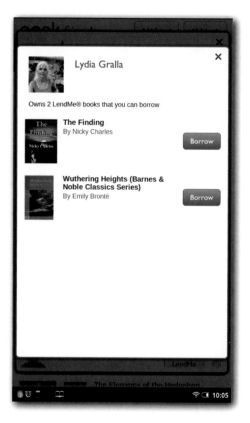

Your friend now gets the request in the three ways outlined on page 192. When he accepts the request, the book shows up in your Library with a Borrowed badge on it, and the number of days still left in the borrowing period next to it. After 14 days, the book disappears from your Library.

> **TIP** You can return a book before the 14-day period is up. For details, see page 200.

Once you develop borrowing-and-lending friendships with people, you'll find that they'll often offer to lend you books they think you might like. So someone may offer to lend you a book, and you'll find out about it in all the ways outlined on page 192.

If you get the request via email, click the View My Offer button and you're sent to your Barnes & Noble account on the Web, where you can accept or decline the offer. (You may need to log into the account first.) Similarly, when you click on the offer on Facebook, you're also sent to your Barnes & Noble account on the Web. Click Accept next to any book you want to borrow, and Reject next to any you don't.

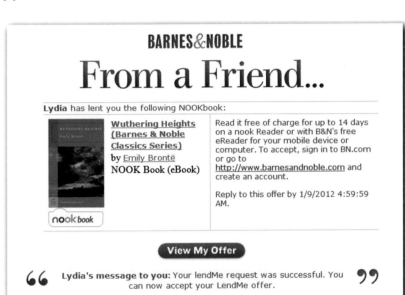

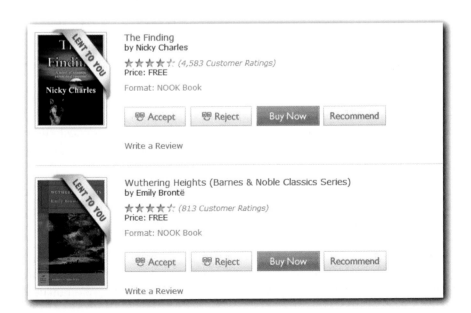

To see all the books that people have offered to lend you, go to the NOOK Friends app, tap LendMe, and go to the "Offers from friends" bookshelf. Tap to accept the offer or decline it.

Returning Books Early

When you've borrowed a book from someone, he can't read it for the 14 days that you have it. But if you finish the book before that time, or decide you don't want to read it anymore before the period is up, you can return it. Why bother? Remember, when you have the book, your friend can't read it, so he gets access to the book sooner if you return it early.

To return a book, log into your Barnes & Noble account, tap NOOK Books, and you see your entire Library, including books that you've borrowed. Tap Return next to any book you want to return early.

Wuthering Heights (Barnes & Noble Classics Series)
by Emily Brontë

★ ★ ★ ★ ✩ (813 Customer Ratings)
Price: FREE

Format: NOOK Book

| Download | Return | Buy Now | Recommend |

Write a Review

Borrowing Books from the Library

Just as you can borrow printed books from libraries, you can borrow NOOK books as well. You don't have to go to your local library to borrow the book; instead you head to the library's Internet site.

Not all libraries have NOOK books available for lending, and the way you borrow may vary from library to library. This section, though, covers the most popular way, and should go a long way to help you borrow whatever is available. Before you borrow, here's what you need to know:

- **You can borrow a book for 14 days.** As with books you borrow from friends, at the end of the borrowing period, the book automatically gets returned to the library.

- **Not all books can be borrowed for the NOOK.** Publishers make far fewer books available for lending for the NOOK than they make available in print. They worry that it's easier to borrow a NOOK book than a print book, because it doesn't require going to the library. So don't be surprised if you can't find your favorite book for the NOOK at the library, or if there are fewer copies for the NOOK than there are for the printed version.

> **NOTE** At this writing, some publishers don't make any of their books available as eBooks you can borrow from the library. Simon & Schuster, for example, doesn't make its books available as borrowable library eBooks, although that may change at some point.

- **Only one copy of a library eBook can be borrowed at a time.** Just as with a physical book, only one copy can be out at a time. Libraries typically have far fewer copies of a book in eBook format than in print, so you may have to wait to borrow an eBook you want.

- **You need a library card to borrow books.** Want to borrow a NOOK book from the New York Public Library? You need a New York Public Library card. You can't borrow books from libraries that let only residents borrow books if you're not a resident. Check with your local library for details.

- **There may be limits on how many eBooks you can borrow at one time.** Your local library may limit you to a maximum number of eBooks—five, for example.

- **Look for eBooks in the EPUB or PDF formats.** Those are the common formats your NOOK Tablet can read, so when browsing or searching, look for them.

How to Borrow and Read NOOK Books

As mentioned previously, libraries may have different methods for lending out eBooks, and for you then to transfer them to your NOOK. Typically, though, you must download the free Adobe Digital Editions software, and then register it. Without first doing so, you may not be able to borrow books.

Head to *www.adobe.com/products/digitaleditions* and install the software. You must also register for an Adobe ID to use the software and borrow books from a library. If you don't have one, head to *www.adobe.com/account.html* and create one. Then, when you're asked to activate your computer after the Adobe Digital Edition software is installed, enter that ID and password.

Now that you've got the software activated, it's time to borrow a book. Ask your library for the website it uses to lend eBooks, and ask to have a user name and password set up. Also check for any special lending policies, and whether the library offers online help.

Once you do all that, you're ready to go. Head to your library's eBook-lending website. Different libraries organize their eBook collections differently; you may be able to search and browse or only one of the two.

Look for the NOOK section. If there seems to be one, look for books in EPUB and PDF formats. Those are the ones you can borrow.

TIP For excellent all-around help with borrowing eBooks, head to the NOOK eBook Central site run by Google and the New York Public Library (*https://sites.google.com/a/nypl.org/ebook-central/home/device/nook*). Although much of what's there is specifically for borrowing books from the New York Public Library, it's a good overall resource for advice about how to borrow books from any library using your NOOK Tablet.

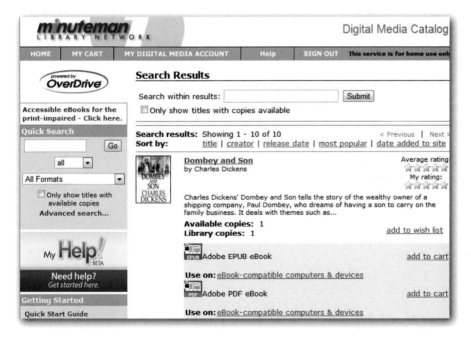

Once you've found a book you want to borrow, follow these steps:

❶ **Follow the site's instructions for downloading the book.** Typically, you'll click the book's link, follow a checkout procedure, and then download the book. Make sure you remember where you saved the downloaded book. It will end in .acsm, such as DombeyandSon9781775410713.acsm, or in .pdf.

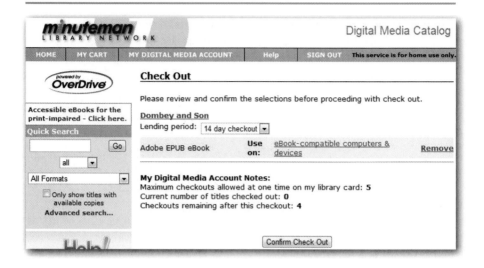

❷ **Double-click the file.** The book opens in Adobe Digital Editions. If you want, you can read the book in that program.

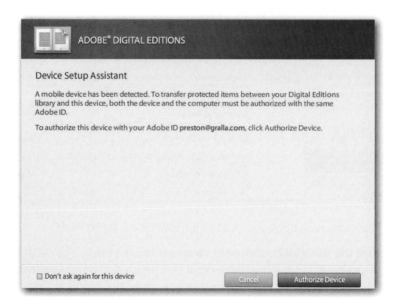

❸ **Connect your NOOK Tablet to your computer.** A screen on your computer appears, telling you that you need to authorize the NOOK to use Adobe Digital Editions. Click Authorize Device. After a moment, your NOOK is authorized.

A new shelf appears on the Adobe Digital Editions screen titled My NOOK.

❹ **Drag the book you just borrowed to this shelf.**

❺ **Disconnect your NOOK Tablet from your computer.** The book won't appear on a shelf in your Library. Instead, you have to open it as a file. In the Library, tap "my stuff"→My Files, and in the My NOOK section, you'll see a Digital Editions folder. Tap it.

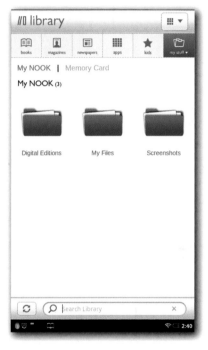

❻ **Look for the file name of the book you just transferred,** for example, Dombey_and_Son.epub. It will end in .epub or .pdf. Tap it.

The book opens. You can now read it just as you can any other book on your NOOK.

Remember, you can borrow the book for only 14 days. After that, it automatically gets returned to the library.

NOTE Even when you have the book on your NOOK Tablet, you can continue to read it on your computer using Adobe Digital Editions.

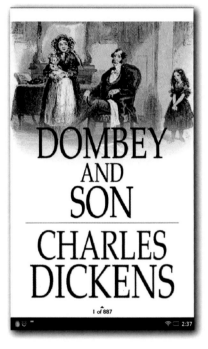

PART **IV**

Apps, Movies, TV Shows, Music, Photographs, and Files

CHAPTER 8
Streaming Media: Pandora, Netflix, and Hulu Plus

CHAPTER 9
Downloading and Using Apps

CHAPTER 10
Music, Pictures, Video, and Documents

CHAPTER 11
Transferring Files Between Your NOOK Tablet and Your Computer

Streaming Media: Pandora, Netflix, and Hulu Plus

YOUR NOOK TABLET IS a superb eReader, of course, but it's also a great entertainment machine for watching movies and TV shows and listening to music. Its high-resolution screen gives you crisp, clean video. And using the NOOK Tablet's headphone jack, you can listen to music or movies in glorious stereo on headphones or an external speaker. So check out the rest of this chapter to learn how to do all that and more.

Understanding Streaming Media

Netflix, Hulu Plus, and Pandora all use a technique called *streaming*, which means the movies, TV shows, and music aren't stored on your NOOK Tablet or played from there. Instead, they live on big computers called servers owned by those services, which send the video wirelessly to your NOOK Tablet—when it's connected to a WiFi network. So if you're not connected to a WiFi network, you can't use those services or other streaming media services like Grooveshark or Rhapsody.

Furthermore, if your WiFi connection isn't a strong one, you may experience hiccups when watching movies or TV shows and listening to music. So if you find blips and delays, try to find a better WiFi connection. If you're at home, try repositioning your router, or moving to a different seat or room. If you're using a public WiFi service, try moving to a different location.

Streaming Media on the NOOK Color

Your NOOK Color may not come with Netflix, Hulu Plus, or Pandora built into it. And it may not let you watch TV on Hulu Plus or Netflix. That's because the software built into the original NOOK Color couldn't handle those streaming services.

An update to the NOOK in late 2011 and early 2012 changed that—it let you use Netflix. The update was delivered automatically to NOOK Color users via WiFi. But that update only gave you the ability to use Netflix; it didn't actually download the Netflix *app* to your NOOK Color. If you'd like to use Netflix on your NOOK color, go pick up the Netflix app at the NOOK Store (page 50).

There's a chance that your NOOK Color may not have received the Netflix update. Fear not; you can install that update on your own. For details, see page 435.

At this writing, the update to the NOOK Color did *not* let it use Hulu Plus. But Hulu and Barnes & Noble are working on giving the NOOK Color Hulu Plus capabilities as well. So head to the NOOK Store and search for Hulu Plus. If you find it, you can download and use it, otherwise you'll have to wait for a bit as Barnes & Noble and Hulu work out any kinks.

As for Pandora, it should be built into your NOOK Color. If it isn't, head to the NOOK Store and download it.

Using Netflix

Netflix is a two-pronged video service—with it, you can have DVDs delivered to your home or stream videos straight to your computer, NOOK Tablet, or any other device that supports the use of Netflix.

Because it's a two-pronged service, it can be easy to get confused about what you're buying exactly when you subscribe to Netflix, and what can be streamed versus what can be delivered to you on DVD.

It's really pretty simple, though. You can subscribe to the streaming-only service, the DVD-only service, or a combination of the two. The unlimited streaming service and the DVD-only service are your least expensive options. The combination service charges different rates, depending on whether you want to have one, two, three, or four DVDs out simultaneously.

To use Netflix on your NOOK Tablet, you need to subscribe to the streaming-only service or one of the combo services.

To watch movies or TV shows on your NOOK Color using Netflix, go to the Apps screen, and then tap the Netflix icon. You'll come to a login screen. Tap in your login information, or if you haven't yet subscribed to Netflix, tap the Netflix.com link to set one up. You can also set up a Netflix account by heading to *www. netflix.com* on a computer's browser.

At the top of the screen, in the Continue Watching area, you'll see any movies or TV shows that you've started watching on your NOOK Tablet, your PC, or anywhere else. Each will have a red arrow on it. That's one of the niftiest things about the Netflix app—you can start watching on your computer and continue watching on your NOOK Tablet, and vice versa. To watch something you were previously watching, just tap it. You can also scroll through the Continue Watching area by swiping with your finger.

Once you tap a show to watch, make sure to turn your NOOK Tablet horizontally, since Netflix always plays in landscape mode. When your TV show or movie begins, the bottom of the screen has a variety of controls for playing it (see page 215 for details). Those controls vanish after a second or two. To make them appear again, tap the screen.

The Netflix screen also shows you movies and TV shows in a variety of categories, depending on what you've watched before. So you may see a Top 10 list customized to your taste, French Movies (if you've rented them before), Crime Movies (again, if you're watched them before), and so on. Swipe sideways in any category to see more movies and TV shows. Scroll down to see more categories. Make sure to scroll to the bottom to see the New Releases and "Newly Added to Netflix" categories if you want to find out what's new. And look for the Instant Queue, which has the movies in your Netflix queue that you can watch on the NOOK Tablet.

> **NOTE** The Netflix app lets you watch streaming movies and TV shows, but it doesn't include ordering DVDs to be delivered to your home.

Tap any of the movies or TV shows and you'll come to a screen that tells you its title, release date, cast, director, rating you're likely to give it based on your past ratings, and other movies or TV shows you might want to watch. To watch it now, tap the arrow icon on the shows picture. To add to your instant watching queue, tap "Add to Instant Queue." If you already have it in your queue and want to remove it, tap "Remove from Instant Queue."

If you tap a TV series, you'll see a list of multiple episodes at the bottom of the screen. Tap any to play it.

Watching a Movie or TV Show

When you tap a movie or TV show, the NOOK's orientation changes to landscape, the movie or show starts playing, and you'll briefly see a series of controls and information onscreen. To make the controls go away, tap the screen. To make them appear again, tap the screen again.

Here's what each does:

Play/Pause   Title   Time Remaining

Rabbit Hole

0:01:51   -1:29:37   11:20

Time   Slider   Back   Choose Audio   Display
Elapsed   and Subtitles   Subtitles

- **Title.** Shows the title of the movie or TV show, including the season and episode number if it's a TV show.

- **Play/Pause.** Plays the movie or TV show or pauses it.

- **Time elapsed.** Shows how much time has elapsed.

- **Slider.** Lets you move forward or back.

- **Time remaining.** Shows how much time is left.

- **Back.** Takes you back to the screen where you were previously.

- **Choose audio and subtitles.** Brings up a screen that lets you choose whether to use subtitles (if any are available) and the language of the audio track (if more than one is available).

- **Display subtitles.** If subtitles can be turned on or off, tap this to turn them on, and tap again to turn them off.

NOTE Not all movies give you control over subtitles or let you choose different languages. For example, many foreign films can't have the subtitles turned off.

Control the volume using the NOOK Tablet's normal volume controls.

TIP You may find some movies and TV shows can play audio only at a low volume, no matter how high you turn it. To get around the problem, plug headphones or external speakers into the headphone jack. Also, the NOOK Tablet's built-in speakers are monaural rather than stereo, so if you want stereo sound, you must use external speakers or headphones.

Browsing and Searching for Movies and TV Shows

Netflix has thousands of movies and TV shows you can watch, not just those that show up on the screen when you log in. To browse all categories, tap the Browse button at the top of the screen, and then tap a category. You come to a variety of subcategories, like Classic Dramas, Courtroom Dramas, Newly Added, "Suggestions for You," and so on. Swipe through each, or scroll through the entire list of subcategories. Tap the movie or TV show in which you're interested, and then tap to watch it or add it to your queue.

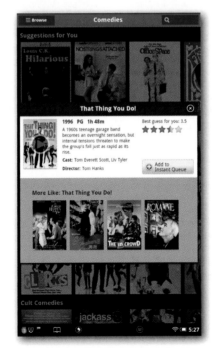

To search for a movie, tap in the search box and type in your search term. As you type, the results narrow. When you find a movie or TV show you want to watch, tap it, and then follow the usual routine for watching or adding to your queue.

Managing Your Netflix Queue

There's one thing missing in the NOOK Tablet's Netflix app—the ability to manage your queue or Netflix account. As explained before, you can add movies and TV shows to your queue, or remove them, but that's the extent of what you can do. If you want to reorder what's in your queue, change your subscription, or order DVD rentals, head to the Web.

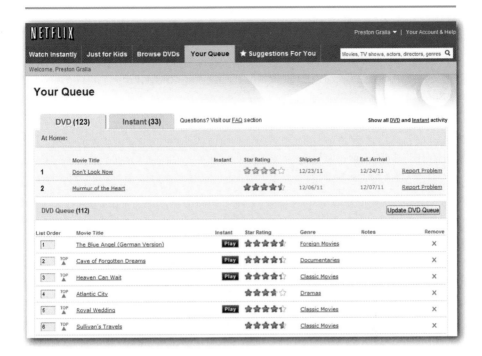

Using Hulu Plus

Hulu Plus isn't as well known as Netflix, but it's a great way to watch TV shows, movies, and other video from a wide variety of sources. Current TV shows are well represented, but there are plenty of old favorites as well. Like Netflix, Hulu Plus streams video to your NOOK Tablet.

> **NOTE** Hulu Plus lets you view movies as well as television shows, but it has a very limited selection of them. Netflix is far better for movie watching than Hulu Plus.

Hulu offers both free and paid services, but on the NOOK Tablet, you can *only* use the for-pay version. At press time, it costs $7.99 per month, and it gives you a wider range of TV and video, including streaming access to full seasons and past seasons of TV shows. (The non-pay version, which you can watch on the Web, typically offers single episodes or clips.)

To watch TV or video on your NOOK Color using Netflix, go to the Apps screen, and then tap the Hulu Plus icon. You'll come to a login screen. Tap in your login information, or if you haven't yet subscribed to Hulu Plus, tap the icon to sign up. You can also subscribe to Hulu Plus by heading to *www.hulu.com* on a computer's browser.

> **TIP** If you decide not to subscribe to Hulu Plus, you can still watch a small selection of video. Tap the Free Gallery icon when you launch Hulu Plus.

Once you've signed up and logged in you come to a screen with these options:

- **TV.** Shows you a selection of TV shows to watch.

- **Movies.** Shows you the movies you can watch.

- **Queue.** A list of TV shows, movies, and other video that you've lined up for later viewing.

- **History.** Lists what you've watched on Hulu Plus. You can rewatch a show from here as well.

- **More.** Gives you access to your account information, a search tool, a favorites list, and a logout screen.

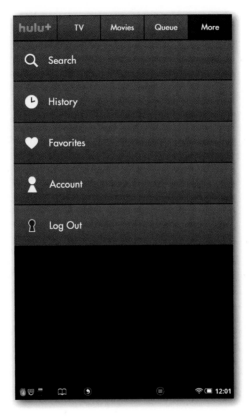

At the bottom of the screen you see two buttons: a Back button for returning to where you just were, and a Menu button that brings up the same set of options as when you tap the More button. So why have the Menu button? So that when you're in another part of Hulu Plus—browsing TV shows, for example—you can quickly get to those options.

Tap the TV or Movies icon, and you come to a list of TV shows or movies to watch. At the very top of the screen are navigation buttons for TV, Movies, Queue, and More. Just below those icons you see a highlighted TV show or movie, and then beneath that all the movies and TV shows you can watch.

NOTE Shows and episodes sometimes expire on Hulu Plus so you can't watch them after a certain date. If that's the case, you see a notice next to the show.

In the list, you find not just full TV shows and movies, but also trailers and clips. If you'd like to only see the full shows and movies, or only trailers and clips, tap the All Videos button and you can choose which you want to see.

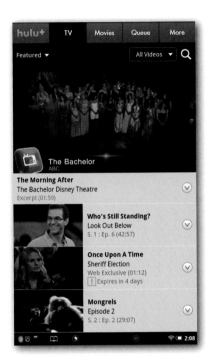

When you tap a movie or TV show, the NOOK's orientation changes to landscape. If you tap a TV show, you may see an ad or two before it starts, and sometimes while you're watching as well. (Don't try to fast-forward through the ads—you can't do it.) Then the TV or movie starts playing, and you briefly see a series of controls and information onscreen. To make the controls go away, tap the screen. To make them appear again, tap the screen again. Control the volume using your NOOK's volume control. And if you can't hear even with the sound turned all the way up, use headphones or external speakers as described in the tip on page 20.

Here are the controls and information you'll find:

Back Button   Title   Options Button

Time Elapsed

Pause/   Slider Bar   Time
Play   Remaining

- **Title.** Displays the title of the movie or TV show.

- **Play/Pause.** Plays the movie or TV show or pauses it.

- **Time elapsed.** Shows how much time has elapsed.

- **Slider bar.** Drag the bar and you move forward or back through the show.
  You can also tap to jump to a different spot in the video.

> **NOTE** When you're watching an ad, you can't use the slider bar to move through it.

- **Time remaining.** Shows how much time is left in the video.

- **Back.** Takes you to the previous screen.

- **Options.** Brings up a screen that lets you change the video quality of what
  you're watching. You can choose from High, Medium, and Low. Generally,
  you should choose High, but if you're having a problem with hiccups or
  other streaming video problems, choose Medium or Low, and see if that
  solves the problem.

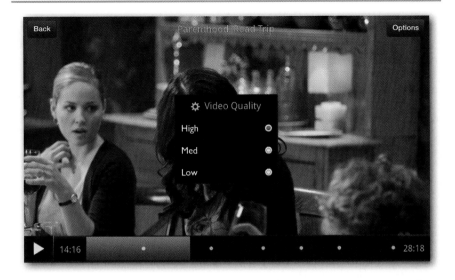

More Options for Handling Movies and TV

When you're browsing through TV and movies and you tap the down arrow next to any video, a series options appears. Tap the arrow, and here are your choices:

- **Watch.** Starts playing the TV show or movie.

- **Queue.** Adds it to your queue for later watching (page 228).

- **Video.** Provides more details about the show or movie, including the name, date it was aired, network that aired it, episode number, and description. You can then watch the show from the screen that appears, put it in the queue, or see more information about the series, as described in the next bullet.

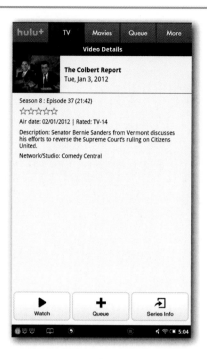

- **Series info.** Takes you to a screen where you can tap buttons to see more episodes of the show, view clips of the show or movie, add the episode to your queue, and put it in your Favorites by tapping the heart button. If you tap the Episodes button, you'll see more episodes of the show.

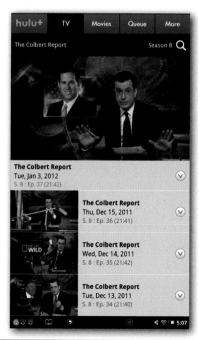

Browsing and Searching for TV and Movies

As you browse through TV and movies, they appear in what Hulu Plus calls *Featured* order, which means that Hulu determines the order in which they're displayed. But if you tap the Featured arrow at upper left, you can display them in a different order—by most popular, recently added, alphabetical, by network (for TV shows), by studio (for movies), and so on.

> **NOTE** For legal and licensing reasons, you may not be able to view all the video choices on your NOOK Tablet that you can on the Web. So you may come across an occasional TV show that tells you that you'll have to watch the show on the Web, not on your NOOK Tablet.

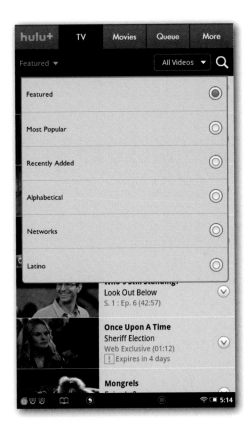

To search for a TV show or movie, tap the search icon and type in what you're searching for. Then tap any results to watch or tap the arrow next to it to get more details.

Using the Queue and History List

The Queue and History List work just as you'd expect. Tap the Queue button at the top of the screen, and you'll see all the shows you've put into your queue. The same holds with the History List. Tap More

Using Pandora

Wish you had a personalized music station that would play exactly the kind of music you want, without obnoxious radio announcers and interruptions? How about your own personal jukebox, playing any kind of music you want at the tap of a button—rap for one mood, techno for another, jazz for another, opera for another, and so on? And what if it played you music that you've never heard before, but that fit right in with your tastes?

Stop wishing. You've got Pandora built into the NOOK Tablet. This free, fabulous music service may forever change the way you think about and listen to music.

You may already know Pandora from the Web; it started life as a web-based music service. But it's expanded into Android as well, and now you can use it on your NOOK Tablet. Head to Apps and tap the Pandora icon, and then sign up for an account. If you already have an account, just sign in once you've downloaded and installed it.

Once you've got your account set up, the fun begins. Tap the Add Station button at the bottom of the screen, and then type in the name of an artist, a song title, or a composer that's closest to the kind of music you want to create a station for. As you type, Pandora lists possible matches. Tap a match, or keep typing until you type in the full name. Then Pandora goes about creating the station for you and starts playing the music.

As the music plays, a graphic of the album from which the song is taken is displayed, along with the title of the album, the title of the song, and the name of the artist. Beneath that is a slider that shows you the progress of the current song. (Unfortunately, you can't move forward and backward through the song using this slider; it just shows you the progress.)

> **NOTE** If you switch to something else on your NOOK Tablet while you're listening to music on Pandora—reading a book, say—Pandora keeps the music playing. To make it stop, tap the small Pandora icon in the Notification bar, and then tap the Pandora notification that appears. That switches you to Pandora. Tap the stop button to stop the music.

Want to know why Pandora chose the current song for you? Tap the little information button to the right of the slider, and Pandora gives you the details. You may or may not understand what it's telling you, but it's well worth checking out. For example, when playing the Tom Petty song "Love is a Long Road," Pandora might say it chose the song for you because "it features rock song structure, a subtle use of vocal harmony, a vocal-central aesthetic, extensive vamping, minor key tonality, electric rhythm guitars, a dynamic male vocalist, and many other similarities identified in the Music Genome Project." What "extensive vamping" means is anybody's guess...point is, Pandora usually succeeds in playing music you're sure to enjoy.

NOTE The Music Genome Project is an attempt to understand music at its most fundamental level, based on its core musical components—its "genome." It's the core of Pandora's technology.

At the bottom of the screen is a set of buttons for controlling Pandora. The buttons are fairly self-explanatory. The thumbs-down button tells Pandora that you don't like the current song. When you tap it, the song stops playing—and Pandora has learned something about your musical tastes. Based on that, it stops playing songs with some of the characteristics of that particular song. The thumbs-up button tells Pandora that you like the current song, and so it plays more songs with its characteristics. The middle button lets you bookmark a song or artist. You can't use these bookmarks on your NOOK Tablet, though; instead, you have to head to the Web and click Profile. From there, you can see the artists or songs you've bookmarked, and use them in a variety of ways, such as getting lyrics, seeing similar tracks, playing a sample of the song, and more.

The other two buttons are the usual controls for pause/play and skip.

To switch to another Pandora station, tap the My Stations button at the bottom of the screen. Tap any to play it. If you have a long list, scroll through it as you would any other list. Tap Edit, and you can remove any station from the list.

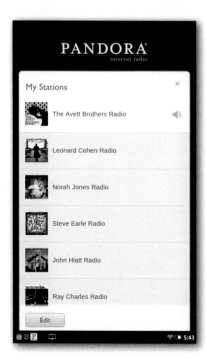

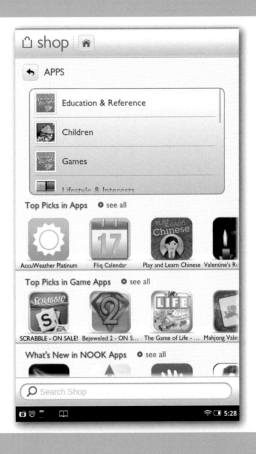

CHAPTER 9

Downloading and Using Apps

THE NOOK TABLET IS called a *tablet* for a reason. Just like other tablets, it can do lots of things other than letting you read books—notably running apps. Just as with all tablets and smartphones, the NOOK lets you download apps to do all kinds of nifty things, from playing music to playing games or keeping track of your diet. Bottom line: Anything you can do on a traditional tablet, you can do on your NOOK Tablet and NOOK Color. (And yes, that includes Angry Birds.)

NOTE The NOOK Color runs apps as well, although it may not run *all* the apps that the NOOK Tablet can. For example, as of this writing, it cannot run Hulu Plus, although by the time you read this, that may have changed.

In this chapter, you'll learn all about how to get apps, how to install them, how to manage them, and how to use them—including the built-in apps on your NOOK Tablet. You'll also get advice on some great apps to download.

Running Apps

The NOOK Tablet runs the Android operating system, even though its interface doesn't look like other Android tablets or smartphones you've seen. That's because Barnes & Noble has customized the Android operating system for eReading and other purposes.

NOTE The Android operating system was created by Google, which makes it available free of charge to tablet and smartphone manufacturers.

Because the NOOK Tablet is built on Android, it runs Android apps. But unlike many tablets and smartphones, it doesn't give you the power to download just *any* Android app. Apps must get the OK from Barnes & Noble to run on the NOOK Tablet because of the company's operating system customizations. The only apps you can run are those built into the NOOK Tablet or the ones you can download from the NOOK store. You'll find you can't download apps from the Android Market (*http://market.android.com*).

NOTE You can, if you wish, *root* the NOOK to make it work like an ordinary Android device and give to run any Android app. When you do that, though, you may damage the NOOK Tablet, you void the warranty, and you get no support from Barnes & Noble. You also lose all of the eReader capabilities described in this book. Barnes & Noble also has made it very difficult to root the NOOK Tablet and NOOK Color. For details, see Chapter 17.

Running an app is simple. Press the NOOK button, tap Apps to see the apps in your Library, and then tap the app you want to run. You can also tap Apps on the Media bar to see the most recent apps you've run. Tap any to run them. Tap "My library" to see the rest of your apps in the Library. And you can, of course, tap an app on your Home screen, or any one on the Daily Shelf.

When you run an app and want to quit it, most the time you don't need to shut it down. Just press the NOOK button to get to the Quick Nav bar and perform another task, or press the NOOK button twice to get to the Home screen.

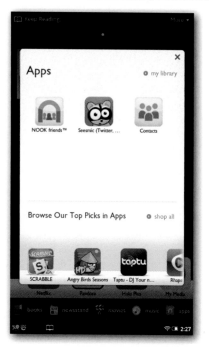

Managing and Deleting Apps

Got an app that you love so much you want it always to be just a tap away? Then put it on your Home screen. You can do that and plenty more, including deleting it, adding it to a Library Shelf, and other nifty things as well. To do it, hold your finger on an app and from the screen that appears, choose the following:

- **Open.** Runs the app. Of course, you could have just tapped the app's icon, without going to all the trouble of opening this menu.

- **View details.** Shows you details about the app. It's the same information you saw on the screen before buying and downloading it.

- **Recommend.** Lets you recommend the app to a friend. Turn to page 240 for details.

- **Add to Home.** Puts a shortcut to the app on your Home screen.

- **Add to Shelf.** Lets you add it to a shelf that you've created in My Shelf. (See page 161 for details.)

- **Remove from Shelf.** Lets you remove it from a shelf.

- **Archive.** Moves it off of your NOOK, but still keeps it accessible whenever you want to use it again. See page 171 for details.

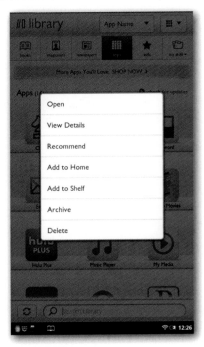

- **Delete.** Deletes the app from your NOOK. Be very careful when doing this, because unlike with archiving, you can't retrieve the app if you change your mind later. If you decide you want to use it again, you have to buy it again.

> **NOTE** If you hold your finger on an app built into the NOOK Tablet, you won't get every one of these options. You can choose only from Open, View Details, "Add to Home," "Add to Shelf," and "Remove from Shelf."

Built-in NOOK Apps

The NOOK Tablet comes with a number of built-in apps, including for Netflix, Pandora, Hulu Plus (Chapter 8), Contacts (Chapter 15), playing music, viewing pictures and videos (Chapter 10), and more. For the full rundown on those apps, check out the chapters where they're covered. The following pages tell you about three other notable apps built into the NOOK Tablet.

> **NOTE** Depending on when you bought your NOOK Color, it may not come with Netflix or Hulu Plus on it, and may not be able to run Hulu Plus. See the tip on page 49 for more info on how you can get these apps onto your NOOK Color.

- **Crossword.** You have a NOOK Tablet, so no doubt you're a book lover. There's a good chance that you're a crossword lover as well, so try out this app. Fight the urge to tap the Hint button—that's cheating!

- **Sudoku.** With your NOOK Tablet, a good Sudoku puzzle is always within easy reach. You can choose from several levels of play, and there's even a timer to track how long it takes to do a puzzle, so you can watch your skills improve. For help as you learn the game, there are Undo and Redo buttons and also a Hint button that you can use as a last resort.

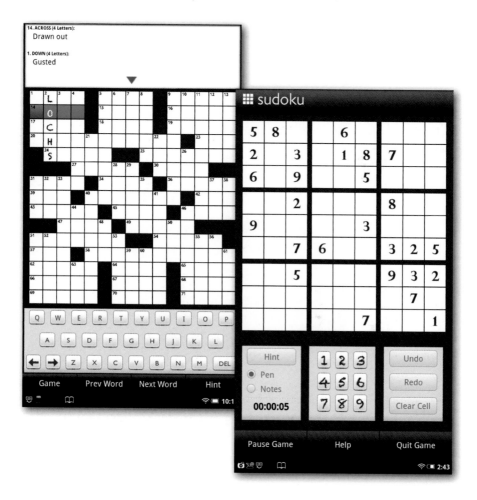

- **Chess.** Want to play chess but don't have a partner nearby? You've got one on your NOOK Tablet. To play, drag a piece to the spot where you want to move it. It's a nice app for a quick chess game, but it doesn't let you play online against others, and doesn't include extras like changing the difficulty level.

Getting Apps in the NOOK Store

To get more apps, head to the NOOK Store by pressing the NOOK button and tapping Shop. On the top part of the screen, underneath "browse the NOOK Store," you'll usually find links to apps or sometimes also to categories of apps.

Tap the apps icon, and you'll come to the main screen of the Apps store. At the top is a scrollable list of app categories, and beneath it are various lists, such as "Top Picks in Apps," "Top Picks in Games Apps," and others. Tap any category to see apps in that category. You may see subcategories, and in these subcategories you'll usually see lists of apps at the bottom of the screen.

> **NOTE** On the main screen of the NOOK Store, you'll also find lists of apps, which change over time —"Top Picks in Apps," "What's New in NOOK Apps," and possibly others.

At some point when browsing the subcategories, you'll see a list of all apps in the subcategory. Scroll through them until you see an app you're interested in, and then tap the app for more details.

Tap an app, and you come to a screen that includes the name of the app, version number, app maker, description (supplied by the maker), price (or a button labeled Free), and a Share button. Tap the Share button to recommend it to others via email, Twitter, or Facebook (you can also Like it on Facebook). You also see the average rating of the app on a five-star basis, and how many people have rated it.

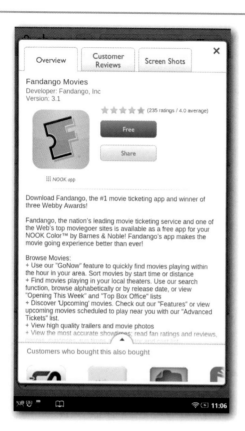

TIP When deciding whether to pay for and download an app, be careful about using the ratings and reviews as your guide. For example, if there are only a handful of reviews and they're all positive, the developers (or their friends) may be doing the rating. If there are dozens of reviews or more, it's less likely that the developers and their friends are behind them all.

If you're looking for other apps you might be interested in, tap the small up arrow at the bottom of the screen to see what other apps purchasers of this app also bought.

NOTE To download apps, you need a Barnes & Noble account with a valid credit card (page 37).

Tabs across the top let you read individual reviews and see screenshots. You can filter reviews in multiple ways, including those rated most helpful by others, the most recent reviews, and so on. Just tap the drop-down menu in the upper right of the screen.

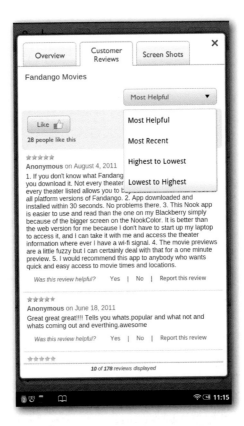

If you decide you want to pay for the app and download it, tap it the green price (or Free) button. The button turns into a gray Confirm button. Tap the button to download it; if the app was for-pay, the credit card associated with your Barnes & Noble account gets charged. A small green bar on the app's icon displays the download progress. After it downloads, the button displays the word Open. Tap to run it now; later, you can run it the way you'd run any app (page 234).

Back and Menu Buttons in Apps

When you use an app, you may notice two small icons in the Notification bar that you don't normally see. The one shaped like an arrow is a back button; tap it to go to what you were doing before opening the app. The other one, with a series of lines, is a menu button. Tap it for various options specific to the app. For example, in the Fandango movie app, the menu lets you go to your account, or switch to a view that shows movies or a view that shows theaters. Not all apps have these buttons.

Got an app you love so much that you want it always to be just a tap away? Put it on your Home screen—hold your finger on the app, and from the menu that appears, select "Add to home."

Five Great Apps to Download

There are thousands of great apps you can download, and you'll want to spend lots of time browsing for them. The five described in this section are ones you might want to give a whirl, though—they're among the best in class.

Pulse News

Are you a news junkie? Then you'll want the great, free news app Pulse. It grabs articles from newspapers, magazines, and websites. Using Pulse, you grab articles and information from all over the Web and display them in a big tablet-friendly format with lots of photos and graphics. You customize exactly what kinds of stories and publications you want to show.

TIP Geeks will want to know that the underlying technology that allows Pulse to accomplish all this magic is RSS, which stands for Really Simple Syndication, a format that lets websites and blogs publish updates, and apps like Pulse grab them.

Tap any story to read it. To share the story, tap the Facebook or Twitter icons at the bottom of the screen. You can also share via email and in other ways by tapping the double-headed arrow icon. At the top of the screen, you can change your view of the story—either with or without all the fancy design elements. Tap the "me" button, and you get more features, including syncing your stories to other tablets, smartphones, and computers (if you use Pulse on them).

Pulse is already set up to grab a variety of news feeds from around the Web, but it's easy to change that to your own selections. Tap the settings icon at upper left to add or remove news sources. Tap the + button, and you come to a screen that lets you add new sources. You can also add an entirely new page of stories from this screen by flicking to the right and adding more news sources.

There's a lot more to Pulse as well. It's free and it gives you great sources of information, so if you're a news junkie, or even if you're not, give it a try.

Evernote

If you suffer from information overload, here's your remedy. Evernote does a great job of capturing information from multiple sources, putting them in one location, and then letting you easily find them—whether you're using your computer, your tablet, or another Android device.

Not only that, it's free.

You organize all your information into separate notebooks, and can then browse each notebook, search through it, search through all notebooks, and so on.

No matter where you capture or input information, it's available on every device on which you install Evernote. So if you grab a web page from your PC and put it into a notebook, that information is available on your NOOK Tablet, and vice versa.

You can capture information from the Web, by taking photos, by speaking, and by pasting in existing documents. And you can also type notes as well.

The upshot of all this? Evernote is the best app you'll find for capturing information and making sense of it all.

Fandango

Wonder what's on at your local movie theater tonight? Like to find out what other people have thought about the movies? Want to buy tickets before you go?

Fandango does all that, plus more, and it does it for free. Launch the app, and then tap Movies to see a list of currently playing movies. Tap a movie, and you come to a page that lists the name, running time, rating, synopsis, overall rating, trailer, and theater where it's playing. If the theatre lets you, you can buy tickets as well. Tabs at the top of the page lead you to more information, including reviews and director and cast information.

You can also see all the theaters near your home, find out their movie schedules, and buy tickets. When you launch the app, it doesn't know your location, so it can't give you those details accurately. Tap the small Menu icon at the bottom of the screen, select My Account, tap Location, and then enter your location. After that, you'll be just fine.

Words with Friends

You've got a NOOK, so you're clearly a word person. If your love extends to word games, and you want to play with other word lovers, then you'll want to get the popular Words with Friends app. (It's a for-pay app, not a free one.)

It's a game similar to Scrabble that you play against friends from Facebook, your Contacts List, Twitter, or other places. The app can even find random opponents for you to play against. One of the many great things about it is that you don't need to play an entire game at once. You can start, play for a few minutes, go off and do something else, pick up the game where you left off...games can last for several days if you like, or you can play straight through. And you can also play multiple games at the same time.

Trip Advisor City Guides

Traveling to a city for business or pleasure? Then you'll want to get the free City Guides from Trip Advisor. There are separate ones for different cities, so in the NOOK Store, type the name of the city you plan to visit along with the words *City Guide* to find it, like this: *San Francisco City Guide*.

You'll get a great free app that tells you everything you want to know about visiting a city—what restaurants and sites to visit, what hotels are good, information about neighborhoods, local transportation, history, culture, architecture...even an interactive map. You'll find ratings, individual reviews, directions and more.

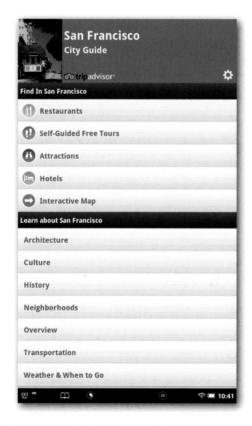

There are guides from around the world. In fact, you may want to download some just to imagine visiting. Paris, anyone?

Troubleshooting Apps

In a perfect world, apps would never misbehave. Unfortunately, it's not a perfect world. An app may quit the moment you launch it, or cause your NOOK Tablet to restart, or do any number of odd things. If that happens, try these steps:

- **Launch the app again.** There's no particular reason why relaunch should work, but it often does. When you launch the app again, it just may work properly.

- **Archive or delete and reinstall**. There may have been an oddball installation problem. So archive or delete the app, and then reinstall it. That action sometimes fixes the problem. When to archive and when to delete? If it's a for-pay app you'll want to archive rather than delete it, or else you'll have to pay for it again.

- **Restart the NOOK Tablet.** Just as restarting a computer sometimes fixes problems for no known reason, restarting the NOOK Tablet may have the same effect.

If none of this works, then it's time to uninstall the app. Don't fret; there are plenty more where it came from.

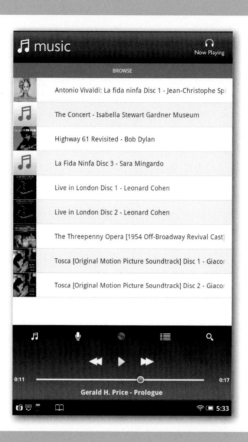

CHAPTER 10

Music, Pictures, Video, and Documents

YOUR NOOK DOES MORE than work as a great eReader and entertainment player—it's also a great device for listening to music, viewing pictures, playing videos, and even reading work documents such as PDF files and Microsoft Office documents. Everything you need to do all that is built right into the NOOK itself. Read on to learn how to do it all.

Getting Files into Your NOOK

Before you can listen to music, view movies or pictures, or read documents, you have to get them into your NOOK Tablet. You can get them there in three different ways:

- **Via email.** Someone can send you the files via email, and you can save them on your NOOK Tablet (page 339).

- **From the Web.** As you browse the Web, you can download files to your NOOK Tablet (page 273).

- **Transferring them from a computer.** Connect your NOOK Tablet to your computer via the USB cable, and you can drag them to your NOOK's internal storage, or to a microSD card if you've installed one (page 277).

Playing Music and Audio Files

You play music and audio files on your NOOK Tablet using the built-in Music Player. To launch it, press the NOOK button, tap Apps, and then tap Music Player. You can also tap the music button on the Media Library and then tap Music Player. However you get there, the player launches.

The Music Player has two modes—Browse mode and Now Playing mode. When you're in Browse mode, you'll see a list of artists, songs, or albums through which you can browse. Tap the Now Playing icon at upper-right to switch to the Now Playing mode. When you're in Now Playing mode, you see just the song you're playing. To switch to the Browse mode, tap the Browse icon at upper-right. You can only be in the Now Playing mode when you're actually playing music.

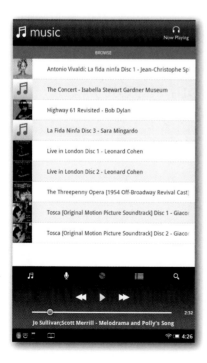
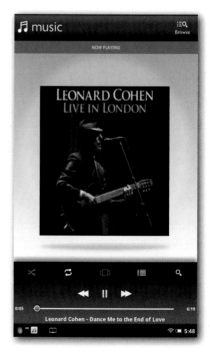

You can also browse the music files on your NOOK Tablet manually, and then listen to any that you choose. To do that, in the Library, tap "My stuff"→My Files and tap My NOOK or Memory Card, depending on where you've stored the files. Assuming you've stored your music files in the Music folder, tap My Files→Music. Then browse to any files and tap any to play it. The Music Player launches, and starts playing the file.

In the Browse mode down at the bottom of the screen, just above the slider for moving through a track and controls for playing music, you'll see a row of five icons, giving you five different ways to browse and find music:

- **List.** Lists individual songs, and includes their titles, singer, and length. They're organized alphabetically, by the name of the file. Scroll through them in the usual way. There's an even faster way: As you scroll, a scroll icon appears on screen. Drag it up and down to scroll faster. To the left of each song you'll see a re-sort button. Using it, drag a track to a different location. It will stay there permanently. Tap any track to play it.

- **Artist.** Organizes songs by artists' names. Next to their names is the number of albums you have of theirs. Tap the sideways-facing arrow and you'll see each album, including album art (if available) and the number of songs on it. Tap an album to see a list of songs on it. Tap a song to play it.

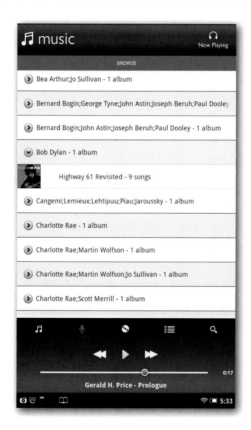

- **CD.** Organizes songs by album. It includes artwork (if available), and lists the name and artists. Tap an album to see all the tracks on it. Tap a track to play it.

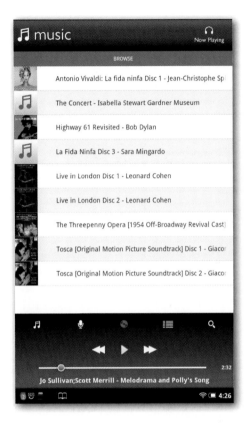

- **Playlist.** Shows all your playlists. Even if you haven't created a playlist, one will be there—Recently Added—which shows all the songs you've recently added. Tap any playlist to see all the songs on it and play them. For more details about playlists, see page 262.

- **Search.** Tap this and you can search your music collection. As you type your search term, the results narrow.

When you find a song you want to play, tap it. You immediately pop into Now Playing mode, and the music plays. If artwork is available, it takes up most of the screen.

NOTE The NOOK Tablet's speakers play only mono sound, and at times can be hard to hear. Plug headphones or external speakers into it, though, and you'll get full, rich stereo sound.

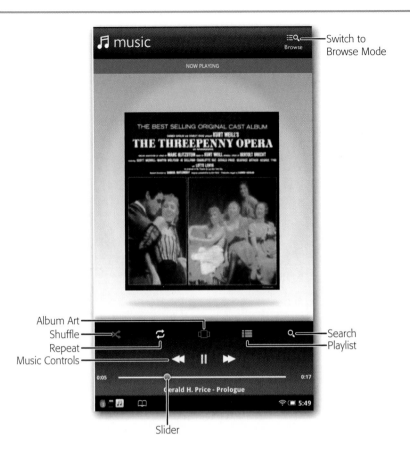

Album Art
Shuffle
Repeat
Music Controls
Slider

Switch to Browse Mode
Search
Playlist

At the bottom of the screen you'll see the usual controls for playing and pausing music, moving to the next track, and previous track and scrolling through the track. Just above that, you'll see a row of icons—the red icon shows you which view you're in. Here's what each section does:

- **Shuffle.** Plays songs in a random order.

- **Repeat.** Tap it to repeat all your songs; double-tap to repeat the song you're currently playing. When you tap twice to repeat the current song, the number 1 appears.

- **Album art.** Shows you album art, if any is available; this is the view you normally see when music is playing.

- **Browse.** Shows a list of songs from the current album.

- **Search.** Lets you search for music.

More Options for Playing Music

When you're browsing for music, press and hold your finger on a song or album, and a menu pops up with these choices:

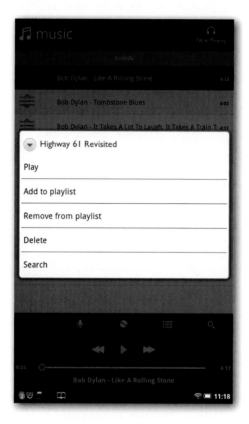

- **Play.** Plays the song or album.

- **Add to playlist.** Adds it to an existing playlist, or lets you create a new playlist and add it to that one. (See page 262 for more details about playlists.)

- **Remove from playlist.** Removes it from its current playlist.

- **Delete.** Deletes the song.

- **Search.** Searches for the song on the Internet using the browser or on the Music Player. Of course, you can do the same thing more easily by holding your finger on the song in the Music Player, but isn't it nice to have other options?

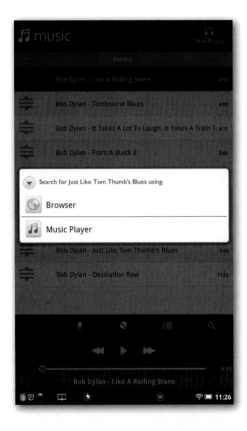

TIP What if you don't want to make any of the choices when the menu appears? There appears to be no way to back out and get back to the Music Player. There's a hidden trick, though: Swipe with your finger from right to left along the Notification bar and the menu goes away.

Creating and Managing Playlists

At first glance it's tough to figure out how to create a playlist on your NOOK Tablet. There seems to be no button to tap to create one. It's simple to do, though. As just detailed, hold your finger on a song or album, and then tap "Add to playlist" from the menu that appears. A screen appears that shows you any playlists you've already created, as well as one that the NOOK Tablet automatically creates for you—"Current playlist", which contains the songs you've most recently added.

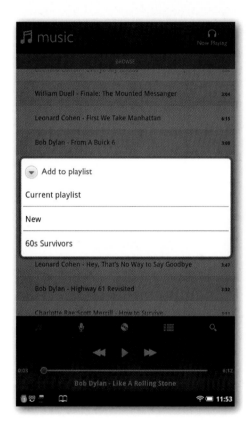

To create a new playlist, tap New, type the name of the playlist you want to create, and then tap Save. The playlist is created, and it'll contain the song you've just added.

NOTE If you hold your finger on an album to create a new playlist, when you create the playlist, it'll contain all the tracks from that album.

Keep adding songs to your playlist this way. To play a playlist, go to Browse mode, and then tap the Playlist icon to see a list of them. Press and hold your finger on any playlist, and from the menu that appears tap Play. The first song in the Playlist starts up in Now Playing mode. Control music as you would normally. Each song in the playlist plays, one after another.

To see all the tracks in a playlist, tap it (instead of holding your finger on it). But you won't see the playlist's name anywhere. Tap any song to play it; the rest of the songs from that point on in the playlist play in succession.

There's no way to edit the playlist directly by adding or removing songs. Instead, remove a song by pressing and holding your finger on it, and then selecting "Remove from Playlist." To add songs, you have to go to the song or album, as described at the beginning of this section. To delete or rename a playlist, hold your finger on it, and then select either option from the menu that appears.

Listening to Podcasts and Audiobooks

Your NOOK Tablet can play more than just music; it can also play podcasts and audiobooks, as long as they're in a file format it can recognize. (For a list of audio file formats, see Table 10-1.)

First, subscribe to podcasts as you normally would, using your PC, Mac, iPhone, iPad, iPod, Android tablet or smartphone, or similar device. Then when the podcast is on your computer—for example, in iTunes—copy it to the Music folder of your NOOK Tablet, just as you would copy music (page 253). Make sure that you subscribe to the podcast in MP3 or another NOOK Tablet-friendly format.

Looking for software for your PC or Mac that will let you subscribe to podcasts so you can transfer them to your NOOK? The free Juice app (*http://juicereceiver.sourceforge.net/*) is a good bet.

As for audiobooks, again, make sure that they're in a format your NOOK Tablet can play, such as MP3. Then just transfer them to your NOOK Tablet's Music folder.

Alas, Audible fans: The audiobooks from Audible.com are in a file format that the NOOK Tablet can't read.

There are plenty of places on the Internet you can find audiobooks to download:

- **Barnes & Noble Audio Books** (*http://bit.ly/ycmq2d*)**.** You'll find a big selection here, especially of bestsellers and newly released books.

- **Audiobooks.org** (*www.audiobooks.org/*)**.** Nice selection, including free ones.

- **Simply Audiobooks** (*www.simplyaudiobooks.com*) **and Audiobooks.com** (*www.audiobooks.com*)**.** Top-notch services that let you rent audiobooks rather than buy them.

Table 10-1. The NOOK Tablet can play many, but not all music and audio files. The primary file type that's missing from the list or Windows Media Audio (.wma) files. So if you've got music and audio in those formats, you're out of luck. You'll have to convert them to one of the formats the NOOK can handle if you want to play them.

AUDIO FILES
.aac
.amr
.mid
.midi
.mp3
.mp4a
.ogg
.wav

Using the My Media App for Viewing Photos and Playing Video

The NOOK Tablet has an extremely good high-resolution screen, ideally suited for viewing photos and playing video. As with music and audio files, you'll first have to get them on your NOOK Tablet via email (page 339), downloading from the Web (page 273), or transferring them from your computer (page 282).

Once you've got them on your NOOK Tablet, you view them using the built-in My Media app. To launch it, press the NOOK button, tap Apps, and then tap My Media.

NOTE You can also browse the photos and video files on your NOOK Tablet manually, and then view any that you choose. To do that, in the Library, tap "My stuff"→My Files and tap My NOOK or Memory Card, depending on where you've stored the files. Assuming that you've stored your music files in the Pictures folder, tap My Files→Picture. If you've stored your videos in the Videos folder, tap My Files→Videos. Then browse to any file and tap any to play it. The My Media app launches and starts playing the file.

The My Media app opens into the Grid view, which shows you all your pictures and videos in a neatly spaced arrangement. Flick through them to see them all. It displays both photos and videos; videos have a small rightward-facing arrow on them.

Tap a photo to view it. For a moment, you'll see not just the photo, but also a row of icons across the bottom of the screen for doing things with the photo—cropping it, setting it as your wallpaper, and more. After the icons go away, you can make them come back by tapping the middle of the photo. When they're onscreen you can make them go away by tapping the middle of the photo again.

Some photos display better horizontally than vertically, so turn your tablet 90 degrees, and the orientation changes. Turn it back if you want to view the photo vertically. To view the next photo in the Gallery, tap the right side of the screen; to view the previous one, tap the left side. To return to the Grid view, tap the middle of the screen to bring up the icons, and then tap Grid at top right. When you're in the Grid view, tap Picture to see the last photo you were viewing.

When you're in Picture view, here's what you can do by tapping any of the icons across the bottom of the screen:

- **Slideshow.** Plays a photo slideshow, displaying each photo for a few seconds before moving on to the next. Stop the slideshow by tapping the screen.

- **Wallpaper.** Sets the current photo as your NOOK's wallpaper. When you tap, a movable highlighted box appears inside your photo, representing the portion of the photo that will become your wallpaper. Move the box around until you've got the part of the photo you want to use as your wallpaper, and then tap Save. Tap Discard if you change your mind. When you tap Save, the cropped photo now appears as your Home screen's wallpaper. (To change your wallpaper back to the previous one, or to another photo, see page 65.)

- **Crop.** Tap this option, and a highlighted box appears onscreen. Drag any side of it, and arrows appear that let you select the portion of the photo you want to save. Tap Save to crop the photo to its new dimensions, and tap Discard to leave your photo in its original uncropped condition.

- **Left.** Rotates the photo to the left 90 degrees. Each time you tap it, it rotates 90 more degrees.

- **Right.** Rotates the photo to the right 90 degrees. Each time you tap it, it rotates 90 more degrees.

- **Delete.** Removes the photo from your NOOK.

If you tap a video instead of a photo, it starts running in a video player. You'll see the usual controls for playing, pausing, and moving through the video. Tap the screen to make the controls disappear; tap again to bring them back.

Table 10-2. The NOOK Tablet can view and play many but not all picture and video formats.

PICTURE AND PHOTO FILES
.jpg
.gif
.png
.bmp
VIDEO FILES
FLV and F4V (Adobe Flash)
.3gp
3g2
.mkv
.mp4
.m4v

Working with Office Documents

Your NOOK Tablet can do double-duty as a work tablet, letting you view Office documents including Word files (.doc, .docx, .docm, .dotx, .dotm), Excel files, (.xls, .xlsx, .xlsm, .xltx, .xltm), PowerPoint files (.ppt, .pptx, .pptm, .pps, .ppsx, .ppsm, .pot. potx, .potm), and plain text files. (txt).

As with audio files, pictures, and videos, you'll first have to get them on your NOOK Tablet via email (page 339), by downloading from the Web (page 273), or by transferring them from your computer (page 282).

To view the files, you don't first launch an app. Instead, you browse to where you've put them. To do that, in the Library, tap "My stuff"→My Files and tap My NOOK or Memory Card, depending on where you've stored the files. So if you've stored your files in the Documents folder, tap My Files→Documents to get to a list of them.

TIP   If you've downloaded files from the Web, you'll find them on the NOOK Tablet's built-in memory, not on its microSD card. Get to them by tapping My Files→My Downloads.

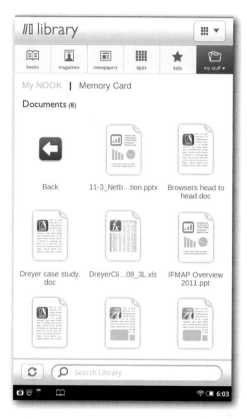

Tap any file, and it opens in an app built into the NOOK Tablet called Quickoffice Lite. This app lets you view Office files, but not edit them. Two small icons appear at the bottom of the screen. The left one is a back button; the right one pops up a menu that has different features depending on the file you're viewing. For example, in a Word document you can search within the file, go to a specific page number, change the view between print mode and draft mode, and get more information about the file (file name, author, size, and so on). On a PowerPoint document you can jump to a specific slide number or play an entire presentation.

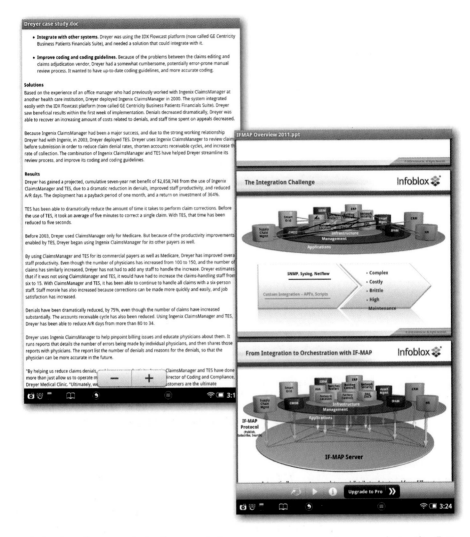

If viewing documents isn't enough for you, you can pay to upgrade to the Pro version, which costs $14.99. Download it from the NOOK Store, or tap the menu icon at the bottom of the screen and tap "Upgrade to Pro."

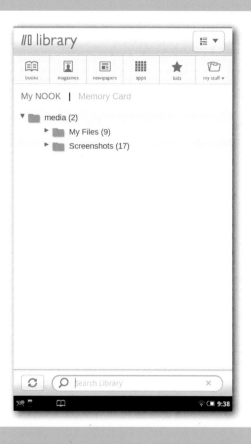

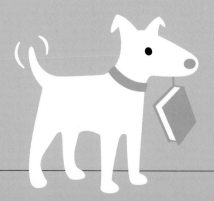

CHAPTER 11

Transferring Files Between Your NOOK Tablet and Your Computer

YOUR NOOK TABLET'S 16 gigabytes of memory goes a long way. You've got twice as much room for books, periodicals, files, and apps than with any competing eReader. But sometimes that 16 GB doesn't go far enough and you want more.

Unlike other eReaders, your NOOK Tablet has a built-in slot for a microSD card, which means you can expand its storage, and add lots of it. There's plenty you can do with that storage, adding space for music, Office documents, video, and more. This chapter tells you how to do that, from installing an SD card, to transferring files and then learning how to manage them.

 NOTE The NOOK Color and $199 NOOK Tablet have 8 GB of built-in storage, not 16 GB.

Installing an SD Card

Most of the storage built into the NOOK is for Barnes & Noble content and for the NOOK's Android-based operating system. 1 GB is available for non–Barnes & Noble content. That's where the NOOK's SD card comes in. You can put an SD card with up to a whopping 32 GB of memory in it, with room for literally thousands of books, magazines, newspapers, and files.

How many you can actually fit depends on what you put there. Figure that an SD card can store about 1,000 books for every gigabyte of storage space, so a 32 GB SD card can hold an astounding 32,000 books! Even if you're a nonstop reader, that should last you several lifetimes.

Of course, you'll likely store more than books on the SD card. You may store magazines and newspapers as well. And that's where your mileage will vary. Highly interactive magazines with plenty of high-resolution photos can weigh in at an astounding 1 GB each. And if you store music files, they can add up as well.

Types of SD Cards You Can Use

When buying an SD card, make sure you buy one of the two formats that the NOOK supports—microSD or microSDHC. What's the difference? It's right there in the name. The HC in microSDHC stands for *high capacity*. Cards 4 GB or over are called microSDHC, while cards under that capacity are microSD.

Since microSDHC cards can hold more than microSD cards, and the cost difference isn't enormous, there's little reason not to spring for the HC variety. You can generally find a 32 GB microSDHC card for $40 or under, so that size gives you the most bang for your buck.

Make sure when buying a card that it is formatted with the FAT32 file system. As a general rule, most or all are, but it doesn't hurt to check.

NOTE MicroSDHC cards are rated by their class—Class 2, Class 4, and Class 6. Class 2 is the cheapest, and Class 6 is the most expensive. If you don't see a class rating on the packaging, it's a Class 2 card. The higher the class, the more quickly you can transfer files to it, but the class rating has absolutely nothing to do with how quickly you can *display* books from the card. Class 6 cards tend to be significantly more expensive than Class 4 cards, and some people have had problems with them. To be on the safe side, stick with Class 4.

Installing the Card

If you haven't installed a microSD card before, don't fret—it's a piece of cake. Here's how:

❶ **Put your NOOK face down on a clean surface.** Look down at the bottom right of your NOOK near the curved notch for a gray diagonal lid labeled Nook.

❷ Pull the lid open gently with your fingertip and fold it against the back of the NOOK. You've exposed a small slot.

❸ Holding the card between your thumb and forefinger, with the logo side up, insert it gently into the slot.

❹ **Push the card gently until it clicks into place.**

❺ **Snap the gray lid back into place.**

If you haven't used the card before, you may need to format it before you can use it. If that's the case, you'll see a dialog box telling you that the card needs to be formatted. Tap Format Now. You'll get a warning, telling you that formatting the card will delete all its contents. Tap the Format Now button again, and the NOOK formats the card. (If you don't get the alert telling you that the card needs to be formatted, don't worry—that just means it's already formatted and you're ready to go.)

Once the card is installed, you'll see two new links in the Media bar of your Library, one labeled My NOOK, and one labeled Memory Card. Tap the Memory Card link to see and use its contents.

> **NOTE** The NOOK Tablet can play media files up to 2 GB.

Removing the Card

Removing an SD card is as easy as installing one. Place your NOOK face down and open the card slot as described in the steps on page 26. Push gently against the memory card with your fingertip and then release it; part of the card pops out. You can then slide the card out of the slot and snap the gray lid back into place.

Table 11-1. You don't want to waste your time transferring files that will merely sit on your NOOK, unloved and unused. This table details what kinds of files work with it.

BOOK FILES, MICROSOFT OFFICE FILES, AND MULTIMEDIA FILES
EPUB (the main book format for the NOOK)
PDF
Word (.doc, .docx, .docm, .dotx, .dotm)
Excel (.xls, .xlsx, .xlsm, .xltx, .xltm)
PowerPoint (.ppt, .pptx, .pptm, .pps, .ppsx, .ppsm, .pot. potx, .potm)
Plain text (.txt)
HTML (.htm, .html, .xhtml)
Comic book archive (.cbz)

MUSIC FILES
.aac
.amr
.mid
.midi
.mp3
.mp4a
.ogg
.wav

PICTURE AND PHOTO FILES
.jpg
.gif
.png
.bmp

VIDEO FILES
Adobe Flash
.3gp
3g2
.mkv
.mp4
.m4v

NOTE Want to hear some real techie talk about your NOOK Tablet's multimedia prowess? It supports MPEG-4 Simple/Advanced Profile up to 1920x1080 pixels, and H.263 up to 352x288. It also supports H.264 Baseline/Main/High Profile up to 1920x1080 pixels, and WEBM VP8 up to 640x480 pixels. What does all that mean? If you have to ask, you don't need to know.

Transferring Files to Your NOOK Tablet

Before you can enjoy your music, videos, eBooks, and work documents (okay, maybe not enjoy...), you have to get them onto your NOOK Tablet, and that's what this section is all about. It's a breeze to transfer files between your PC or Mac and your NOOK.

Once you transfer files to your NOOK, you don't need even to know what apps on your NOOK handle each of these file types—the NOOK is smart enough to know. So when you tap one of the files, the right app automatically jumps into action and launches itself, opening the file. But if you're curious about whether a specific file will work on the NOOK Tablet, see Table 11-1. You don't want to waste your time transferring files that will merely sit on your NOOK, unloved and unused. This table details what kinds of files work with it.11-1.

As a general rule, EPUB files open in the main NOOK reader; Microsoft Office files open in Quickoffice (page 273); and picture, music, and video files open in the NOOK's built-in media player.

> **TIP** Even if you don't have a SD card, you can transfer files to it; you take the same steps.

Transferring with a PC

First connect your NOOK to your PC with the micro USB cable that came with the NOOK (page 23). Don't use any other cable; Barnes & Noble warns that if you use a different cable, you might damage your NOOK. Connect the micro USB plug into your NOOK, and plug the normal-sized USB plug into your computer's USB port.

When you connect your NOOK to your PC, the NOOK puts itself into *USB mode*. Your screen displays a notice telling you that it's in that mode, and that you can go ahead and transfer files. But when your NOOK is connected to your PC or Mac, you can't do anything with it—the screen doesn't respond to taps. At that point, it's essentially a USB drive connected to your computer. Once you unplug it from your computer, it returns to its true NOOK identity.

> **NOTE** When you unplug your NOOK from your PC or Mac, it takes a few seconds for the SD card to be ready to use. You'll get a notification that it's being prepared. Also, when you unplug it, you may hear a momentary musical chime—that's just your NOOK telling you that all is right in the world, and it's preparing itself to do your bidding.

Transferring files from your PC or Mac to your NOOK is sometimes called *side loading*.

After you've connected it to your PC, launch Windows Explorer. Your NOOK now shows up as a removable disk, just like any USB drive. You can now use your NOOK as if it were any USB flash device—copying files to and from it, creating folders, and so on.

If you haven't installed an SD card, you'll see only one new drive, labeled MyNOOK if you have a NOOK Tablet, and MyNOOKColor, if you have a NOOK Color. If you've installed an SD card, you'll also see another drive, just labeled Removable Disk.

The folder structure of MyNOOK (or MyNOOKColor) and the Removable Disk (which is the SD card) is similar in some ways. MyNOOK and MyNOOKColor has a variety of folders you don't need to worry about, such as B&N Downloads, DCIM, and LOST.DIR, so don't pay any attention to them. Instead, use Windows Explorer to go to the My Files folder. That's where you'll be placing your files.

Here are the folders you'll find:

- Books
- Documents
- Magazines
- Music
- Newspapers
- Music
- Photos
- Videos
- Wallpapers

Unless you're a true nonconformist, you'll put your books in the Books folder, Microsoft Office files in the Documents folder, Music files in the Music folder, and so on. (See Appendix Bfor details about file types.) Keep in mind that you're not required to use this folder structure; and you can put files wherever you want, and you can even create new folders. But for simplicity's sake and for over-all good housekeeping, you're best off staying with the folder structure that's already there.

The NOOK uses the EPUB file format for books, so when you're borrowing books from a library, or downloading them from the Internet, make sure to look for files in that format. After you've got them on your computer, just drag them over to the Books folder.

Your SD card (labeled Removable Disk when you look at it on your PC) has the same folder structure, and you'll store files in the My Files area, just as on the NOOK itself.

Once you've dragged files from your PC to your NOOK, disconnect the USB cable, and you're ready to start using the files. When the card is inserted properly, a small icon of a card appears in the Notification area, telling you that you've got a card in your NOOK. Tap it and a screen pops up reading "SD card inserted. Click to browse SD card content…" Tap this notification, and you arrive at the area of your Library that lets you browse the contents of the card. You can also get to this area by heading to the Library and then tapping "My stuff"→My Files→Memory Card. For details about what you can do with the files once they're on your card, turn to page 287.

 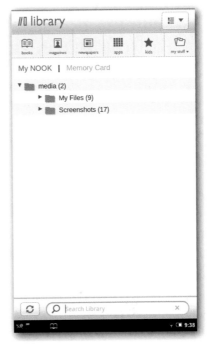

NOTE Wondering what the LOST.DIR folder is for? If the NOOK determines that you've moved any files to it that are corrupted or have other kinds of problems, it moves them (or copies of them) here.

Transferring with a Mac

Just as with a PC, to transfer files to your NOOK from a Mac, connect your NOOK to your Mac using the micro USB cable that came with the NOOK. You may find that when you connect it, iPhoto immediately launches. Close it down; you won't need it.

Instead, launch Finder. Browse it using the Finder as you would any other USB storage device to transfer files to your NOOK by dragging them.

Finding Books Online to Transfer to Your NOOK Tablet

Above all, your NOOK is an eReader, so you'll likely want to find books to transfer to it. One of the simplest ways is to check with your local library. Many libraries have programs that lend out books in the EPUB format that the NOOK uses. (For details, see page 176.)

> **NOTE** Some websites of local bookstores sell eBooks in the EPUB format. Check with your local stores to see if it does.

When you find eBooks online in the EPUB format, you want to make sure that they can legally be distributed for free. The best way to do that is to go to a reputable website known for distributing free books without copyright violations. The best one is Project Gutenberg (*www.gutenberg.org*).

Keep in mind that if you're looking for free eBooks, the NOOK Store (page 146) is an excellent place to look, because you'll find many high-quality free books there. When you get free eBooks from the NOOK Store, you won't have to download them to your PC and then transfer them to your NOOK. They're downloaded straight to your Library.

Browsing and Managing Files on your NOOK Tablet

To browse the files on your NOOK Tablet, go to the Library, and tap "My stuff"→My Files. You come to a screen that's divided in two—on the left you find My NOOK, and on the right, Memory Card. Tap My NOOK to browse the folders built into the NOOK's main memory, and tap Memory Card to browse the memory card. If you haven't installed a memory card, only My NOOK appears.

Tap the folders as described on page 285. So to look at your Music files, head to Music, for example. If you'd like to see all the files you downloaded from the Web to your NOOK, tap My NOOK, and then go to My Files→My Downloads. Tap any file to open it in the Gallery.

To delete a file, hold your finger on it, and then select Delete from the menu that appears.

The Web and Email

CHAPTER 12

Surfing the Web

THE NOOK TABLET IS more than just the best eReader on the planet. It's also a pro at browsing the Web, with a great built-in browser. You can do anything on it that you can do with big-boy browsers on your PC or Mac—visit anywhere on the Web, bookmarks web pages, use web forms, and so on. The screen may be smaller than your desktop display, but it's big enough and clear enough to give you a satisfying web experience wherever you go. How to do it all? That's what this chapter is for.

A Tour of the NOOK Tablet's Browser

To access the Web, press the NOOK button, and choose Web from the Quick Nav bar. The NOOK Tablet's browser launches.

NOTE If the button for the Web is grayed out and sports a Disabled badge, it has been turned off and you can't browse the Web. Fear not; you can easily turn it back on—turn to page 325 to learn how.

The NOOK's browser has plenty of goodies, much like those in a computer browser, including bookmarks, AutoComplete for web addresses, cookies, password memorization, the ability to save pages...just about the whole nine yards. However, the browser itself is fairly barebones, and its simplicity can be off-putting at first. But once you know your way around a bit, you'll be browsing at warp speed. Here are the main controls you need to know about:

- **Address bar.** Here's where you enter the URL—the web address—for a page you want to visit.

- **Bookmarks.** Tap this button, and you'll add the current page to your Bookmarks list and also be able to see pages you've visited frequently, and the history of your web browsing. See page 302 for more details.

- **Options menu.** Tap this button to the far right of the address bar to get at many of the browser's features, including going forward, opening a new browser window, seeing and managing your bookmarks, finding text on a page, and more. To see all your open windows, and to close any that you don't want open anymore, tap Windows. To reload the current web page you're visiting, tap Refresh. (You may want to refresh the page to see if there's new content on the page since you first visited, or if the page didn't load completely and you want to try again.) There's also a Forward button, and a More button, with plenty more options, as you'll see on page 313.

- **Back button.** Tap here to go to the page you last were on.

The Address Bar

The address bar is the box at the top of the browser where you type the URL of the website you want to visit. To type a URL into the address bar, first tap the text box in the bar. The current URL gets highlighted in green. To delete the current URL, tap the X that appears on the right side of the screen. However, when the URL is green, you don't really need to do that, since when you start typing, the current URL vanishes and is replaced by what you type.

Then use the keyboard to type an address. As you type, the NOOK displays sites you've visited that match the letters you type. So when you type the letter *C*, for example, it might display Computerworld.com, CNN.com, and so on. It may be a very long list.

As you continue to type, the list narrows down and matches only those sites that match the letters you're typing. So if you type *com*, *cnn.com* no longer appears on your list, but *computerworld.com* does. When you see the site you want to visit, just tap its listing; you head straight there. If there's no match on the list, you have to type the entire URL. After you type the URL, tap the Go button to the right of the address bar or on the keyboard.

You may find it easier to type URLs if you rotate the NOOK 90 degrees. That way, the keys are much larger, and you'll be able to see more of the URL as you type. When you type this way, matching sites and terms show up in boxes just above the keyboard, rather than in a list.

TIP Don't bother to type the *http://* part of a web address. The NOOK knows to put that in for you. You must, however, type the .com or other ending, such as .edu. After you've typed the address, tap the Go button to the right of the address bar or on the keyboard, and you head to the page.

You can also use the address bar to search the Web. Just type your search term, but don't add a .com ending. Your browser searches the Web for the term using Google.

When you head to a page, a small green progress bar appears just above the address bar, showing you how much of the page has been loaded, and indicating how much is left to go. An X also appears in the place of the Bookmark icon. Tap the X if you want to stop loading the page.

Navigating a Web Page

Head to a web page, and most of the time you see an entire page, laid out with the same fonts, links, pictures, and so on, as if you were visiting it using a computer with a larger screen. Move around the page by using the normal NOOK gestures. Of course, looking at an entire web page on the NOOK's screen isn't the same thing as looking at a web page on a 21-inch monitor. The type and photos are small, and the links can be difficult to tap on. But letting you see the entire screen at once makes a good deal of sense, because at a glance, you can see what section of the page you want to view.

That's where the fun begins. You can use the NOOK's zooming and scrolling capabilities to head quickly to the part of the page you want to view, and then zoom in.

You've got four ways to do so:

- **Rotate the NOOK.** Turn it 90 degrees to the left or to the right. The NOOK changes the orientation of the website to fill the wider view, and while doing so, zooms in.

- **Use the two-finger spread.** Put two fingers on the NOOK's screen on the areas where you want to zoom in, and move your fingers apart. The web page stretches and zooms in. The more you spread, the greater the zoom. Pinch your fingers together to zoom back out. You may need to do the two-finger spread or pinch several times until you get the exact magnification you want.

- **Double-tap.** Double-tap with a finger on the section of the page where you want to zoom. Double-tap again to zoom out. You can't control the zoom level as finely with the double-tap as you can with the two-finger spread.

Double-tap ——

- **Use the + and – signs**. As you move around the page, two buttons appear on the lower-right portion of the screen, + and –. Tap the + button to zoom in and the – button to zoom out.

Once you've zoomed in, scroll around the web page by dragging or flicking your finger—the same kind of navigation you use for other apps on the NOOK.

Tapping Links

When it comes to links, the NOOK Tablet's web browser works largely like any computer browser, except that you tap a link rather than click it. Tap the link, and you get sent to a new web page.

NOTE Sometimes when you tap a link, instead of loading a web page, the NOOK may take a different action. For example, if the link is to an email address, it opens the email app, with a new message addressed to the link's email address.

But this is the NOOK, so there's a lot more you can do with links than just tapping them. Hold your finger on a link, and a menu appears with these options:

- **Open.** Opens the linked page in the current window.

- **Open in new window.** Opens the linked page in a new window.

- **Bookmark link.** Puts the link into your Bookmarks list.

- **Copy link URL.** Tap to copy the link's URL to the Clipboard, so you can paste it somewhere else, such as in a document or an email.

TIP   If you hold your finger on a graphic that's also a link, a "Save image" option appears, which lets you save the graphic. See page 314 for details.

Multiple Windows

The NOOK Tablet's browser doesn't confine you to a single window—you can use multiple ones and easily switch among them. In fact, you may have multiple windows open without even knowing it.

NOTE   The NOOK Tablet uses Adobe Flash Player, so you can watch the Flash videos you find on websites such as YouTube and many others.

To open a new window, tap the Options menu, and from the menu that appears, tap "New window." A new window opens, and your old one appears to go away. (Don't worry; it's still there, lurking in the background.) When you open a new window, it opens to a Barnes & Noble page welcoming you to the NOOK. You can change that, however; for details, see page 306. On the new page you've just opened, head to the website you want to visit. You've now got two web pages open, even though you only see one of them. You can keep opening web pages like this, and have multiple pages open, although you'll see them one page at a time.

How to switch to another window? Tap the Menu button and tap windows. You see a list of all the browser windows you have open. Tap any you want to switch to. To close a window, tap the X button at its far right. To open a new window, tap the windows icon 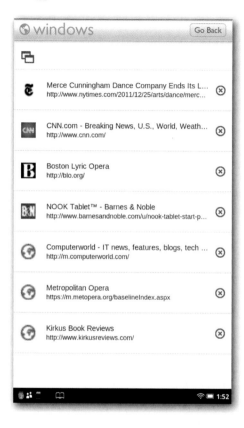 at the top of the screen.

Bookmarks

Just as with computer-based browsers, the NOOK's browser lets you save your favorite sites as bookmarks—sites you can easily visit again without having to retype their URLs. In fact, before you even use your browser, it has bookmarks for a few popular sites, including BN.com, Facebook.com, Twitter.com, and YouTube.com, among others.

Whenever you visit a web page you want to add as a bookmark, tap the Bookmark button ★ on the right side of the address bar, and the Bookmark screen appears. You'll see all your bookmarks, and on the upper left of the screen you'll see the page you were on when you tapped the button, with the word "Add" on it. Tap it and the "Add bookmark" screen appears, with the name of the page you were on, and its address.

Tap OK, or else edit the screen (for example, to change the title). Here you can edit the name or the actual URL of the bookmark. In the Name box, type a different name if you want one, and in the Location box, type a different location. Then tap OK. Or you can just leave it as is and tap OK. The bookmark is added to your list. To go back to the browser, tap the Go Back button.

NOTE If you edit the URL, and the new URL differs from the page you wanted to bookmark, you'll go to the URL you typed in, not the original one you planned to bookmark.

When you're in the browser, to see the bookmarks, tap the Options Menu and then tap Bookmarks. You see all your bookmarks. To head to any, just tap it and you're there.

NOTE Most of the time when you add bookmarks, and then go to your bookmark screen, you see thumbnails of the pages you've added. However, in some instances instead of seeing a thumbnail, you see a generic icon representing a Web site. The bookmarks pre-added to the NOOK all show up with the generic icons until you visit them; after you visit them they generally appear with thumbnails of the websites.

Managing Bookmarks

The NOOK Tablet lets you do more than just go to bookmarks. You can delete them, edit them, and more. To do it, head to the Bookmarks screen and then hold your finger on the bookmark you want to edit or manage. A menu appears with the following choices:

- **Open.** Opens the bookmarked site in the current window. So let's say you're on *www.google.com*, you go to your bookmarks, and then hold your finger on the *www.bn.com* bookmark. Now, *www.bn.com* opens in the window where *www.google.com* had previously been open.

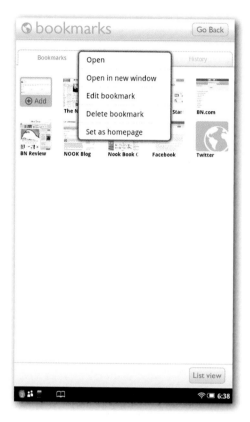

- **Open in new window.** Opens the bookmarked site in a new window. So if you're at *www.google.com*, open your bookmarks, and then hold your finger on *www.bn.com*, *www.bn.com* opens in a window of its own.

- **Edit bookmark.** Brings up a page that lets you edit the name and location of the bookmark. It's the same page for adding a bookmark.

NOTE If you sometimes find yourself with a slow WiFi Internet connection and wish there was a way to browse the Web faster, here's a bookmark you should add to your list: *http://google.com/gwt/n*. It hides most graphics and lets you browse the Web much more quickly on a slow connection.

- **Delete bookmark.** Deletes the bookmark. After you tap it, you get a warning that you're about to delete the bookmark, just in case you want to reconsider, or if you tapped this option by accident.

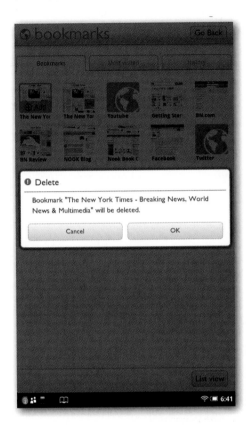

- **Set as homepage.** Tap this, and from now on whenever you open a new window, it opens to that site.

Most Visited and History Lists

When you go to your Bookmarks, you see two more ways to browse sites that you've been to before—"Most visited" and History. The NOOK Tablet keeps track of sites you've visited, and puts these two lists together based on that. They're great ways, in addition to Bookmarks, to head back to sites you've visited before without having to type—or even remember—the web addresses. The "Most visited" list shows the sites you've visited most often, with the most visited sites at the top. The History list shows all the sites you've visited, in the order you've visited them—today, yesterday, and so on. Just tap the corresponding tab to see the list.

The lists are scrollable, so flick through them to see more lists off the bottom of the screen.

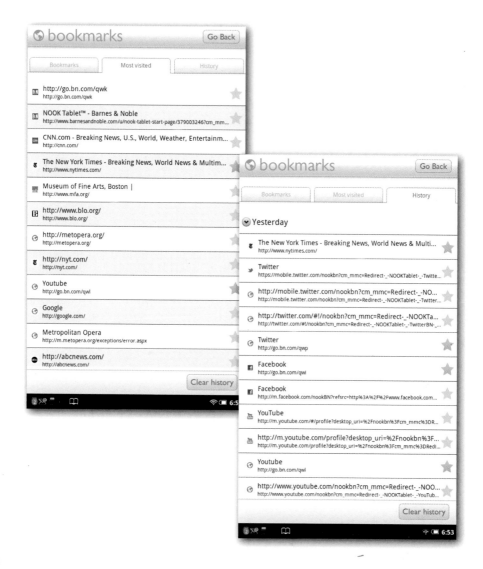

Using the Most Visited List

The "Most visited" list works much like the Bookmarks list—tap the site you want to visit and you immediately get sent there. You'll notice one difference between these lists and the Bookmarks list: The sites all have stars to the right of them, some gold, some gray. A gold star indicates that the site is on your Bookmarks list. Tapping a gray star adds that site to your Bookmarks (and turns the star gold). To remove a site from your Bookmarks list, tap a gold star. It turns gray, and the site gets removed from your Bookmarks list. Whenever you add or remove a site from your Bookmarks list in this way, you'll get a brief onscreen notification.

Just as with Bookmarks, you can edit and manage the "Most visited" list. Hold your finger on the site you want to edit or manage, and a menu appears, similar to the one you see when you hold your finger on a site in Bookmarks.

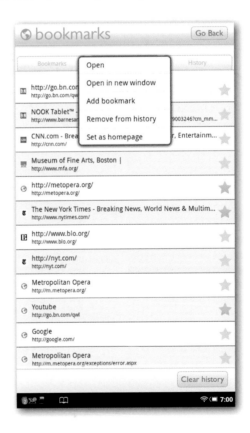

The lists are nearly identical, with a few minor differences:

- **Add bookmark** is included in the "Most visited" menu so you can add the site to Bookmarks. It's easier to simply tap the gray button to do this, but if you like your NOOK so much that you enjoy holding your finger on it, you can do it this way as well.

- **Remove from history** removes a site from the "Most visited" list as well as from your History list.

> **NOTE** If you press and hold a site in your "Most visited" list that's in your Bookmarks list, you'll have the option of removing it from Bookmarks as well.

If you want to clear out your entire "Most visited" list and History list, tap "Clear history" at the bottom of the screen.

Using the History List

The history list is organized slightly differently from the other two lists—you can see the sites you've visited in groups—Today, Yesterday, Last Seven Days, Last Month, and so on. Tap the button next any of the groups, and the group expands so you can see all the pages you visited today, for example. Tap it again and the list collapses.

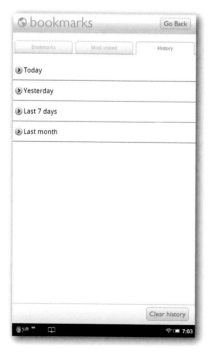

As with the "Most visited" list, tap a star next to a site to add it to your Bookmarks, and the star turns gold. Tap a gold star to remove it from your Bookmarks, and the star turns gray. Tap any site to get the same set of options that you do when you hold your finger on the site in the "Most visited" list. You can also clear your history by tapping the "Clear history" button at the bottom of the screen.

> **NOTE** Tapping a site in the History list won't send you to that site. Instead, you'll have to hold your finger on it and then select Open or "Open in new window."

Finding Text, Getting Page Information, and More

When you browse the Web, you may be on a mission of sorts—looking for a specific piece of information. You might be looking for a specific word or phrase within a web page. And when you're on a page, you may be looking for more information about it. The NOOK browser can do all that and then some. To do it all, press your finger somewhere on the web page that's not a graphic or link. A menu appears with these options:

- **Find on page.** Looking for text on a page? Tap this option, and a search box appears, along with the keyboard. Type the text or phrase you're searching for, and the NOOK finds the text, sends you to its location on the page, and highlights it in green. To find the next time the text or phrase is mentioned, tap the right arrow. To find a previous mention of it on the page, tap the left arrow. To exit the search, tap the X to the right of the search box.

The original version of the NOOK Color software gave you an additional option—the ability to copy text to the NOOK Clipboard. But when the NOOK Color software was updated in late 2011 and early 2012, that feature was taken away. The NOOK Tablet never had the feature. However, it's possible that a software upgrade may make it available again.

- **Page info.** Tap to see basic information about the page—title and web address. Tap Back to make the window disappear.

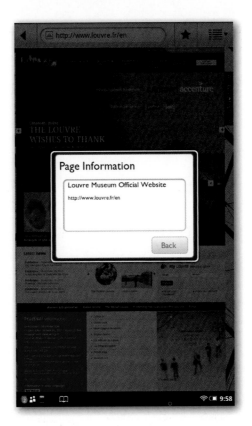

- **Settings.** Here's how you can change countless browser settings, including the size of the text displayed, privacy controls, and so on. See page 320 for details.

- **Downloads.** As explained on page 287, this will bring you to the folder that has all your downloaded files.

- **Bookmark this page.** Tap this option and then add the bookmark in the usual way (page 302).

Refreshing Pages, Going Forward, and More

Two things appear to be missing on the NOOK Tablet's browser that you'll find on a computer's browser—Forward and Refresh buttons. You may not see them, but there's a simple way to go forward or to refresh a web page. Tap the Options menu, and then select Refresh to refresh the page, or Forward to go forward. That's all there is to it.

There are other things you can do when you tap the Options menu, covered elsewhere in this chapter: Head to bookmarks (page 302), and see and manage your open windows (page 300). And if you tap More Options, you'll be able to do even more: Add a bookmark, find text on a page, get page info, view your downloads (all on page 273), and adjust your settings (page 320).

Saving Online Images

When you're browsing the Web, sooner or later you'll come across a picture you'd like to save. For example, if a friend posts a picture from your birthday party on Facebook, you can save it on your NOOK Tablet and then share it with others.

There's a quick and easy way to save that image. Hold your finger on the picture for a second or two, and a menu appears with the following options:

- **Save image.** Downloads the picture to your NOOK. See the next section to learn how to go back and view all the pictures in this folder.

- **View image.** Opens the image in its own page. As a practical matter, this option doesn't do much, because it doesn't make the image any larger or smaller—you're seeing the same image, just on its own rather than on a web page.

If the picture is also a link, the menu shows the usual options for bookmarking the link, saving the link, and so on.

Viewing Downloaded Images

When you download an image, you'll get a brief alert that the file is download-ing. A small multiheaded arrow will appear in the Notification bar, indicating that a file is downloading. (If the graphic is very small, it may download so quickly that you don't notice the arrow.)

After you've downloaded a picture, tap the Notification bar. You'll see a notifica-tion with the name of the file you just downloaded and the time it was down-loaded. Tap it and you'll open the file in the Gallery. For details about what you can do with a picture once it's in the Gallery, see page 267.

What if you don't want to see the picture right away, or want to see pictures you've previously downloaded? In the browser, tap the Options Menu and select More Options→Downloads.

You come to a list of all your pictures. They're listed by file name, which may or may not give you a clue to their contents. If you see something like Serena_ Williams.jpg, you'll know it's a photo of the tennis great Serena Williams. But if you see something like Wi231qil.jpg, you won't have a clue what it is.

Underneath the name, you'll find the address of the site you downloaded it from, along with the file size and, to the right, the date of download. Tap any picture to view it in the Gallery.

TIP When you download a picture from the Web, it gets downloaded to the NOOK's My Files→My Downloads folder on the NOOK's internal storage. You can head there outside of your browser. In the Library, tap "My stuff"→My Files. Then tap My Files→My Downloads. You'll see a list of all the files you've downloaded. Tap any to open it in the Gallery. (If you haven't yet downloaded any files from the Web, the My Downloads folder won't show up.) You can also see the pictures there by connecting your NOOK to a PC or a Mac, and then browsing to My Files→My Downloads folder on the NOOK.

If you'd like to get rid of the downloaded files, tap the Clear List button at the bottom of the page. You'll get a warning telling you that you're about to clear the list and remove all the files from the browser cache (page 321). In plain English, that means that you're about to delete all the files. So tap OK only if you really want to kill them all.

What if you want to delete some files, but not all of them? In your Library, tap "My stuff"→My Files. Then tap My Files→My Downloads. You'll see a list of all your downloaded files. Hold your finger on any you want to delete, and select Delete from the menu that appears. You may first want to open the file in the Gallery by tapping it, to make sure it's the file you want to delete. You can also delete the files by connecting your NOOK to your PC or Mac, and then using Windows Explorer on your PC or Finder on your Mac to delete the files. See page 287 for details.

Reading PDF Files

The Web is filled with PDF files, documents that often have complex layouts combined with graphics. These files can't be read directly by your browser. It's easy to read them on your NOOK, though. When you tap a link to a PDF file, it gets downloaded in the same way that a picture does, and you view it the same way as well. So just follow the instructions for viewing pictures, and look, instead, for the PDF file you downloaded. Then tap it, and it opens in Quickoffice, an app that ships with your NOOK and that lets you read PDF files in addition to Microsoft Office documents such as Word, Excel, and PowerPoint files.

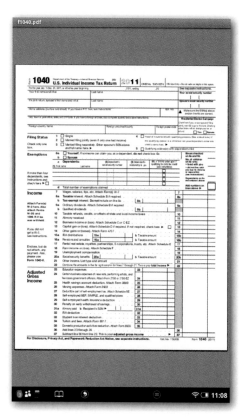

Web Pages Designed for Mobile Devices

As you browse the Web, you may come across sites that differ significantly when viewed on the NOOK Tablet compared with the exact same sites viewed on a computer. That's because web designers have created pages specifically designed to be viewed with mobile devices such as the NOOK and smartphones, taking into account that mobile devices have smaller screens than computer screens.

ABC News for example, has sites designed especially for mobile viewing. Head to the same site at the exact same time of day with a smartphone and a computer, and you see very different pages, even though the content of the pages is the same.

These pages are formatted to be read on the phone, so very often they don't include complex layouts, and instead present articles and other information in scrollable lists. They generally don't let you zoom in and zoom out. You'll navigate primarily by scrolling and clicking links.

The websites know which kind of page to display by detecting what kind of device you're using. Sometimes, though, the websites get confused, and so you may visit the website one day and get delivered a page designed for a mobile device, and another day and get one designed for a large computer monitor.

Odder still, sometimes the type of page switches depending upon the orientation of your NOOK Tablet. Visit a page when you're in the vertical orientation, and it displays the page for a mobile device; turn the NOOK horizontally to landscape mode and the page displays for a full-blown computer monitor. Turn it back to vertical, and it switches to the mobile site again.

TIP There are a few things you can try if you come across a page that displays for a mobile device that doesn't look good on your NOOK. Try changing the orientation; sometimes that works. You may also want to look around the page to see whether there's a link you can click that will let you display the full version of a page, rather than the mobile version. The techie news site Techdirt.com, for example, includes a link like that.

Online Privacy and Security

Whether you browse the Web with a computer or with your NOOK Tablet, there are potential security and privacy dangers out there—cookies, pop-ups, and malicious websites. The NOOK browser, just like its big—brother browsers on computers, includes the tools you need to keep you safe and protect your privacy when you browse the Web.

You get at all the privacy and security settings via the browser's Settings menu. When you're in the browser, tap the Options Menu and choose More Options→Settings, and then scroll down to the Privacy Settings and Security Settings areas to get at the most important settings.

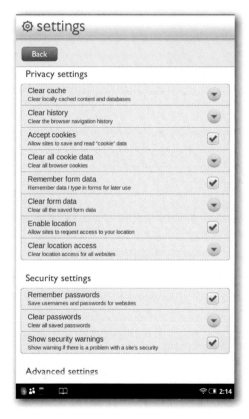

Out of the box, the NOOK's privacy and security settings are configured to make sure that you're safe and secure. So most likely, you won't need to change any settings. But there are a few options and features you might want to know more about, or that can be used to enhance your privacy, as you'll see in the next sections.

Cookies

Cookies are tiny bits of information that some websites store on the NOOK Tablet for future use. When you register for a website and create a user name and password, the website can store that information in a cookie so you don't have to retype it every time. Cookies can also remember your habits and preferences when you use a website—your favorite shipping method, or what kinds of news articles you're likely to read.

But not all cookies are innocuous, since they can also track your web browsing from multiple sites and potentially invade your privacy.

The NOOK browser gives you control over how you handle cookies—you can either accept them or tell the browser to reject them. Keep in mind that if you don't allow cookies on your NOOK, you may not be able to take advantage of the features on many sites.

To bar websites from putting cookies on your NOOK in the Privacy Settings section of Settings, uncheck the box next to "Accept cookies." The checkmark disappears, and from now on, no cookies will be put on your NOOK. You can always turn this setting back on again, if it causes problems with web browsing.

While you're in Privacy Settings, you can also delete all the cookies that have been put on your NOOK so far. Tap "Clear all cookie data." You get a warning that you're about to delete your cookies. Tap OK to clear them, or Cancel if you change your mind.

Other Privacy Settings

There's more you can do in the Privacy section of the browser's settings screen to make sure your privacy isn't invaded. For example, you can clear your browsing history so that others who use the browser can't see where you've been.

You can also tap "Clear cache" to clean out website information your browser has stored on your NOOK Tablet. A *cache* is information the browser stores on your NOOK so it won't have to get that information from the Web the next time you visit that site. The cache speeds up browsing, since it's faster to grab the information—a website image, for example—from your NOOK than from the Web. Tap "Clear cache" if you want to clear all that information out, if you worry that the information there poses a privacy risk.

At many websites, you log in by typing a user name and password, and other information such as your address. The NOOK browser remembers those user names, passwords, and other information, and fills them in for you automatically when you next visit. That's convenient, but it also presents a privacy risk, because someone else using your NOOK Tablet can log in as you.

If that concerns you, there are two actions you can take. First, in the Privacy section, tap the green checkmark next to "Remember form data." When you turn it off, the browser won't remember user names, passwords, and other information you type into forms. You can always turn it on again. To delete all the information already stored on your NOOK, tap "Clear form data." Next, scroll down to the Security Settings area and turn off the checkbox next to "Remember passwords." To clear out saved passwords, tap "Clear passwords."

Pop-Up Blocker

What's top on your list of web annoyances? Most likely at the pinnacle are pop-ups and pop-unders—ugly little windows and ads that either take an in-your-face stance by popping up over your browser so that you have to pay attention, or pop under your browser so that you don't notice they're there until you close the browser window.

Sometimes these pop-ups and pop-unders are malicious, and if you tap them they attempt to install dangerous software or send you to a malicious website. Sometimes they're merely annoying ads. Sometimes, though, they may actually be useful, like a pop-up that shows a seating chart when you're visiting a ticket-buying site. The NOOK browser includes a pop-up blocker, and like all pop-up blockers it can't necessarily distinguish between bad pop-ups and pop-unders and good ones, so it blocks them all.

However, if you're on a website that uses pop-ups that you want to see, you can turn off the pop-up blocker. Head to the Page Content section of the browser settings, and tap the green checkbox next to "Block pop-up windows." When you leave the site and want pop-ups blocked again, go back to the setting and tap it to turn it on. The green checkmark will reappear next to the setting, and you'll be protected.

NOTE When you turn off the pop-up blocker, it stops blocking pop-ups in all your browser windows, not just on one site. So be careful when you browse other places on the Web when the pop-up blocker is turned off.

Changing Your Home Page, Text Size, and More Settings

There are plenty of other things you can do on the settings page, many of which are too esoteric to bother with. Right out of the box, the NOOK Tablet has been configured very well.

However, there are a few settings worth paying attention to in the Page Content settings:

- **Text size.** Tap here, and choose from five different sizes you want to show on web pages. The choices are somewhat inexact, and range from Tiny to Huge. (Out of the box, the choice is Normal.) Generally bigger is better than smaller, because many web pages were designed with larger monitors in mind than the 7-inch screen of the NOOK.

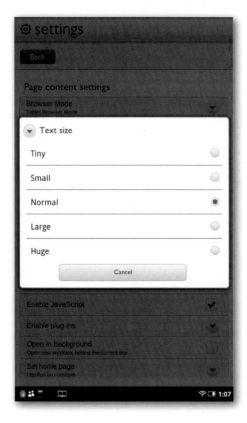

- **Browser mode.** As explained on page 318, some websites check when people visit them to see what kind of device or computer they're using—a full-sized computer, or a smaller mobile device like a tablet or a smartphone. When you visit a website with your NOOK, the site assumes you're using a tablet, and so when possible displays a page suitable for displaying on the tablet. (At least, that's what happens in theory. In practice, websites tend to show the NOOK pages designed for computer monitors, not tablets.) If you'd like to always see the full-blown computer monitor page, you can trick websites into thinking you're using a monitor. Tap Browser Mode and turn on Desktop Browser Mode. Come back here again to change to Tablet Browser Mode if you find it problematic.

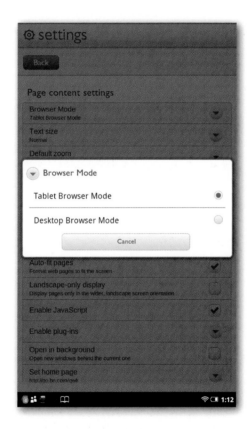

- **Set home page.** Tap here, and a screen appears into which you can type the address of any page you want to be your home page. If you're currently visiting a web page, tap "Use current page" and that page becomes your new home page.

Disabling the Browser

If you worry that your child may use the NOOK Tablet's browser to visit inappropriate sites, you'll be pleased to know that there's an easy way to disable the browser so only those who know the password can use it. It's easy to turn back on—but only if you know the password. Here's how to disable the browser:

NOTE When your browser is disabled, in addition to being unable to surf the Web, you can't use the Look Up feature in Reading Tools to search for terms using Google and Wikipedia. You also can't watch the tutorial videos that come with the NOOK. And finally, you can't search the Web with the search tool in the Quick Nav bar. All of these features depend on the browser.

❶ Press the NOOK button to open the Quick Nav bar, and then tap Settings→Security→Restrictions.

❷ Tap Restrictions, and from the screen that appears, type in a passcode that will be used to disable and enable the browser. Tap four numbers for your passcode. Tap them in again when you're asked to confirm.

❸ **From the screen that appears, tap Browser to turn on the checkbox (turn it green).** The browser is now disabled. On the Quick Nav bar or anywhere else the Web icon appears, it will be grayed out, with a Disabled badge. When you tap it, nothing happens.

NOTE Disabling the browser turns off the browser, but it doesn't disable Internet access. So you can still search for and download apps and books, send and receive email, and share recommendations via Facebook and Twitter.

To enable the browser again, in the Quick Nav bar, tap Settings→Security→ Restrictions. Enter your passcode, and then uncheck the green box next to Browser to enable the browser again.

NOTE You can disable and enable access to the social features of your NOOK such as Facebook in the same way you disable and enable the browser, just by tapping the box next to Social rather than Browser.

From: Grub Street   ⊕

The Rag 2/27/12: All About AWP, Artists, the Muse and the Move

2/27/2012 5:35 PM

Welcome to the latest installment of the *Grub Street Rag*, a newsletter of the Boston literary scene brought to you every Monday from the Lederhosen critics at Grub Street's World Headquarters. As always, if you are receiving this email in horror, please advance to the bottom of the page to unsubscribe yourself.

Put Your Name On a Piece of Grub's New Home

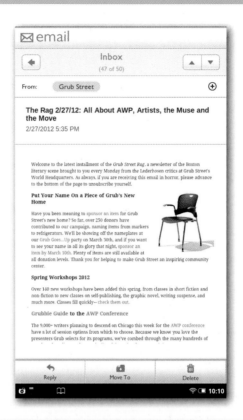

Have you been meaning to sponsor an item for Grub Street's new home? So far, over 250 donors have contributed to our campaign, naming items from markers to refrigerators. We'll be showing off the nameplates at our Grub Goes...Up party on March 30th, and if you want to see your name in all its glory that night, sponsor an item by March 10th. Plenty of items are still available at all donation levels. Thank you for helping to make Grub Street an inspiring community center.

Spring Workshops 2012

Over 140 new workshops have been added this spring, from classes in short fiction and non-fiction to new classes on self-publishing, the graphic novel, writing suspense, and much more. Classes fill quickly-- check them out.

Grubbie Guide to the AWP Conference

The 9,000+ writers planning to descend on Chicago this week for the AWP conference have a lot of session options from which to choose. Because we know you love the presenters Grub selects for its programs, we've combed through the many hundreds of

CHAPTER 13

Using Email

YOU WANT EMAIL ON your NOOK Tablet? You've got it. Your NOOK does a great job of handling email. Want to read attachments like pictures, Microsoft Office documents, and PDFs? The NOOK Tablet can do that. How about working with just about any email service out there? It can do that, too. You can also manage your mail, sync your mail, and plenty more right on the NOOK. It's a great way to have your email always in your pocket. This chapter shows you how to get the most out of email on the NOOK Tablet.

Set Up an Account

To get started, first launch the email app by pressing the NOOK button, tapping Apps, and then tapping Email. If you prefer, tap the apps icon in the Media bar, and tap Email from your list of apps. You're greeted by a Welcome screen that lets you set up an email account on the NOOK Tablet. Type your password and email address, and then tap Next.

What happens next depends upon whether you're setting up a web-based email account such as for Gmail or Microsoft Live Hotmail, or else an account that you get through work or an Internet service provider (ISP). If you're setting up a web-based mail account, your Google Tablet will make sure that your settings are correct, log you in, and immediately begin downloading mail to your tablet.

If you instead are setting up an email account through work or an ISP, the NOOK Tablet asks you to choose your account type, either POP or IMAP. Not sure what kind of account you have? It's most likely a POP account (also called a POP3 account), so try that first, and if it doesn't work, come back and try IMAP. You can also turn to page 334 for more information about POP and IMAP accounts, and how best to use them.

Next, you'll come to a screen full of intimidating-looking techie details. Despair not, though, because there's a very good chance that you won't have to change a thing on it. It has the username and password you just entered, as well as other information, such as your POP3 or IMAP server name, security type, port number, and whether the NOOK Tablet should delete email from the server when it checks for email. In the majority of cases, you won't have to change a thing here, so tap Next.

TIP Make sure that Never is selected in the "Delete email from server" section. If you select "When I delete from Inbox" instead, your NOOK Tablet deletes that email not just from the tablet, but from the server, and you won't be able to read it on your computer.

Next, you're asked to enter information about your outgoing mail server, which has the techie name SMTP server. As with the previous screen, leave everything as is, and then tap next.

You'll now be asked how often to check for new email, whether to notify you when mail arrives, and whether the email account you're setting up should be your default email account. Select your settings and tap Next.

The NOOK Tablet takes a moment or two to check your settings and to log you in. If life is being good to you, you should be all set—the NOOK Tablet starts downloading email to your inbox.

TIP If you're already using an email program on your computer, that means you've already set up the account there, and its settings are in the email program. So go to the account settings on the email software on your computer, and grab the settings from there.

However, as you know, life is not always good. The NOOK Tablet may have trouble logging you in.

NOTE At any point during the setup process, the NOOK Tablet may report it's having a problem setting up your account, so you may encounter problems at several points along the way.

If that's the case, you may have entered your username and password wrong, so try again. If you're still having problems, some of your ISP's email settings may be different from the ones that the NOOK Tablet assumes them to be—for example, the name of the POP3 server, the port number, and so on. So take a deep breath and pick up the phone. Then call your ISP's tech support line and read a good book on the NOOK Tablet while you wait on hold for an hour or three. When a tech comes on the line, explain the problem you're having. Then return to the Welcome screen for setting up an email account, tap Manual Setup, and then select either POP or IMAP; tap OK. That takes you to the screen with all the techie details, including the name of the POP3 or IMAP server, the security type, and port number. Ask the techie for those details, and have him or her stay on the line while you fill them in and make sure you can connect to your email account.

POP3 and IMAP Accounts

Here's what you need to know about POP3 and IMAP accounts for setting up and using on your NOOK Tablet:

- With a **POP (Post Office Protocol)** account, the POP server delivers email to your inbox. From then on, the messages live on your NOOK Tablet—or your home computer, or whichever machine you used to check email. You can't download another copy of that email, because POP servers let you download a message only once. So if you use your account on both a computer and your NOOK Tablet, you must be careful to set up the account properly, as described in the box on page 335, so you won't accidentally delete email. Despite this caveat, POP accounts remain the most popular type of email accounts, and are generally the easiest to set up and use.

- With an **IMAP (Internet Message Access Protocol)** account, the server doesn't send you the mail and force you to store it on your computer or NOOK Tablet. Instead, it keeps all your mail on the server, so you can access the exact same mail from your NOOK Tablet and your computer— or even from multiple devices. The IMAP server always remembers what you've done with your mail—what messages you've read and sent, your folder organization, and so on. So if you read mail and send mail on your NOOK Tablet, when you then check your mail on a computer, you'll see all those changes, and vice versa.

That's the good news. The bad news is that if you don't remember to regularly clean out your mail, your mailbox can overflow if your account doesn't have enough storage to hold it all. If your IMAP account gets full, then when people send you email, their messages bounce back to them.

Keeping Your POP Mailboxes in Sync

The difference between POP and IMAP accounts is that POP email lives only on whatever machine you download it to. With IMAP, a copy automatically remains on the server so you can download it again on another device. Say you read incoming email on your NOOK Tablet, delete some of it, keep some of it, and write some new messages. Later that day, you go to your desktop computer and log into the same email account. You won't see those incoming messages you read on your NOOK, nor the ones you sent from it.

When you're using both your NOOK Tablet and home computer to work with the same POP account, how do you keep them in sync? By making your POP account act more like an IMAP account, so it leaves a copy of all messages on the server when you download them to your home computer. That way, you can delete messages on the NOOK, and still see them in your inbox at home.

How you set it up depends on which email program you use at home. In Outlook 2010, choose File→Account Settings, and then double-click the account name and select More Settings→Advanced. Turn on "Leave a copy of each message on the server." Also turn on "Delete messages from server after they are deleted from this computer," so that you won't fill up the server space allocated to your account.

To get to these settings in earlier versions of Outlook, choose Tools→Email Accounts→EMail→View or Change Email Accounts→[your account name]→Change→More Settings→ Advanced.

In Entourage, choose Tools→Accounts. Double-click the account name, and then click Options.

Reading Mail

Now that you've got an account, it's time to start reading mail. Launch the email app. You see a list of emails, and the list you see depends on what you were doing the last time you were using the email app. As you'll see on page 352, you can set up the NOOK Tablet with multiple email accounts, so the email app will open to the last account you were reading. For example, if the last time you used email you were in your Gmail inbox, you see all the mail in your inbox. If you were viewing mail in a different *label* (the term Gmail uses for a folder), you see just the mail in that label.

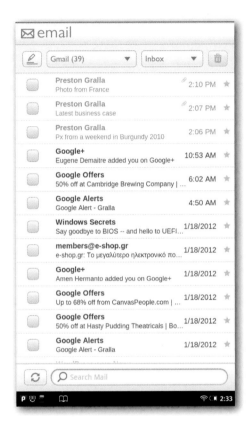

NOTE   While most email programs use folders to let you organize your email, Google uses labels in its web-based email, and that's what you use on the NOOK Tablet.

Most of the time, of course, you'll land in your inbox, which lists all your mail. Mail you haven't read is in black type, and the mail you"ve already looked at is in gray. The top of your screen displays the total number of messages in your inbox, and also the mail account that you're currently using.

Keep in mind that typically, when you view this email, you're only looking at the latest email that has been downloaded to your NOOK Tablet. So if you have older mail in Gmail, it won't show up, and if you have downloaded mail to your own computer, it won't show up, either.

If you've organized your mail into folders on your computer and you have a POP3 account, that organization won't be reflected on the NOOK Tablet. You won't be able to see or use the folders from your computer's email software.

When you're viewing mail in a list like this, each piece of mail shows the following:

- The sender

- The subject line

- The date it was sent, or, if it was sent today, the time it was sent

To open a message, tap it. Scroll up, down, and sideways in the message using the normal NOOK Tablet gestures of dragging and flicking. All the links you see in the email message are live—tap them, and you go to the web page to which they're linked, using the NOOK Tablet's web browser. Tap an email address, and a new email message opens to that address. Tap a YouTube video, and the video plays. In fact, in many instances, the text in the email message doesn't even need to be a link. If you tap a street address, the NOOK Tablet launches your web browser and shows you that location in Google Maps.

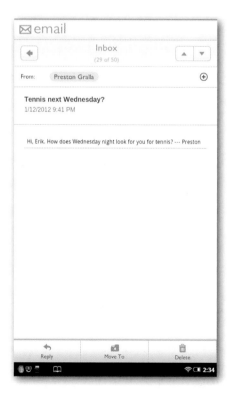

At the top of the screen, you find several important buttons and pieces of information. Right in the center of the screen at the top, you see the folder you're currently in (again, Gmail calls them labels), the number of messages in that folder that have been downloaded to your NOOK Tablet, and where the current email is on that list, for example three out of 25.

To the left of that there's a Back arrow. Tap Back to go back to the enclosing folder. To its right you'll see an up arrow and a down arrow. Tap the up arrow to read the previous mail in the folder; tap the down arrow to read the next.

Handling Pictures in Mail

You'll often get sent pictures in email. Some are embedded in the content of the message itself—for example, a company logo, or when someone has pasted a picture directly into the message. Other times, the sender attaches the image to the messages, like a family member sending you Thanksgiving photos.

If the graphics are embedded in the content of the message, you see a button titled Show pictures. In some cases you don't really need to see the graphics (who cares what a company's logo looks like, really?). In that case, do nothing, However, in other cases, the graphic is an integral part of the message, like a graph or a map. If that happens, tap "Show pictures". You see all the graphics on full display, right in the message.

 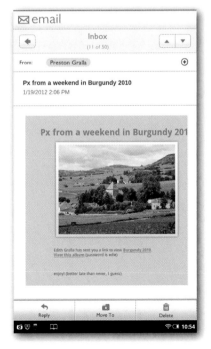

If someone has attached a graphic, you see an icon of a paper clip and an icon representing the graphic, along with the file name and its size. Tap the Open button, and the picture opens in the Gallery (see page 267). The picture also gets downloaded to your Downloads folder so you can view it later on (page 273).

Handling Other Attachments

Your NOOK Tablet can also let you read and save other files, not just pictures, including as Word, Excel and PowerPoint files. It lets you preview those files and other file types as well. (For a list of all the file types the NOOK Tablet can read, see Appendix B.)

The NOOK's email app handles these apps in the same way it does pictures. You'll see an icon of a paper clip, and an icon representing the graphic, along with the file name and its size. Tap the Open button, and the attachment opens. If it's a Word, Excel, or PowerPoint file, it opens in an app called Quickoffice Lite that's built into the NOOK Tablet. As with pictures, the file also gets downloaded to your Downloads folder.

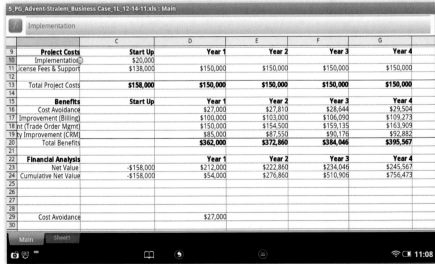

Add the Sender to Your Contacts

If you're reading an email message from someone and want to add her to your Contacts list, tap her name. A screen appears that lets you create a new contact with the sender's name and email address.

Replying to Messages

At the bottom of the screen when you're reading a message, you'll find three icons that do the following:

- **Reply.** Tap this and you get three choices: Reply, "Reply all," and Forward. Reply sends a message to just the sender, while "Reply all" sends the message to everyone who has received it. Forward lets you send the message to someone new. In all cases, the original email message is included at the bottom of the message you send.

- **Move to.** Tap this and you'll see a list of all folders (or in the case of Gmail, labels) in your account. Tap any to move the email to it.

- **Delete.** Tap this to delete the message.

Composing Email

To write an email, get to a folder listing and tap the top leftmost icon . A new, blank message form opens, and the keyboard appears so you can start typing.

Write your message this way:

- **In the To field, type the recipient's address.** As you type, the NOOK Tablet looks through your Contacts list, as well as the list of people you've sent email to in the past, and displays any matches. (It matches the first few letters of first names as well as last names as you type.) If you find a match, tap it instead of typing the rest of the address. You can add as many addresses as you want. You can also tap the small button at the far right of the To field and your list of contacts appears. Tap any to whom you want to send an email.

- **Send copies to other recipients.** Tap Cc:/Bcc: and enter names here. Anyone whose email address you put in the Cc and Bcc boxes gets a copy of the email message. The difference is that while everyone can see all the Cc recipients, the Bcc copy is sent in private. None of the other recipients can see the email addresses you enter in the Bcc field.

NOTE Cc stands for the term *carbon copy* and Bcc stands for *blind carbon copy*. The from those long-gone days in the last century when people typed mail, documents, and memos on an ancient device called a typewriter. To make multiple copies, typists added a sheet of carbon paper and another sheet of typing paper. The force of the keys striking the paper would make an imprint on the second sheet, using the ink in the carbon paper.

- **In the Subject field, type the topic of the message**. A clear, concise subject line is a good thing for both you and your recipient, so you can immediately see what the message is about when you scan your inbox.

- **In the text box, type your message**. Type as you would in any other text field. Note that there's text in the box already, "Sent from my NOOK," which is called a signature. Delete it if you don't want it to appear. You can also change the signature that appears, or not have one appear at all. For details, see page 354.

- **Tap Send (or Cancel).** Tap the send icon at the top right of the screen, and the message gets sent immediately. Tap Cancel to cancel it. You'll then have the option of saving it as a draft, which you can edit later, or abandoning it entirely. To edit the draft message and send it, you'll have to go to your Drafts folder. For details, see page 347.

Managing and Searching Mail

As explained previously, when you're in a folder (or label in Gmail), you'll see a list of your most recent email. Unread mail appears in boldface, and read mail appears in regular face. There's a lot more you can do from this screen than just scroll through your messages.

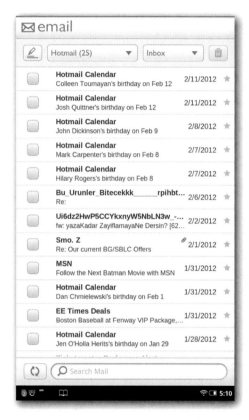

The row of icons across the top of your screen gives you these options:

- **Compose mail.** As detailed in the previous section, tap here to compose a new email.

- **Switch to a new account.** Tap the down arrow on the button to the right of the Compose Mail icon. If you have more than one email account set up on the NOOK Tablet, it shows a list of them all, including how many messages you've got in each. Tap any to go to that account. If you want to see all your email from all your accounts in one place, tap Combined Inbox.

- **Switch to a different folder.** Tap the down arrow on the second button from the right of the screen. It shows you all the folders in your current email account. In POP3 accounts and many web-based mail accounts, the only folder you'll see will be your Inbox, and a Draft folder if you've created a draft of an email message. In Gmail you'll see all your folders. To view mail in a folder, tap it. Tap Draft and you'll be able to see all your drafts. Tap any to open it, edit it, send it, save it, or cancel it.

NOTE You can't create new mail folders or delete old ones using the NOOK Tablet. You'll have to use your computer, or in the case of web-based mail such as Gmail, you'll have to go to the Web to do it.

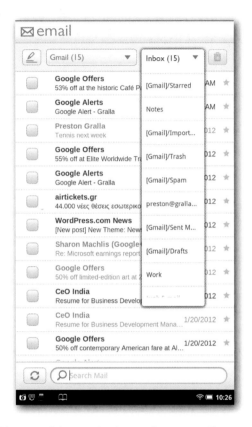

- **Delete mail.** You can delete a single email, or an entire group of them. Tap the box to the left of any mail you want to delete, and a checkmark appears. After you've selected all you want to delete, tap the Delete button.

There are plenty of other things you can do from a folder:

- **Star mail.** Do you have important emails that you want to highlight so you'll always be able to see them? Tap the star icon to the right of any email, and it turns gold. The mail will be put in a special Starred folder. Go to that folder as you would get to any other folder. To unstar a mail, tap the gold star icon so it turns gray. Note that POP3, IMAP, and many web-based mail accounts won't have a star folder, so you can't use starring with them. You can, however, use it with Gmail.

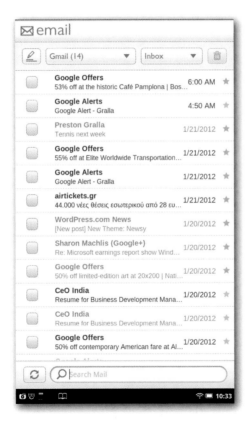

- **Get mail.** To check whether you've got new email, tap the small sync icon at the bottom left of the screen . It checks for new mail, and downloads it if it finds any.

> **NOTE** A Load More Messages button may appear at the bottom of the list of email in a folder. Tap it and you'll get more email—email that's older than the email currently displayed.

- **Search.** Type letters in the Search box at the bottom of the screen. It searches through the current folder. As you type, the search results narrow. Tap any to go the mail. To see them all in a list like in a folder, tap "Show in Panel" and they'll appear just like in a folder, one labeled Search Results. You can manage them just like you can any other mail in a folder.

Press-and-Hold Email Options

Want more ways to manage your mail? It's simple to do. Press and hold your finger on any piece of email, and this straightforward menu pops up:

- **Open.** Opens the email for reading.

- **Delete.** Deletes the email.

- **Forward.** Forwards the email. You can type additional text into the message before forwarding it.

- **Reply.** Replies to the email.

- **Reply all.** Replies to everyone who has received the email.

- **Mark as unread.** Changes the mail from regular-faced to boldfaced, so it appears unread.

- **Cancel.** Does nothing except make the pop-up menu disappear.

Managing Multiple Accounts and Advanced Email Options

Right out of the box, the NOOK Tablet's email app is set up just fine. But if you're the kind of person who likes to fiddle and diddle with options, you've got plenty of ways to customize how it works. And if you have more than one email account, you can customize them on an account-by-account basis—for example, have a different signature appended to Gmail than to a personal account, or having the NOOK Tablet check one account more frequently than others.

To see a list of all your accounts, tap the down arrow on the button to the right of the Create Mail icon and select Accounts. You'll come to a screen that lists them all, including their names, the email address of each, and how much mail is in each account.

To add a new account, tap Add Account and follow the instructions. To delete an account, tap the box to its left so a checkmark appears, and then tap the Delete button.

NOTE When you delete an account, you won't delete the email in it. You'll just remove it from the NOOK Tablet.

To customize the way any account works, tap the gear icon on its far right; the Settings screen appears. Tap what you want to change, fill in the form, and you're done. Here's what you can change, and the effect it will have on your email use:

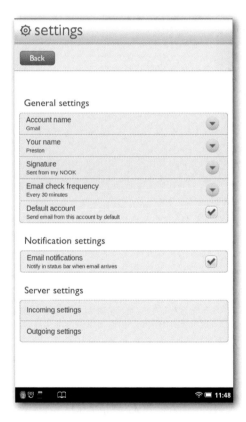

- **Account Name.** Changes the name that shows up in your list of accounts. So if you have a Hotmail account that you would rather have appear as Home, for example, you can change that here.

- **Your name.** Changes the name associated with your account—not the email address, which can't be changed. Think of it as a nickname.

- **Signature.** Changes the signature that's appended to your outgoing email from that account. Tap here, type a new signature, and then tap OK. To go with no signature at all, delete the text and tap OK. You might want to have different signatures for different accounts, one work-related, one family-related, and so on.

- **Email check frequency.** Changes how often the NOOK Tablet checks an account for email. You have it never check, or else check every 5, 10, 15, 30, or 60 minutes.

- **Default account.** When you compose an email, from which account do you want it to be sent? Turn on the box next to any account, and that becomes the default from now on. If you previously had another account that was the default, the checkmark disappears from its Settings screen.

- **Email notifications.** Want to have a notification appear in the Status bar every time an email comes in from the account? Make sure this is checked. If you don't want to be bothered, uncheck it.

- **Incoming settings.** Lets you change the settings related to getting mail from the account's server. For details, see page 330.

- **Outgoing settings.** Lets you change the settings related to sending mail via the account's server. For details, see page 330.

Understanding Gmail's Organization

Gmail has its own terminology and worldview when it comes to handling email compared with other mail accounts. So if you're a Gmail user, you may need help understanding some new some terms and ideas. Here are the most common Gmail concepts:

- **Labels.** Think of these as email folders. Your regular email program has a folder called Inbox, for example, and lets you create other folders, such as Family, Work, and so on. Gmail calls these email containers *labels*.

  That said, there is a slight underlying difference between the way you work with Gmail's labels and how you work with another email program's folders. In your typical email program, you might move mail between folders by dragging them. Not so in Gmail. In Gmail, you affix a label to an email message. When you do that, that email automatically appears when you sort for that label.

  Labels actually give you more flexibility than folders, since you can attach multiple labels to a single email message to have it show up in multiple labels. For example, if you get an email from your brother about advice for your upcoming trip to France, you can add the labels Family and France to the email. That email then shows up in both your Family label and your France label.

> **TIP** The NOOK Tablet's email app is designed to work in concert with Gmail on the Web, but you can't do everything in the Gmail app that you can do on the Web. The NOOK Tablet's email app can't create labels, for example, so to create new ones, you must visit your Gmail account on the Web, using either the NOOK's browser or a computer.

- **Overall mail organization.** Because Gmail uses labels rather than folders, you may find mail in more than one location. Also, unlike some email software, Gmail gives you the option of viewing all mail in one single area titled All Mail, including mail you've archived and all other mail.

- **Archive.** In some instances, you'll get mail that you want to keep around but don't want showing up in your inbox, because your inbox would otherwise get too cluttered. So Gmail lets you *archive* messages. Archiving a message doesn't delete it, but it removes it from your inbox. You can still find the message listed in your All Mail folder. You can also find it by searching.

Gmail's Labels

Labels are an excellent way to organize your email in Gmail, because they're far more flexible than folders, and mail can show up in multiple places. Here are some of the Gmail labels you may see when you use Gmail on the NOOK Tablet:

- **Inbox** contains all your incoming messages.

- **Starred** shows all the messages you've starred (page 349).

- **Sent Mail** lists all messages you've sent.

- **Outbox** shows mail you've created and asked Gmail to send, but that has not yet been sent.

- **Drafts** contains mail you've created but not sent.

- **All Mail** contains all mail, except for Spam and Trash.

- **Spam** contains all mail marked as spam, either by you or by Google.

- **Trash** contains mail you've deleted but that hasn't been removed from the Trash yet because it's not more than 30 days old.

NOTE If you use Gmail's Priority Inbox on the Web, you'll also see a label here called Important, which shows all the messages that Gmail has flagged as being important to you. For details about how Priority Inbox works, and to set it up on the Web, go to *http://mail.google.com/mail/help/priority-inbox.html*.

If you've created any labels other than these using Gmail on the Web, then you see them here as well. You can't create new labels in Gmail on the NOOK Tablet. To create a new label, visit Gmail on the Web using your NOOK Tablet's browser or on a computer.

Getting Social

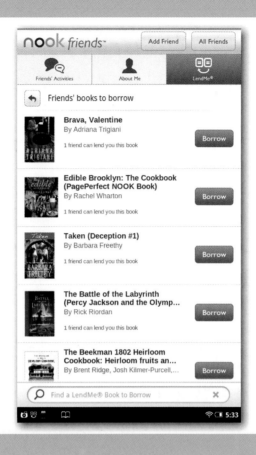

CHAPTER 14

NOOK Friends, Facebook, Twitter, and Beyond

READING, FOR MANY PEOPLE, is more than a solitary experience; it's a social one as well. One of the great pleasures of books is sharing your thoughts about them with others, sharing quotes, sharing reading recommendations, and even sharing books. The NOOK Tablet does all that for you, via the NOOK Friends app as well as its integration with Facebook and Twitter. This chapter shows you how to do that, and plenty more.

What Can You Do with NOOK Friends?

The best way to do all this sharing is via NOOK Friends, the free app built into the NOOK Tablet. If you want to share your reading, it's a spectacular app. Here are its nifty features:

- See your friends' activities, such as their book recommendations and favorite quotes from books they're reading.

- Share your own book recommendations and favorite quotes from books you're reading.

- Lend and borrow books on your NOOK.

Getting Started with NOOK Friends

Who exactly is a NOOK Friend? It's someone who has signed up for a Barnes & Noble account, is in your Contacts list with an email address, and who has accepted your invitation to become a NOOK Friend—or whose invitation you have accepted. It's a reciprocal arrangement; once you become someone's NOOK Friend, he's also yours, and vice versa.

To start, in the Quick Nav bar, tap Apps and then tap the NOOK Friends app. That's it; you don't need to do anything else. The NOOK already knows who you are and your email address, and it doesn't need anything else to begin.

When you first launch the app, you may be surprised to see that even though you haven't added any friends yet or accepted any invitations, you've already got friends and are already tracking your friends' activities. What gives?

If you've linked your NOOK account to your Facebook account, then any Facebook friend who also has a BN.com account is automatically added to your NOOK Friends, and you are added to theirs.

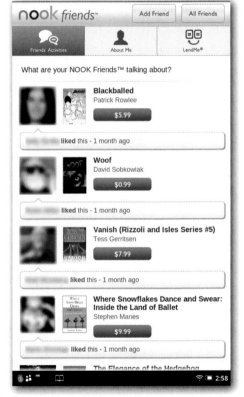

The NOOK Friends app has five buttons on it:

- **Friends' Activities.** A constantly updated screen that presents a stream of news about your friends' recent activities, such as book recommendations and quotes they want to share.

- **About Me.** Your NOOK Friends profile, which includes your name and photo, how many NOOK books you own, and other information.

- **LendMe.** Lets you lend and borrow books.

- **Add Friend.** As the name says, lets you invite someone to be your NOOK Friend.

- **All Friends.** Displays all your NOOK Friends, and lets you borrow books from them if they have any to lend.

Adding Friends to NOOK Friends

The first thing you'll want to do is invite people to be NOOK Friends with you. After all, you can't throw a party if you haven't invited anyone.

NOTE Even folks who don't have a NOOK can still be your NOOK Friends. They won't be able to participate fully—for example, they obviously won't be able to download NOOK books. But they can still get recommendations, quotes from books, and so on. Friends who don't have NOOKs still need a Barnes & Noble account, though. If they don't already have one, they can sign up, either before you send an invitation, or while accepting your invitation.

To invite a friend:

❶ **Tap the Add Friend button.** A screen appears asking whether you want to use the NOOK Contacts app to invite friends, use Facebook, find friends from your Google contacts, or instead invite a friend via email.

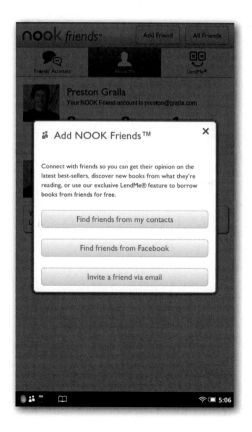

❷ Tap one of the friend sources.

If you tap "Find friends from my contacts," a screen appears with a list of contacts. At the top of the screen are contacts who are already using NOOK Friends, but aren't your friend on it. Beneath that is a list of people on your Contacts who aren't using yet NOOK Friends. Tap Add next to the names of people you want to add, and an invitation gets sent to them.

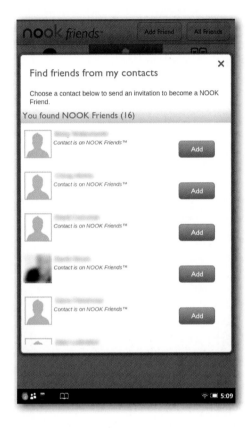

If you tap "Find friends from Facebook," a screen appears with your Facebook friends who also are on NOOK Friends. Tap Add to send an invitation to any to become a NOOK Friend.

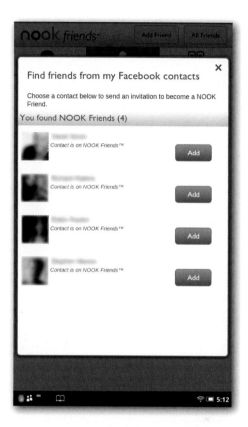

If you tap "Find friends from Google," a screen appears that lets you link your NOOK to your Google or Gmail account. After you link the accounts, the NOOK will import your contacts into your Contacts app (page 392) and will also send you a notification asking if you want to invite any to become NOOK Friends. Tap the notifications, and then tap the name of the person you want to invite to be a friend, and follow the directions for sending an invitation.

If you tap "Invite a friend via email," a screen appears that lets you type in the first name, last name, and email address of someone you want to invite to be your NOOK Friend. Fill in the form, tap Save, and the invitation goes on its merry way.

NOTE If you have already imported contacts from Google into your NOOK's Contacts app, the "Find friends from Google," listing will not appear. You'll receive a notification asking if you want to invite any to become NOOK Friends. Tap the notification, and then tap the name of the person you want to invite to be a friend, and follow the directions for sending an invitation.

When your invitation is accepted, you'll get a notification. Tap it, and you'll see the name of the person who accepted. From there, you can head straight to NOOK Friends and start interacting.

Accepting an Invitation

Other people can invite you to become a NOOK Friend, of course, and how you'll get the invitation varies according to the way it was sent (email, Gmail, Facebook, and so on). But no matter how it was sent, click Confirm Friend, and you'll be connected.

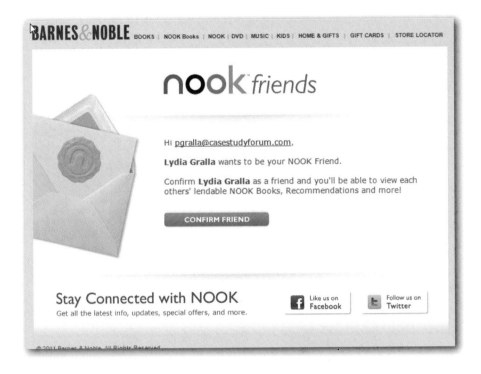

Using and Managing Friends

Once you've invited people to be your NOOK Friend (or you've been invited by others to be theirs), you can see them all by tapping the All Friends button at the top of the screen. You'll see an alphabetical list of all of your NOOK Friends, including photographs if any are available of them (from their Facebook account). If you've got more friends than can fit on one screen (lucky you!), you can scroll through them.

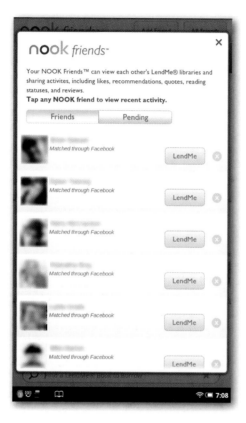

Sometimes even good friends have a falling out, so you can remove someone from your NOOK Friends list by tapping the X next to his name. You'll be asked whether you want to remove him from the list before he's deleted, just to make sure it wasn't a passing fancy.

To see a person's most recent NOOK Friends activities, including books he has recommended, quotes he has shared, and so on (for details, see page 362), tap the person's photograph (or generic person icon if there's no photograph available). To see what books he has available for lending, tap LendMe.

To see all the invitations you've sent that have not yet been accepted, tap Pending. The screen is divided into two sections: Awaiting Confirmation and "Sent invitations." In the "Sent Invitations" section, you'll see names and photos of people to whom you've sent invitations, but who haven't accepted yet. To cancel an invitation, tap the Cancel button. When someone accepts an invitation, they vanish from this area, and show up on your NOOK Friend list.

The Awaiting confirmation section shows all the invitations that have been sent to you that you haven't yet accepted. Tap Accept to become a friend; tap Reject to turn down the invitation.

Using Friends Activities

Once you've got NOOK Friends, you can start sharing with them. One of the key ways is to see what books and periodicals they recommend, and what quotes from books and periodicals they have decided to share with you.

To do that, in the NOOK Friends app, tap the Friends' Activities button at the top left of the screen. You see a scrollable list of the recent activities of your NOOK Friends.

You'll find a variety of activities there:

- Recommendations made directly and privately to you.

- Public recommendations made via Facebook or Twitter.

- Ratings of books, periodicals, and apps.

- Quotes shared publicly via Facebook or Twitter or privately with you.

- Postings of friends' reading status (what book they're currently reading, how far along they are in it, and so on).

- Friends "Liking" a book, periodical, or app on Facebook.

Along with the activity, such as a recommendation, there's also a picture of the book, periodical, or app. Tap its cover or icon to get more details about it. Tap the green button to buy it (or download it if it's free).

Using About Me

Tap the About Me button at the top of the NOOK Friends app, and you see a summary of all of your activity in NOOK Friends with this information:

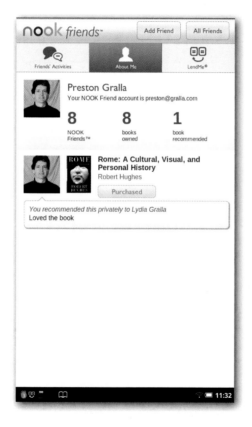

- Your name.

- The email address associated with your NOOK Friends account.

- Your photo, if you've linked the NOOK to your Facebook account (and posted a profile photo on Facebook).

- Your total number of NOOK Friends

- The number of NOOK books you own.

- The number of books you've recommended.

- A scrollable list of all of your NOOK Friends activities, such as your recommendations and, quotes you've shared, either publicly through Facebook or Twitter, or privately.

Using LendMe

If you have NOOK Friends, you'll want to get familiar with the NOOK Friends LendMe feature, because it's a way for you to lend books to your friends and borrow books from them. The feature can be used not only for NOOK Friends, but also for anyone who has a Barnes & Noble account and who uses either a NOOK or a NOOK app on a computer, mobile device, or tablet.

Chapter 7 is entirely devoted lending and borrowing books using your NOOK, but here's a quick recap of what you'll see on the LendMe screen:

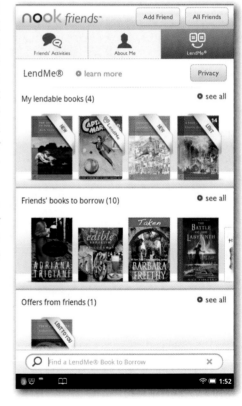

NOTE The LendMe feature is available not just in the NOOK Friends app, but in the Library as well.

- Books you own that you can lend to others.

- Books that your NOOK Friends have that are available for lending.

- Offers to lend books to you.

- Requests from NOOK Friends to borrow books from you.

You can lend or borrow only books whose publisher allows lending. The loan lasts for up to 14 days. When the time is up, you don't need to do anything to return it or to ask for it back—it automatically reverts to the owner. When you lend a book to someone, the digital rights (page 81) for reading it go along with the lending, so if it's a book you've bought, you can't read it while it's lent out. (However, if the book is free from digital rights, you can read it even when you're lending it.)

LendMe Privacy Settings

When you first start using NOOK Friends, every one of your NOOK Friends can see every one of your books available for lending. Whenever you buy a book that can be lent, all your friends know about it.

But what if you don't want them to know what lendable books you have? You can do something about it: Use the LendMe privacy settings to block individual books from being seen, or block the entire list from being seen.

In NOOK Friends, tap LendMe→Privacy, which takes you to the settings screen. If you don't want any friends to ever see any of your lendable books, uncheck the box next to "Show all my lendable books to my NOOK Friends."

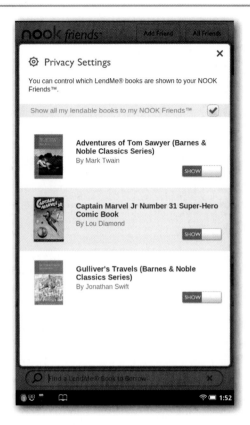

If you only want *some* lendable books to be hidden from friends' view, tap the Show button next to any until it turns into Hide. To unhide a book, tap the Hide button so it turns into Show.

Linking Your NOOK Tablet to Facebook

In order to share book quotes, post reviews, lend and borrow books, and so on with your Facebook friends, you need to first link your NOOK Tablet to your Facebook account. When you link your account, it does more than just let you do all that—you'll also have all your Facebook friend information imported into your Contacts list, so you'll also be able to get in touch via email and more.

It's simple to link to Facebook. First, make sure you're connected to a WiFi network. Then do the following:

❶ Press the NOOK button and select Settings→Social→"Manage your Accounts."

❷ From the Social settings screen that appears, in the Facebook section, tap Link Your Account.

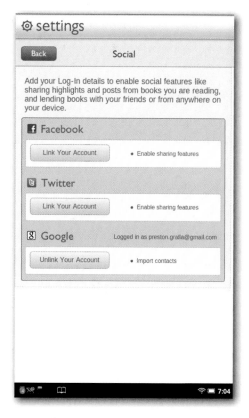

❸ On the screen that appears, type your Facebook user name and password. Then tap "Log In."

❹ **From the screen that appears, tap Allow.** If you instead tap Don't Allow, your Facebook account won't be linked to your NOOK.

You're sent back to the Social settings screen, with an indication that you've linked to Facebook.

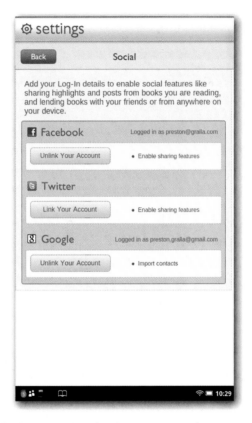

Your NOOK is linked to your Facebook account, and you can start using all of its features as outlined in this chapter and on pages 382-385. In addition, your Facebook contacts start to be imported into the NOOK Contacts app. It may take several minutes for all of them to be imported. To see your contacts, from the Apps area, tap Contacts, and from the drop-down menu that appears, tap Facebook Contacts. They'll be there, and they'll automatically sync as well.

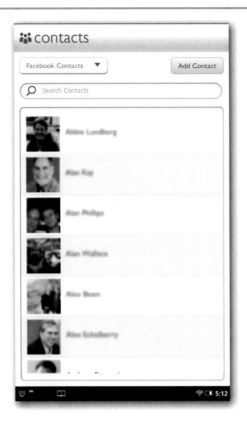

Unlinking Your Facebook Account

If you decide you want to unlink your NOOK and Facebook accounts, first get back to the Social settings screen by pressing the NOOK button and selecting Settings→Social→"Manage your Accounts." Then in the Facebook area, tap Unlink Your Account. When you do so, you'll no longer be able to use the NOOK's Facebook, features. In addition, all your Facebook contacts get deleted from your NOOK. You can easily link again.

Linking Your NOOK Tablet to Twitter

In order to share book quotes, reviews, and do more fun stuff with people on Twitter, you need to link your NOOK Tablet to your Twitter account, in much the same way you do with Facebook.

First make sure you're connected to the Internet by WiFi. Then follow these steps:

❶ **Press the NOOK button and select Settings→Social→"Manage your Accounts."**

❷ **From the Social settings screen that appears, in the Twitter section, tap Link Your Account.**

❸ On the screen that appears, type your Twitter user name and password. Then tap "Authorize app."

You're sent back to the Social settings screen, with an indication that you've linked to Twitter.

Your NOOK is linked to your Twitter account, and you can start using all of its features as outlined in this chapter on pages 382-385.

Unlinking Your Twitter Account

If you want to unlink your NOOK and Twitter accounts, first get back to the Social settings screen by pressing the NOOK button and selecting Settings→Social→"Manage your Accounts." Then in the Twitter area, tap Unlink Your Account. When you do this, you can no longer use all the NOOK's Twitter features. You can easily link again.

Using Facebook and Twitter on Your NOOK Tablet

At this writing, neither Facebook nor Twitter had an app for the NOOK—although you can still link your Facebook and Twitter accounts to the NOOK and use them in concert with NOOK Friends, as already described. But that could change at any time. So it's worthwhile to head to the NOOK Store every now and then and search for Facebook or Twitter to see whether either of their apps become available.

However, there's at least one app that lets you use both Facebook and Twitter on your NOOK Tablet. It's free, it's available now, and it's worth getting. It's called Seesmic, and you can download it from the NOOK Store.

After you download it, press the NOOK button, choose Apps, and then look for the Seesmic icon and tap it; the app launches. Tap "Add an account," and you can add accounts not just for Facebook and Twitter, but for other social networking services as well, including Google+. For each account, enter your username and password, and then tap Sign in.

You can use Seesmic for multiple social networking services, but after you set up your first one, you may think there's no way to set up a second because you seem to be stuck in just that service. Ah, but there's a way: Tap the Menu icon in the Notification bar, and then tap Accounts. You'll come to a list of your existing Seesmic accounts. Tap the + button at the top of the screen to create a new account. Choose the type of account you want to create, enter your username and password, and then tap "Sign in." Create multiple accounts this way and switch among them by tapping the Menu key and then tapping Accounts.

Using Twitter in Seesmic

When you sign into Twitter, you'll see your usual Twitter stream. At the very top of the screen on the right-hand side are icons for tweeting, searching, and refreshing Twitter. The buttons just below show you the most recent posts, replies to your posts, your profile, and so on.

Tap the small menu button in the Notification bar to bring up more options—seeing what topics are trending, changing your settings, and so on. The menu changes according to what you're doing at the time. To the left of the menu button is a Back button.

Seesmic is simple and straightforward—and in some ways easier to use than Twitter on the Web.

Using Facebook in Seesmic

When you sign into Facebook via Seesmic, you can read the news feed from your Facebook Friends, see your friends list, view your Wall, and so on by tapping the appropriate icons at the bottom of the page.

Create an update by tapping the icon at the upper-right portion of the screen, and refresh by tapping the Refresh icon. As with Twitter, Seesmic gives you a useful menu icon at the bottom of the screen.

CHAPTER 15

Managing Your Contacts

AMONG YOUR NOOK TABLET'S many tricks is its ability to keep track of all your contacts, including family, friends, coworkers, and anyone else you want to keep in touch with.

While having your contacts on your NOOK Tablet is certainly a useful feature, there's a more important reason for having them in your NOOK—your Contacts list integrates with NOOK Friends (page 361), Facebook (page 376), and email. So even if you don't plan to use your NOOK Tablet's Contacts app on its own, it pays to know how to use it for all those features. Whatever your reason, this chapter tells you everything you need to know about contacts on the NOOK.

Importing Your Google and Gmail Contacts

First things first: To launch the Contacts app, press the NOOK button, tap Apps, and then tap Contacts. If you prefer, tap the Media bar, and then tap Contacts from your list of apps.

When you first launch the app, it's a bare, empty thing. But if you use Gmail or Google Contacts, there's good news for you—you can easily import them directly into your NOOK's Contacts app. Not only that, but those contacts also sync automatically. So when you add a new contact on your NOOK, for example, it shows up in Gmail and your Google contacts, and when you add a new contact in Google, it shows up on your NOOK.

It's simple to import them and keep them in sync. Here's how to set it up:

❶ **Connect to a WiFi network.**

❷ **Press the NOOK button and select Settings→Social→"Manage your Accounts."**

❸ **From the Social settings screen that appears, in the Google section, tap Link Your Account.**

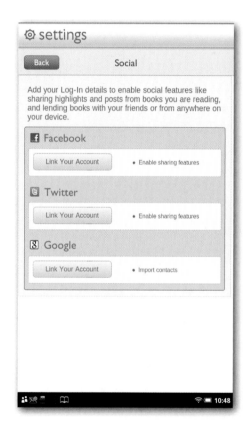

❹ **On the screen that appears, type your Google account email address and password.** If you're a Gmail user, it's your Gmail address and password. Then tap Sign In.

NOTE The NOOK Tablet's Contacts app imports only relevant information from your list of Google contacts. The app doesn't use phone numbers, addresses, and notes, so it doesn't import that informa- tion. Only the first name, last name, and email addresses are imported.

❺ **On the next screen, tap "Grant access."** If you instead tap "Deny access," your contacts won't be imported.

You go back to the Social settings screen, with an indication that you've logged into Google.

TIP   There's another way to import your Google contacts into your NOOK. Launch the Contacts app, and then select Google Contacts from the drop-down menu. From the screen that appears, select Set Up Account. You're prompted to enter your Google account email address and password, as in the steps in this section. From here on in, you'll follow those same steps to complete importing the contacts.

Your contacts start to be imported into the NOOK Contacts app. It may take several minutes for all of them to be imported. To see your contacts, from the Apps screen, tap Contacts, and from the drop-down menu that appears, tap Google Contacts. They'll be there, in all their glory. And they'll automatically sync as well.

Unlinking Your Google Account

If you decide at any point that you don't want to use your Google Contacts on your NOOK, first get back to the Social settings screen by pressing the NOOK button and selecting select Settings→Social→"Manage your Accounts." Then in the Google area, tap Unlink Your Account. When you do this, you delete all your Google contacts from your NOOK. It's easy to get them back again; just follow the directions for linking your account.

Importing Facebook Contacts

If you've got a Facebook account, you can import all your contacts from there as well. To do that, you'll need to link your NOOK Tablet to your Facebook account. For details, see page 376.

When you import your Facebook contacts, their pictures automatically show up in the Contacts app. As with when you import contacts from Google, the only information imported into your NOOK Contacts app is the name and email address of the person.

Creating a New Contact

Whether you import contacts into the Contacts app or not, you'll likely want to create a new contact at some point. It's easy to do:

❶ **Tap "Add contact."**

❷ **On the next screen that appears, type the contact's first and last name and email address.** If the person has more than one email address, tap Add New Email; a second Email line appears. You can keep adding multiple addresses this way.

❸ **If you want to invite the contact to be a NOOK Friend, turn on the box next to "Invite as NOOK Friend."**

> **NOTE** For more information about inviting NOOK Friends, see page 362.

❹ **Tap Save.** That's it; you've just created a contact.

Searching and Browsing Contacts

Finding a contact by browsing and searching is a breeze. Scroll up and down through the Contacts list in the usual way, and when you see a contact whose information you want to see, tap it, and you'll see the same screen that you do when creating a contact, except with the information filled in. You can edit the contact information if you wish, and then save it.

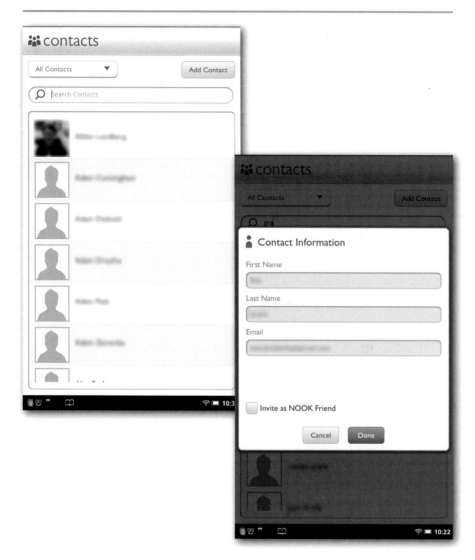

You may notice something unusual when browsing your Contacts list—the names are alphabetized by first name rather than last name. So if you know a lot of Sams and Sallys, they're all next to one another on the list. Why are they alphabetized that way? It's a Google thing. The operating system running the NOOK Tablet is Android, created by Google for smartphones, tablets, and other devices, and Android (and Google's Gmail) alphabetizes contacts by first name rather than last name.

On many Android smartphones and tablets, you can change the way contacts are displayed, and have them show up by last name rather than first name. You can't do that on the NOOK Tablet, though.

The NOOK Tablet offers a simple way to make it easier to browse contacts. Tap the down arrow next to All Contacts at the top of the screen, and you can display a narrower list of contacts—only NOOK Friends, only Google Contacts, only Facebook Contacts, or All Contacts. Any contacts who show up in multiple places also show up on each list, for example, a Google Contact who is also a Facebook friend and a NOOK Friend.

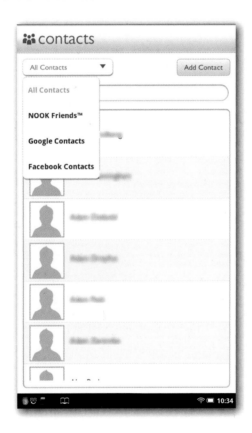

To search for a contact, tap in the "search contacts" box and start typing. As you type, the list of matches narrows. It displays contacts that have the letter combination you're typing anywhere in the name. So start searching for *al* and it displays people whose first names are "Alan," "Alvin," and so on, but also "Dale." And it also displays people with last names of "Palmer," "Carvajal," and others.

When you search, you search only contacts on the list you're currently displaying. So if you're displaying NOOK Friends, you'll see matches only for NOOK Friends on that list.

PART VII

Advanced Topics

CHAPTER 16
Settings

CHAPTER 17
Rooting Your NOOK

⚙ settings

Device Settings

Device Info	›
Wireless	›
Screen	›
Sounds	›
Time	›
Security	›
Power Save	›
Keyboard	›

App Settings

Home	›
Shop	›
Social	›
Reader	›
Search	›

🛡 📖   📖   📶 🔋 6:33

Settings

RIGHT OUT OF THE box, your NOOK Tablet is set up for you and ready to go. But what if you want to change its sounds, customize the way the keyboard works, change the Home screen's settings, and more?

It's simple to do. This chapter tells you all about the NOOK Tablet's settings, and explains what they do for you. To get to the Settings screen, tap the right side of the Notification bar and then tap the Settings button (it looks like a gear) at the upper right of the screen that appears. From there, scroll to the setting you want to change or get information from and tap it. You can also get to the screen by pressing the NOOK button and then tapping the Settings button on the right of the screen.

The top of the Settings screen—titled Device Settings—covers global settings like those for WiFi, sound, and the screen. The bottom of the screen, App Settings, lets you change how individual apps work. Keep in mind that App Settings is generally for apps built into your NOOK Tablet, not those you download from the NOOK Store.

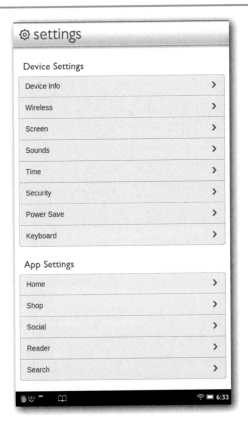

Device Info

Here's where you'll find miscellaneous information about your NOOK Tablet, ranging from battery life to how much storage you've got available, to legal boilerplate you'll never want to read:

- **Battery.** Shows how much life you've got left in your battery, and whether your NOOK Tablet is plugged in and charging.

- **B&N Content Storage Available.** Tells you how much main storage is left for books and other content you purchase from Barnes & Noble, both as a percentage of the total, and in absolute numbers—for example, 95% remaining, with 12.10 GB free out of a total of 12.75 GB available storage.

NOTE Your NOOK Tablet comes with 16 GB of built-in storage, and the NOOK Color with 8 GB. But the content storage available setting shows that you don't have that much total capacity available. What gives? The remaining storage is devoted to the NOOK's Android operating system and to storage you can use for non–Barnes & Noble content.

- **Other Storage Available.** The NOOK Tablet devotes 1 GB of storage to non–Barnes & Noble content, for example, eBooks you take out from the library, or that you find on the Internet and copy to the device. This setting shows you how much you've used and how much you've got left.

- **SD Card.** If you've installed an SD card (see page 277), this section tells you that it's installed. Tap the setting to see how much storage it contains and how much is used. You'll also be able to erase the content of the SD card when you tap the setting. And you can also "unmount" the card—tell the NOOK Tablet that you're about to remove it. It's a good idea to first unmount the card before removing it.

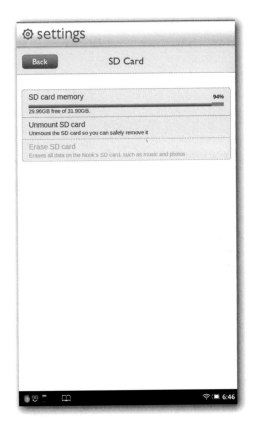

- **About Your NOOK.** Tap this item to get information about your NOOK that you may never need to know, although it may sometimes come in handy, especially if you need to get in touch with tech support. It reports on the name of the owner of the NOOK, the email address of owner, the NOOK's software version, model number, and serial number. There's also something techie called the MAC address. This long, confusing number uniquely identifies the NOOK when it's on the Internet—every Internet-connected device has a unique MAC address.

- **Erase & Deregister Device.** Want to nuke your NOOK? Here's where to do it. Tap here, and a screen appears that lets you delete all information about the NOOK's owner and Barnes & Noble account, and erase all the NOOK's content. The books, though, will remain in your Barnes & Noble account, so you'll still have access to them. Why would you ever use this feature? If you wanted to give your NOOK Tablet to someone else, you'd erase and deregister it, and then the new person can register with his own name.

- **Legal.** Are you the kind of person who likes to while away the hours reading incomprehensible contracts and terms of service? Then Legal is the place for you. If you're not a lawyer, you don't want to read this. In fact, even if you are a lawyer, you probably don't want to read it.

Wireless

Here's where you connect to wireless networks and turn WiFi on and off:

- **Wi-Fi.** Move the slider to the right to turn off WiFi and to the left to turn it on. When it's turned on, the button is green. If you're out of range of a WiFi network and want to save power, turn WiFi off.

- **Wireless Networks.** Lists WiFi networks in range as well as any WiFi networks to which you've connected in the past. It shows you the network to which you're currently connected. (For more details about how to connect to WiFi, turn to page 38.) Tap any network listed here, and you see more details about it, including whether you're connected, whether it uses security and if so what type, signal strength, the speed at which you're connected, and your NOOK Tablet's IP address. If you want to disconnect from the network, tap Forget. That not only disconnects you, but also means the next time you're in range of the network, your NOOK won't connect to it automatically.

Screen

Here's where you control how the NOOK Tablet's screen behaves:

- **Auto-rotate screen.** If you want the NOOK to automatically switch its screen orientation when you rotate it, make sure this box is turned on.

NOTE In some apps and instances, the NOOK won't rotate its screen to match the direction in which you've turned the NOOK. If you're watching a video on Netflix, for example, it plays only in the horizontal (landscape) orientation. And if you're on the Home screen, no matter how you rotate your NOOK, it always stays in vertical (portrait) mode.

- **Brightness.** Tap here and a slider appears that lets you change your screen brightness. Tap OK when you're done.

- **Screen timeout.** Shows how long should the screen stays on before the NOOK darkens it and puts it to sleep. Tap here, and choose 2 minutes, 5 minutes, 15 minutes, or an hour. The shorter the interval, the longer your battery will last on a charge.

Sounds

Head here to customize how sounds work:

- **Mute.** Turn on this box to mute sounds; uncheck it to unmute. Note that it doesn't apply when you play media.

- **Media.** Tap here, and a slider appears that sets the volume for when you play music and videos.

- **Notification.** Here's where you control the volume of your notifications. There's really no need for this setting, though, because you can do the same thing by using the volume along the top-right side of your NOOK.

Time

You can change these two time settings:

- **Use 24-hour format.** Turn on this checkbox if you're a fan of 24-hour format, the same as used in the military and many places overseas—14:00 instead of 2 p.m., for example.

- **Select time zone.** What's your time zone? Select it here.

NOTE Out of the box, the NOOK only displays U.S. time zones. If you want to see time zones from around the world, check the box next to "Show all world time zones" at the bottom of the Time Zone screen, and then select your time zone from those that appears.

Security

You've got two security settings on your NOOK Tablet:

- **Device lock passcode.** If you're worried that unauthorized people may get their hands on your NOOK Tablet, tap here and from the screen that appears, type a four-digit passcode. From now on, whenever your screen locks, entering this code is the only way to unlock it. So make sure you remember the passcode.

- **Restrictions.** If you're worried about your children or anyone else using your NOOK in a way that might concern you, you can turn off the browser and the NOOK's social features, such as Facebook. Tap here and type a passcode; a screen appears that lets you turn off those features. Uncheck this box if you don't want the restrictions in place anymore.

Power Save

There's only a single, lonely setting in this section:

- **PowerSave Mode.** Turn on this checkbox to turn this mode on. It dims your screen and makes a number of minor changes as a way to save power.

Keyboard

Three settings let you make sure the keyboard works the way exactly you'd like:

- **Keyboard sounds.** Are you nostalgic for the sound of a typewriter? (That is, if you've ever used one.) Even if not, turning on this box lets you hear a click every time you tap a key.

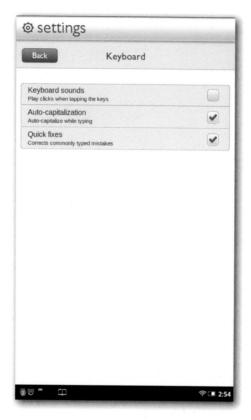

- **Auto-capitalization.** Automatically capitalizes the initial words of sentences and names. Oddly, it works only when you're writing recommendations and reviews (page 95). Otherwise, like when writing email, you're on your own.

- **Quick fixes.** Tap here, and your NOOK Tablet automatically fixes common typos.

Home

Here's where you customize how the Home screen works, and there are plenty of ways to do it:

- **Set wallpaper.** Tap here to change the Home screen's wallpaper—its background image. You can choose from wallpapers built right into the NOOK, or from any photographs you have on the NOOK. For details, see page 65.

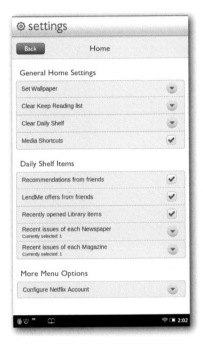 

- **Clear Keep Reading list.** At the top of the Home screen, you'll find the name of the most recent book you were reading. Tap it to open the book to the last page you were reading. If you want to clear that name so that it doesn't appear, tap here and then tap OK. The next book you start reading will show up on the list.

- **Clear Daily Shelf.** Cleans out the Daily Shelf—the list of books you've most recently been reading and the apps you've been using (page 56). Then, as soon as you start reading books and using apps, they'll show up on a fresh Daily Shelf.

- **Media Shortcuts.** Media shortcuts are the small icons on the Home screen, just above the Notification bar, and below the Daily Shelf. The goal of their existence is to help you buy books, periodicals, movies, music, and apps. If you want them out of the way, turn off this box. You can always add them back by turning the box back on.

The next section, **Daily Shelf Items,** has five separate items that let you fine-tune what appears on the Daily Shelf: "Recommendations from friends," "LendMe offers from friends," "Recently opened Library items," "Recent issues of each Newspaper," and "Recent issues of each Magazine." Turn off the boxes on the first three items if you don't want them to appear on the Daily Shelf. For the final two items, tap the down arrow to choose how many recent issues of newspaper and magazines you want to show up. Out of the box, you see only one, but you can instead choose to display two, three, all, or none.

The next section, **More Menu Options,** varies according to which apps you have installed. For example, your Netflix account, if you have one, shows up here. Tap it if you want to unlink your NOOK from your Netflix account, which means you can't watch Netflix from that particular account.

Shop

Here's where you go to customize the way the NOOK Store works:

- **Require Password for Purchases.** Normally, you don't need to type a password when you buy anything in the NOOK Store. However, if you're worried that a child or another family member may go to town using your credit card, or if you want to make yourself think twice before buying something, tap here and then enter a password. After that, the password is required any time someone tries to make a purchase on your NOOK.

- **Manage Credit Card.** Tap here to add a credit card to your NOOK if you haven't already, or to change the credit card you already have. (You can use only one credit card at a time on the NOOK Tablet.)

- **Gift Cards.** If you've been lucky enough to get a gift card, here's where you go to enter the card number so you can use it. You can also check how much money you've got left on any cards.

- **Clear Recent Shop Searches.** When you search in the NOOK Store, it keeps track of your searches, so that the next time you start searching, it shows you past searches that match the first letters of your current search. If you'd prefer those past searches not show up, here's where you can clear them.

Reader

There's only a single setting here:

- **Animate eBook page turns.** If this box is turned on, then when you turn pages in an eBook, the pages slide across the screen. If you turn this feature off, you get the new page without any fancy animation.

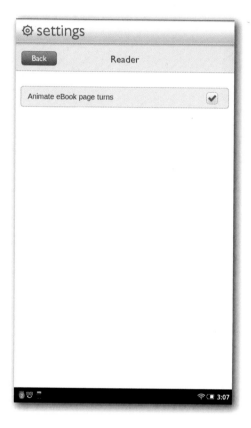

Search

You've got two ways to customize how search works:

- **Searchable items.** Tap here to tell the NOOK what to look for when you perform a search. Choices include the Web, your apps, and your music. No matter what you do, the NOOK always searches your Library and the NOOK Shop, which is why you can't turn off those checkboxes. Depending on the apps you've downloaded, you may also be able to search them with the NOOK's search tool, and turn their searching on or off from this screen. If an app is searchable, it shows up here. For example, the note-collecting app Evernote can be searched. (See page 246 for information about Evernote.)

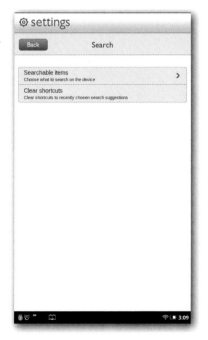 

- **Clear shortcuts.** Your NOOK remembers past searches you've performed, and if you start to type the first letters of them in a new search, it will show them so you can choose from them. If you want to clear them out, tap here.

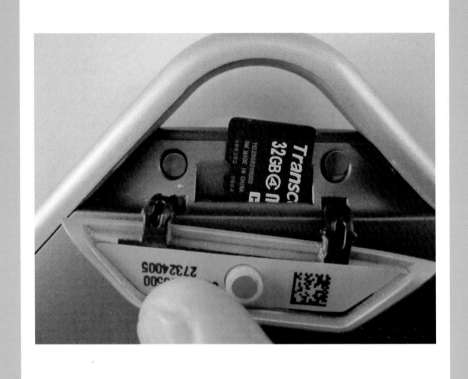

CHAPTER 17

Rooting Your NOOK

AS YOU'VE FOUND OUT throughout this book, your NOOK Tablet and NOOK Color are much more than just eReaders—they've full-blown tablets that let you browse the Web, read email, keep track of your contacts, watch TV and movies, and download apps that let you do even more.

Both tablets are on Google's Android operating system, which Google gives away for free, letting companies do whatever they want with it. Barnes & Noble used Android 2.3 (also called Gingerbread) as the basic operating system for the NOOK Tablet and NOOK Color, and then performed some magic and turned them into combination eReaders and Android tablets.

Along the way, Barnes & Noble made so many changes that the NOOK Tablet and NOOK Color in many ways don't work like other Android devices. If you compare the NOOKs to all-purpose Android tablets such as the Motorola XOOM or Samsung Galaxy Tab, you'll notice that the NOOKs simply don't look like other Android tablets. Even though companies like Samsung have made changes to Android, the interface is still recognizable as Android on their tablets. That's not really the case with the NOOKs.

Those changes are more than just skin deep; they're baked into the operating system. Most notably, the only apps you can download onto them are those available through the NOOK Store. Unlike with other Android tablets, you can't download apps from Google's Android Market or directly from websites. That means there are countless thousands of apps that you can't download.

For those who aren't faint of heart and are willing to get down and dirty with their NOOK, there's a way to turn your NOOK Tablet or NOOK Color into a full-blown Android tablet. It's called *rooting* the device, and essentially it means replacing the NOOK's built-in software with a version that runs Android rather than the software built into the NOOK.

Barnes & Noble frowns on this practice, which is why doing it voids the warranty. And Barnes & Noble does more than frown on it; it also employs ways to make it harder to root the NOOK Tablet and the NOOK Color, as you'll see in this chapter. Also, rooting your NOOK could theoretically end up *bricking* it, meaning that it no longer works.

> **NOTE** So far, this author hasn't *heard* of an instance of bricking a NOOK by rooting it, but in theory it could happen. Caveat rooter.

Understanding Rooting

When you root your NOOK, you replace its operating system with a version of Android that lets you install any app you want (via the Android Market), something you can't normally do with the NOOK. When you do that, you give the NOOK the power to do anything that Android can do. On the other hand, you sacrifice the many benefits of the NOOK's operating system, such as the excellent eReader and other built-in apps, although you can always download a version of the NOOK eReading software (the note on page 426).

The NOOK is based on version 2.3 of the Android operating system, and at this writing, 2.3 is also the version you can *install* when you root the NOOK. However, people are already working on figuring out a way to install later versions of Android onto the NOOK, notably version 3.0, called Honeycomb, which is built specifically for tablets.

There are two ways to root your NOOK:

- **Boot your NOOK into Android from a microSD card.** When you use this method, you don't replace the NOOK's operating system with a new one. Instead, you insert a microSD card into the NOOK that has the Android operating system, and run the operating system from there. That way, you don't alter the NOOK in any way. When you want to run the normal NOOK software, just take the microSD card out of the NOOK and restart it.

- **Replace the NOOK's software in its flash memory.** The *flash memory* is the memory built right into the NOOK hardware. When you use this method, you're directly replacing the NOOK's operating system with version 2.3 of Android. This voids your warranty. And if you change your mind and want to return your NOOK to its original state, bear in mind that while it's theoretically possible to unroot your NOOK (page 429), there's no guarantee that it'll work.

There are pros and cons to each method of rooting, but most people who want to root their NOOKs are better off using the microSD card method. Here are the pros and cons:

- **Using the microSD method doesn't void your warranty** because you're not altering the NOOK itself. You also don't risk bricking your NOOK.

- **Using the microSD method makes it easy to switch between Android and the NOOK's built-in software.** Boot into Android from a microSD card, and then when you want to use the NOOK's built-in software, take out the card and restart your NOOK.

- **Rooting the NOOK's built-in flash memory makes the NOOK run faster** compared with the microSD method. That's because built-in flash memory is faster than the memory on a microSD card, and so running Android from it is faster than running it from a microSD card.

What You Need to Know about the NOOK Software and Rooting

When the NOOK Color was first released, it was relatively easy to root. That's because Barnes & Noble didn't notice that people were trying to root the device. By the time the NOOK Tablet came out, though, Barnes & Noble had taken notice and built anti-rooting technology into the NOOK Color. But the NOOK Tablet was left alone and was still relatively easy to root.

All that changed in late 2011 and early 2012, however. That's when Barnes & Noble updated the operating system of both the NOOK Tablet and the NOOK Color to version 1.41. That update gave the NOOK Color new features, making it work much more like the NOOK Tablet. But it also added anti-rooting features to both devices. Since all NOOKs receive automatic updates, there's a very good likelihood that your NOOK uses version 1.41 or later of the operating system as you read this, which makes it difficult to root.

NOTE   To check which software version you have, press the NOOK button, tap Settings→Device Info→About Your NOOK, and on the screen that appears, look in the "Software version" section. That tells you what version of the NOOK software you have.

Never underestimate the creativity of tinkerers who love mucking around with hardware and software, though, because by early in 2012, they had come up with several different ways to root the NOOK Color and the NOOK Tablet.

This book doesn't cover in precise detail how to root the NOOK's built-in flash memory. On the Internet, many people have posted ways to root the NOOK's built-in flash memory; however, the instructions are not always clearly explained and don't always work. In addition, they require that you download software and files online, and by the time you read this, those files many no longer exist (and downloading software from a source you don't know is always risky). And every time the NOOK software is updated, the hackers have to start over and find new ways to root it. You can search the Web for *NOOK Tablet rooting* and see what comes up, but you're taking your chances.

Instead, this chapter focuses on the simpler and safer way of rooting your NOOK Color or NOOK Tablet—using a microSD card. It also shows you how to get started with the Android Market, which is presumably the reason you wanted to root your NOOK in the first place. If you insist on trying to root the NOOK's built-in flash memory, the end of the chapter gives the general steps for rooting (and unrooting) your NOOK via this method.

Rooting Your NOOK Temporarily with a MicroSD Card

As explained at the beginning of this chapter, this method doesn't touch the NOOK's built-in flash memory. Instead, you boot into the Android operating system from a microSD card and run the Android operating from there. When you want to run the NOOK as you would normally, turn the NOOK off, take out the card, and then turn it on again, and you're running the normal NOOK software, with no muss and no fuss.

NOTE   Your NOOK runs more slowly using this method than if you root the NOOK's built-in software.

While it's possible to create your own bootable microSD card to root your NOOK, there's a much simpler solution: Buy a microSD card that already has the software installed on it. You need to buy a microSD card to root your NOOK anyway, and a microSD card with the rooting software already on it doesn't cost much more. The company n2Acards (*www.n2acards.com*) offers reliable cards for both the NOOK Tablet and NOOK Color. The customer service is also exemplary.

The cards range in price from $34.99 to $79.99, depending on the amount of memory. An 8 GB card runs $34.99, a 16 GB card $49.99, and a 32 GB card $79.99. There are separate cards for the NOOK Color and NOOK Tablet, so make sure to choose the right one. As I write this, there was no card available that could root the 8GB version of the NOOK Tablet, but by the time you read this, it might be available.

> **TIP** When you boot from your microSD card, you also use the card to store your data, so it makes sense to buy a card with plenty of memory up front.

Booting Up from a MicroSD Card

Once you buy the card, booting up the NOOK from it is a breeze. You follow the same instructions whether you're rooting a NOOK Color or NOOK Tablet. Here's what to do:

❶ **Turn off your NOOK.**

❷ **Insert the microSD card with the rooting software into your NOOK's microSD slot.** See page 26 for details.

❸ **Turn on your NOOK.** After a short while you may see a screen that tells you to press a key if you want to go to a boot menu. Ignore that message. After a minute or so, you'll see a screen with the N2A card logo. Wait for between 3 and 5 minutes while your NOOK loads the Android operating system.

❹ **When you see an arc-shaped bar, swipe it to the right, and tap Accept from the screen that appears.** You now boot into Android. Voilà—instant Android tablet!

Booting into Android, though, is just the start of what you can do. You've got yourself a full-blown Android tablet, and can do pretty much anything you can with a tablet.

Using the NOOK as an Android Tablet

You first see a screen full of apps; tap any to run it. To see more apps, tap the small square toward the bottom of the screen, and the App tray appears, chock-full of even more apps. You'll likely have the game Angry Birds on it already. And there's also a NOOK app, so you can read your NOOK books using that app.

> **TIP** If you don't see the NOOK eReader, or ever need to reinstall it, simply go to *www.bn.com* and type *NOOK for Android* in the search box. You'll find a link for downloading the free software from the Android Market.

At the bottom of the screen, you see a series of icons. The house icon brings you back to the main Home screen. Just to the right of that is the Menu key; tap it to bring up a menu. It's context-sensitive, so it displays different options depending on where you are. To the right of the Menu icon is an arrow icon—the Back button. And to the right of that is the magnifying-glass search button; tap it to search the Internet or your tablet.

Just to the right of the magnifying glass is an up arrow; tap it to display any alerts you may have.

> **TIP** For more help using your NOOK as an Android tablet, consider buying *Motorola Xoom: The Missing Manual*. Although that book is specifically for the Motorola Xoom tablet, the Xoom uses a basic Android operating system, similar to what you'll see on the NOOK when you root it, so you may find much of it helpful.

Getting to the Android Market

Now that you're familiar with the tablet, there are a few things you should do to really get the most out of it. First, you need to connect to a wireless network. Back on the Home screen, tap the "WiFi settings" icon. That shows you any wireless networks within range. Tap any to which you want to connect, fill in any required information such as user name and password (which you can get from the network's owner), and you'll connect.

To download apps, you have to get them from the Android Market. But you can't do that quite yet; you need to take a few more steps first. First you need to add your Google account to the rooted NOOK (or else create a new one and add it to the NOOK). Here's how:

❶ **On the Home screen, tap the Menu key and select Settings→Accounts & Sync.**

❷ **At the bottom of the screen, tap "Add account."**

❸ **On the screen that appears, tap Google.**

❹ **Follow the directions onscreen for adding an account.** If you already have an account, tap "Sign in" when you get to the right screen. If you don't have an account, tap Create.

NOTE   When you sign into your Google account, your rooted NOOK syncs up with your Google information. So, for example, all your Google contacts are automatically added to your rooted NOOK, the calendar on your rooted NOOK syncs with your Google calendar, and so on.

You end up back on the screen where you first set up your Google account. At this point, you have access to your various Google services, such as Gmail and Google Calendar. Another thing that happens when you add a Google account: The Android Market is installed on your rooted NOOK. If you're using a NOOK Tablet, you're ready to use the market. But if you're using a NOOK Color don't try the Android Market yet; you're not quite out of the woods. There are a few more steps you need to take:

❶ **On the Home screen, tap the Manage Apps icon.**

❷ **On the top of the screen, tap the All tab.** You see a list of the apps on your tablet.

❸ **Scroll down until you see Google Services Framework. Tap it.**

❹ **On the screen that appears, tap "Clear data," and then tap OK.**

❺ **Tap the Back button at the bottom of the screen.** You come to the list of apps again.

❻ **Scroll down to the Market icon and tap it.** On the screen that appears, tap "Clear data," and then tap OK, exactly as you did before.

❼ **Hold down the NOOK's power button and select reboot from the screen that appears.** Make sure you don't remove the microSD card.

The NOOK reboots back into Android, and you can then use the Market to download apps. Tap the Market icon on the Home screen.

Your rooted NOOK has the same software but not the same *hardware* as many other Android tablets—for example, there's no GPS. So you may not be able to use all the apps normally written for Android tablets. And your rooted NOOK also isn't a phone, so you don't get to use the various phone features of many Android apps.

When you use the rooted NOOK as a tablet, the apps that come with Android (like the Contacts app), and any apps you download, along with all the data in those apps, is downloaded to the microSD card in your NOOK, not into the NOOK's main memory. So when you boot back into your normal NOOK, you won't have access to all those apps and that data. The apps disappear, the contacts disappear, and so on. That's why you should consider buying as large a capacity microSD card as you can afford.

When you want to use your NOOK again as a normal NOOK, press the power button, and from the screen that appears, select Power Off. Then remove the microSD card and start up your NOOK as you would normally. You'll be back with your familiar friend.

Rooting the Built-in Flash Memory

Rooting the NOOK's built-in flash memory is more problematic than just buying a bootable microSD card. If you plan to do it, head over to *http://forum. xda-developers.com*, because that's where rooters tend to hang out, and that's where you can find the latest instructions. Another good place to check is *http:// nookdevs.com/Main_Page*.

There are plenty of places on the Internet that give instructions on rooting the NOOK Color and NOOK Tablet. Many for the NOOK Color require that you first "roll back" the 1.41 or later operating system to version 1.40. Using this method, after rolling back the NOOK Color, you need to install software that allows hidden settings to be tweaked, and then install special drivers on it, and then finally root the tablet. As for the NOOK Tablet, you generally don't roll back the software.

Rooting the NOOK's flash memory involves a several-step process. But the devil is in the details, and each of these steps may be a lengthy, several-step process. Make sure when you find instructions that you read any discussions about them, in case people have uncovered problems with them, or have further advice. In general, though, here's what you'll do:

❶ **Download software to your PC.**

❷ **Use that software to create a disk image on a microSD card, and then copy a file in the .zip format to the microSD card.**

❸ **Put the microSD card into your NOOK.**

❹ **Restart your NOOK and follow the onscreen instructions.**

At that point, you'll have Android 2.3 running on your NOOK, and you can then use it like an Android tablet, including installing software from the Android Market.

Unrooting Your NOOK

What if after you root your NOOK you decide you'd like to go back to the NOOK software instead of Android? You may be able to do it. Again, do an Internet search. Some people have reported success using an Android app called NOOK Tablet unrooter. You download the app and then use it to unroot the NOOK. You can find instructions and a file to download here: *http://forum.xda-developers. com/showthread.php?t=1380235*. You can find another way to do it here: *http:// www.addictivetips.com/mobile/unroot-nook-tablet/*. Again, though, keep in mind that when you root your NOOK, you may or may not be able to unroot. When you unroot, you'll generally lose all the data on the device.

Appendixes

Maintenance and Troubleshooting

THEY MAY NOT LOOK like it, but the NOOK Tablet and NOOK Color are at heart computers—computers with a special purpose, but still, computers. And like any computers, they sometimes require special care. This appendix gives you advice on what to do when you run into trouble.

Unfreezing a Frozen NOOK

There may come a time when your NOOK Tablet or NOOK Color may become unresponsive—it may freeze no matter what you do. It's generally easy to fix:

❶ **Press the power button, hold it down for 20 seconds, and then release it.** That turns off the NOOK.

❷ **Wait a minute and press the power button for 2 seconds.** That turns it back on again. All should be well.

What if your NOOK simply refuses to turn on? It may be that your battery is out of juice, so recharge it. Keep in mind that the battery can be so low that it may take several minutes for it to get enough of a charge to restart. So if you plug it in and it still won't start, go away for several minutes, and then return and restart it.

Fixing SD Card Woes

If you're having trouble with installing the NOOK's SD card, or have had trouble after installation, there are several things you can do.

First, make sure it's the right type of card. The NOOK handles either a microSD or a microSDHC card. MicroSDHC cards are higher capacity than microSD cards. If you have another type of card, it won't work. The NOOK can handle cards with up to 32 GB capacity.

If you have the right card type, make sure that you've installed it properly and that it isn't loose. (For details about how to install an SD card, see page 26.)

Try removing the card and then reinstalling it. Before removing the card, you need to unmount it. To do that:

❶ **Press the NOOK button to bring up the Quick Nav bar.**

❷ **Tap Settings→Device Info→SD Card.**

❸ **Tap Unmount SD Card.**

It's now safe to remove the card. For details about how to do it, see page 26. After you remove the card, you can reinstall it as detailed on page 277.

Cleaning Your NOOK's Screen

After all the tapping, touching, and swiping you do, your NOOK's screen over time will get dirt and grime on it. It's a good idea to regularly clean it off, not only so that you can see more clearly, but because if dirt and grime build up, the NOOK might not work properly—it may not respond to taps, or it may think you're tapping it when you're not.

Clean the NOOK's touchscreen with a lint-free, microfiber cleaning cloth. Some cloths for cleaning reading glasses work well on the screen. Make sure that you don't use chemicals, liquids, or moisture, or abrasive cloths on the screen, because you could damage the screen or the device itself.

Updating the NOOK's Software

Barnes & Noble regularly updates your NOOK's software without your having to do anything, over your NOOK's WiFi connection. You'll know that it's been updated because a small green notification icon appears in the Notification bar. Tap the icon, and you see a notification telling you the new version number of the software.

However, if for some reason yours doesn't have the latest update, you can manually update it yourself. Also, sometimes Barnes & Noble makes a manual update available before it automatically updates the NOOK via WiFi, so if you absolutely must have the latest update, you can install the update yourself.

First check the version number of your NOOK software, and then see whether Barnes & Noble has a newer version available. To do it:

❶ **Press the NOOK button to bring up the Quick Nav bar.**

❷ **Tap Settings→Device Info→About Your NOOK.**

❸ **Look at the number beneath "Software version."** That's the version of the NOOK software you have.

❹ **Go to the NOOK Tablet Support page on the Web at** *http://bit.ly/z3rAk7.*
If that URL is out of date, go to the Barnes & Noble website and from the
navigation bar at the top of the page, click Nook Support.

❺ **Look for the section of the page that covers your device.** The NOOK
Tablet and NOOK Color don't use identical software.

❻ **Underneath your device listing, click Software Updates.** You'll see the
latest version of the NOOK software listed. If it's the same version as yours,
there's no need to do anything else. If it's newer, however, you can manually update your software, as you'll see in the following instructions.

If it turns out that your NOOK software is out of date, you can update the software yourself. Here's what to do:

❶ **On the support page for your device, click the + sign next to "Get Version 1.41 (or whatever the newest version is) Today."** Look for the text that says "click here for the software update file," and then click it.

NOOK Tablet™: Software Updates

Questions about NOOK? Find Instant Answers™ here 🔍

NOOK Tablet Support	
Getting Started	⊞ Software Updates - Version 1.4.1
Software Updates	⊞ Get Version 1.4.1 Today
Video Tutorials	
FAQs	⊞ What's new in Ver 1.4.1?
Protection Plan	
Terms of Service	⊞ How do I get Version 1.4.1?
	⊞ Will I be prompted to start the automatic download over Wi-Fi?
	⊞ How do I know I have received the update?

❷ **Save the file to your computer, and note where you've saved it.** Don't change the name or try to open it. It will be a file in the .zip format.

> **NOTE** Before attempting an update, make sure that your NOOK has a battery charge of at least 20 percent. To check your battery life, press the NOOK button, and then tap Settings→Device Info. At the top of the screen, you'll see how much battery juice you've got left.

❸ **Connect your NOOK Tablet to your computer with a USB cable and then drag the .zip file you just downloaded to the main directory of your NOOK.** For details about how to connect a NOOK Tablet to a computer and transfer files, see Chapter 11. Don't create a new folder for it, or rename the file.

❹ **Disconnect your NOOK from your computer.** When your NOOK goes into sleep mode, it will begin the process of installing the update. Make sure not to turn off your NOOK while it's performing the installation.

When the installation is done, the NOOK will restart, and you're sent to the unlock screen. You'll see a green "n" in the Status bar telling you that the update has been successful.

⑤ **Tap the notification to see the version number of the update, which will match the number you saw on the Web.**

Warranty and Repair

Your NOOK comes with a one-year warranty, for itself as well as for its charger and USB cable. The warranty isn't transferrable, so if you give or sell your NOOK to someone, or get it or buy it from someone, the warranty doesn't follow along.

NOTE However, if you got the NOOK as a gift, you, as the gift recipient, get the warranty. It says so right on the gift receipt.

The usual caveats apply to the warranty: If you've misused the device, damaged it by accident, tampered with it, and so on, the warranty is no good any longer.

If the NOOK goes on the blink during the warranty period, and you need Barnes & Noble to take care of it, call 1-800-THE-BOOK (1-800-843-2665) to make your claim. Barnes & Noble will either repair it and send it back to you, or send you a refurbished or new device.

Where to Get Help

If you've got questions about the NOOK, there are several places you can turn. Start off at the Barnes & Noble website, in the Support area for the NOOK Tablet or NOOK Color. From the *www.bn.com* website, click NOOK, and from the page you get to, click the Support link toward the top of the page. On the page you come to, underneath the NOOK Tablet and NOOK Color, you'll see links to frequently asked questions and video tutorials. Click either of them and see if there are answers to your questions. In the frequently asked questions area, you can also search for answers. There's also a chat link on the page; click it to chat with tech support.

There are also other useful places on the Web to go to:

* **B&N Community (***http://bookclubs.barnesandnoble.com/***).** This Barnes & Noble community area has discussion forums devoted to the NOOK Tablet, NOOK Color, and other versions of the NOOK. Check out the discussions, and post any questions you have.

- **nookTalk (***www.nooktalk.net***).** This site has news, tutorials, and forums where NOOK owners discuss problems and solutions. You can post questions here, as well as look for others who have solved your problem.

- **AndroidTablets.net (***www.androidtablets.net/forum/nook/***).** This site, devoted to Android tablets, has forums devoted to the NOOK Tablet and NOOK Color.

NOOK Accessories

There are plenty of accessories to help you get the most out of your NOOK Tablet and NOOK Color. In most instances, the same accessory will work with both devices, but it's always a good idea to check before buying, especially because some will work with a NOOK Tablet, but not a NOOK Color.

A good place to get them is from the NOOK Accessories area of the NOOK online store on the Barnes & Noble website; get to it at *http://bit.ly/zv5GeF*. (If that URL doesn't work, go to *www.bn.com*, click the NOOK heading, and then look for the NOOK Store; click it and head to the Accessories area.) You can also buy many accessories at the NOOK area in any Barnes & Noble store.

The accessory you'll probably want most is a cover to protect the NOOK and its screen. There are plenty of kinds from which to choose. You'll also find chargers, USB cables, reading stands, car-charging kits, and SD cards. For SD cards, you may be better off buying at an online electronics store such as *www.newegg. com*, because the cost and selection can be better than at the Barnes & Noble website. If you want to avoid scratching the NOOK screen, pick up a transparent screen protector.

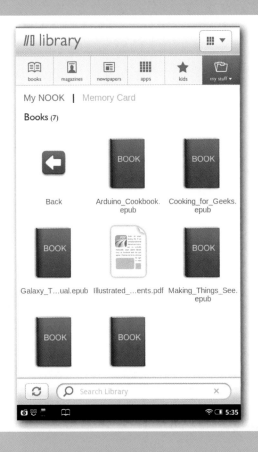

File Formats

THE NOOK IS MORE than just an eReader; it's also a general-purpose tablet that can play media files, let you read Microsoft Office documents, and more. Here's a list of the file types it can handle:

BOOK FILES AND MICROSOFT OFFICE FILES
.epub (the main book format for the NOOK)
.pdf
Word (.doc, .docx, .docm, .dotx, .dotm
Excel (.xls, .xlsx, .xlsm, .xltx, .xltm)
PowerPoint (.ppt, .pptx, .pptm, .pps, .ppsx, .ppsm, .pot. potx, .potm)
Plain text (.txt)
HTML (.htm, .html, .xhtml)
Comic Book Archive (.cbz)

MUSIC FILES
.aac
.amr
.mid
.midi
.mp3
.mp4a
.ogg
.wav

PICTURE AND PHOTO FILES
.jpg
.gif
.png
.bmp

VIDEO FILES (THE NOOK TABLET CAN PLAY MEDIA FILES UP TO 2 GB.)
Adobe Flash
.3gp
.3g2
.mkv
.mp4
.m4v

NOTE Here are more details about the how the NOOK handles multimedia files: It can handle MPEG-4 Simple/Advanced Profile up to 1920 × 1080 pixels, and H.263 up to 352 × 288. It can also play H.264 Baseline/Main/High Profile up to 1920 × 1080 pixels, and WEBM VP8 up to 640 × 480 pixels.

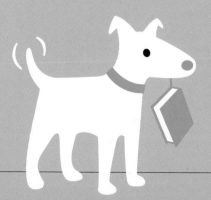

Visiting B&N with Your NOOK Tablet

YOU'LL FIND IT WORTH your while to visit a Barnes & Noble store with your NOOK Tablet, because when you do that, you get extras, notably the ability to read many NOOK books for free for an hour.

When you go into a Barnes & Noble store, your NOOK Tablet automatically finds the store's WiFi network and connects to it. For this to work, of course, WiFi needs to be turned on; for details see page 38.

When you're in the store, turn on your NOOK; a screen appears telling you that you're connected. Click Connect to Shop, and then follow the directions for finding any special offers or browsing for books to read for free.

If the screen doesn't appear, or if you move away from the screen and can't get back to it, don't despair; you can still easily find books to read for free. Go to the NOOK Store (page 146) and in the Popular Lists scrolling area you'll find a new entry—Read in Store. Tap it, and you'll come to a list of books with the In Store badge. Scroll through the list until you see one you want to read. Tap the book, and you'll see the usual details page, with one addition—a Read in Store button. Books in that list aren't the only ones that you can read for free. Many other books can be read for free for an hour as well Just browse and search as you would normally, and look for books with the Read in Store banner.

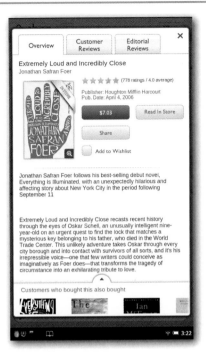

Tap the button, and you'll get a notification that you can read the book for free for an hour. The book downloads to your NOOK; a green bar shows the download progress. When the green bar stretches all the way across, the Read button turns green. Tap it. For the next hour, as long as you stay in the store, you can read the book using all the normal NOOK Tablet reading features. After that, you'll no longer be able to read it. You can also buy the book by tapping the Buy Now button at the top of the screen.

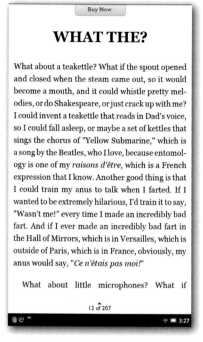

After an hour, a screen appears, telling you that your time is up. At that point, you can buy the book, add it to your wish list, or simply stop reading.

Index

Cloud (Cloud storage), 171

confirming purchases from Nook Store, 157

connecting
to computer, 24–25
to home network, 38–39
to WiFi network, 34–35

Contacts app
about, 15
browsing and searching, 392–395
changing display of contacts, 393
creating new contact, 392
importing contacts from Facebook, 392
importing Google and Gmail contacts, 387–391
unlinking Google account, 391

Contacts list, adding sender to contacts, 341

Contents icon, on Reading Tools menu, 84, 89, 99

Cookies, 321

copying files to NOOK, 254

cropping pictures, 271

Crossword app, 237

current date, in Quick Settings, 54

customer
ratings, 153
reviews, 154

customizing
Daily Shelf, 57–58
email settings, 353–355
Home screen, 60–64
text and display, 96–98

D

Daily Shelf
about, 56–57
customizing, 57–58

deleting items from, 58–59
moving items to Home screen, 59
opening eBooks from, 79
settings, 416–417

Delete icon, email, 343

deleting
apps, 236
bookmarks, 306
email, 348
email account, 353
email options, 331
highlighting, 105
items from Daily Shelf, 58–59
kids books recordings, 138
notes, 105

deregister NOOK, 404–405

details about WiFi connections, 39

device information, 400–404
battery setting, 400
B&N Content Storage Available, 401
deregister NOOK, 404–405
erase NOOK, 404–405

dictionary, Merriam-Webster Collegiate Dictionary, 100

Digital Rights Management (DRM), 81

Discover icon
on Reading Tools menu, 86

display, changing, 96–98

documents
getting on NOOK, 253
working with, 272–274

double- tap gesture
about, 43
back button, 46
cleaning up Home screen, 43
seeing details about Library items, 43

downloading

settings, 414–415

special characters, 48–49

tasks and changes in, 47

using, 46–49

kids books

backing up recordings, 139–140

buying, 126–127

deleting recordings, 138

editing, 137–138

navigating, 132–133

Read and Play feature, 126, 131–132

Read by Myself feature, 126, 128–131

reading comic books, 122

reading interactive, 12

Read to Me feature, 126, 131–132

record reading, 133–136

tips for recordings, 138

zooming in, 129–130

L

Labels (email)

understanding Gmail, 355–356

vs. Folders, 338

lending books

about, 187–194

using NOOK Friends app, 374–376

lending period, 191, 194

LendMe

badge on book covers, 147

borrowing and lending books using, 182–184

notifications indicator on Status bar, 52

privacy settings for, 375

using in NOOK Friends app, 374–376

letter P, on Status bar, 52

libraries (public), borrowing books from, 201–207

Library

button on Quick Nav bar, 49

Kids Books section, 131

Library items. *See also* eBooks (books)*; See also* magazines*; See also* newspapers

about managing, 159–160

archiving, 171–172

changing view, 166–167

Daily Shelf and, 57

on SD card, 176

options, 163–164

organizing using shelves, 167–172

re-sorting, 166–167

searching, 72, 74–75

line spacing, changing book, 96

links

in eBooks, 112

in web browser, 298–299

Load More Messages button, 350

locking

NOOK, 22

screen orientation, 109, 110

LOST.DIR folder, 286

M

MAC address, 35

Mac computer

reading books on, 177

transferring files to, 286

unplugging SD card from, 282

magazines

archiving, 171–172

browsing, 157

buying, 56, 159

get latest issue, 57, 58

information on last read, 55

opening, 63

reading, 13, 113–118